READING THE BEATLES

READING THE BEATLES

CULTURAL STUDIES, LITERARY CRITICISM, AND THE FAB FOUR

Edited by

Kenneth Womack
and
Todd F. Davis

STATE UNIVERSITY OF NEW YORK PRESS

Published by
State University of New York Press, Albany

For information, address State University of New York Press,
194 Washington Avenue, Suite 305, Albany, NY 12210-2384

Production by Marilyn P. Semerad
Marketing by Fran Keneston

Library of Congress Cataloging-in-Publication Data

Reading the Beatles : cultural studies, literary criticism, and the Fab Four /
edited by Kenneth Womack, Todd F. Davis
    p. cm.
    Includes bibliographical references (p.) and index.
    ISBN 0-7914-6715-5 (hardcover : alk. paper) — ISBN 0-7914-6716-3
(pbk. : alk. paper)
    1. Beatles. 2. Rock music—England—History and criticism. 3. Music—Social
aspects. I. Womack, Kenneth. II. Davis, Todd F., 1965–

ML421.B4R43 2006
782.42166'092'2—dc22
                                                                            2005011240

ISBN-13: 978-0-7914-6715-5 (hardcopy : alk. paper)
ISBN-13: 978-0-7914-6716-3 (pbk. : alk. paper)

10 9 8 7 6 5 4 3 2 1

For Fred Womack

Tomorrow Never Knows

CONTENTS

Acknowledgments xi

Introduction: "Dear Sir or Madam, Will You Read My Book?" 1
  Kenneth Womack and Todd F. Davis

Part I
"Speaking words of wisdom": The Beatles' Poetics

1. "I am he as you are he as you are me and we are all together":
   Bakhtin and the Beatles 9
    Ian Marshall

2. From "Craft" to "Art":
   Formal Structure in the Music of the Beatles 37
    John Covach

3. "Love, love, love":
   Representations of Gender and Sexuality in
   Selected Songs by the Beatles 55
    Sheila Whiteley

4. Painting Their Room in a Colorful Way:
   The Beatles' Exploration of Timbre 71
    Walter Everett

Part II
"A splendid time is guaranteed for all": Theorizing the Beatles

5. Mythology, Remythology, and Demythology:
   The Beatles on Film   97
   Kenneth Womack and Todd F. Davis

6. *Vacio Luminoso:*
   "Tomorrow Never Knows" and the Coherence of the Impossible   111
   Russell Reising

7. The Spectacle of Alienation:
   Death, Loss, and the Crowd in
   Sgt. Pepper's Lonely Hearts Club Band   129
   William M. Northcutt

8. We All Want to Change the World:
   Postmodern Politics and the Beatles' *White Album*   147
   Jeffrey Roessner

Part III
"We can work it out": The Beatles and Culture

9. "The rest of you, if you'll just rattle your jewelry":
   The Beatles and Questions of Mass and High Culture   161
   Paul Gleed

10. A Universal Childhood:
    Tourism, Pilgrimage, and the Beatles   169
    Kevin McCarron

11. "Baby You're a Rich Man":
    The Beatles, Ideology, and the Cultural Moment   183
    James M. Decker

12. Spinning the Historical Record:
    Lennon, McCartney, and Museum Politics   197
    John Kimsey

Afterword: I Want to Hold Your Hand   215
        Jane Tompkins

Bibliography   221

List of Contributors   233

Index   237

ACKNOWLEDGMENTS

We owe a special debt of gratitude to the many friends and colleagues who helped make this volume possible. We are particularly grateful for the encouragement and advice of Lori Bechtel, James Decker, Jeanine Lumadue, Ian Marshall, Kjell Meling, Dinty Moore, Gary Weisel, Sheila Whiteley, Michael Wolfe, and Andrew Womack. The efforts of Nicole Adu, Carole Bookhamer, Barb Brunhuber, Kristina Cole, Richard Jester, Jean Kelley, Kate Latterell, Jennifer K. Lynn, Amy Mallory-Kani, Drew McGhee, Deb Shandor, Alexis Shevenock, David Villani, and Deb Wilshire are especially appreciated. We would also like to thank James Peltz, Marilyn Semerad, and the staff at SUNY Press for their invaluable work on behalf of this volume.

INTRODUCTION

"Dear Sir or Madam, Will You Read My Book?"

KENNETH WOMACK
AND TODD F. DAVIS

O N A CLOUDY, frigid afternoon in January 1969, the Beatles performed their final, impromptu concert on the rooftop of their London office building. In the ensuing months, they recorded their brilliant swan-song *Abbey Road* (1969), saw their personal relationships dissolve into bitter litigation, and seemingly walked off their considerable global stage forever. Yet in the decades since their disbandment, they have continued to exert a substantial impact on the direction of Western culture. In 2000 alone, the surviving Beatles debuted a restored print of their much-ballyhooed film *A Hard Day's Night* to renewed critical acclaim; published a lavish, best-selling coffee-table book titled *The Beatles Anthology*; and released a compilation of their greatest hits that topped the musical charts in thirty-four countries and vastly outsold contemporary music's other popular boy groups, 'N Sync and the Backstreet Boys. As Edna Gundersen recently observed in *USA Today*, "Though defunct for the past 31 years, the Beatles still deliver the rock of ages—all ages" (E1). Perhaps even more remarkably, the Beatles continue to influence our conceptions of gender dynamics, the nature and direction of popular music, and the increasingly powerful and socially influential con-structions of iconicity and celebrity.

The reasons behind the phenomenon of the Beatles and their sustained success are as multifarious and as eminently complex as Western culture itself. Beatlemania emerged on a postwar British landscape pocked with poverty and craters—the literal scars of the socioeconomic havoc wrought by the long

1

reach of World War II. Vast unemployment and stultifying class disjunction were in the air, but younger Britons had simply had enough. They no longer wanted to hear about the Great Depression or the Blitz. As events would so clearly demonstrate, they wanted to bathe themselves in the sounds of "Please Please Me" and "She Loves You"—and they wanted to hear the words of love and possibility over and over again. Things could not have been more different in the United States, of course, where Americans were winning the peace during one of the nation's most sustained periods of economic growth and expansion. Clouds were on the horizon, to be sure—the realities of the cold war had been rendered all too clear by the missiles of October 1962. But nothing could have prepared Americans—indeed, the world—for the devastation of the Kennedy assassination and its attendant effects on a nation's belief in itself and in the possibilities of the future. But then, like a proverbial breath of fresh air, the Fab Four arrived on the scene in February 1964, and a nation in mourning became transfixed by "I Want to Hold Your Hand" and the notion—pleasant relief that it was—of meeting the Beatles.

Their Englishness no doubt played a central role in their initial charm—their North Country accents soaring above a deft blend of Mersey beat music and African-American rhythm and blues. Armed with their ready wit and unflinching smiles, the Beatles were simply too much for Americans to resist. Overstating George Martin's role in fashioning the sound that first caught the attention of British and American ears, that transformed the Beatles into the stuff of history, is nearly impossible, of course. The A&R (Artists & Repertoire) men at Decca may have genuinely believed that guitar-oriented music was on its last legs, but Martin clearly heard something different in the unpolished, stage-honed thrashings of John, Paul, George, and Ringo. With his guidance, the Beatles dared to experiment with their sound, to revivify it with irony and nostalgia, to adorn it with a string quartet, a full-blown orchestra, and even a sitar. Martin afforded them with the courage and the knowledge to tinker with their sound as far as their artistry would take them. And, as history has shown, their fecund imaginations traversed well beyond the boundaries of their musicality, transmogrifying Western culture's conceptions of hope, love, and the idea—whimsical as it may seem—of an everlasting peace.

Reading the Beatles: Cultural Studies, Literary Criticism, and the Fab Four addresses the enduring nature of the band's many sociocultural achievements. But the volume also pointedly examines the Beatles' considerable *literary* accomplishments. And why not? Little argument exists among musicologists and literary critics alike about the Beatles' inherent literary qualities. After all, their songs—like our greatest works of literature—almost exclusively concern themselves with the human condition and the dilemmas that confront us regarding the interpersonal relationships that mark our lives. The Beatles' albums offer a range of decidedly literary characters, from Mean Mr. Mustard, Eleanor Rigby, and Polythene Pam to Billy Shears, Bungalow Bill, and Rocky

Raccoon. These personages, in addition to the psychological dimensions of the band members' personalities themselves, imbue their works with a particularly literary texture. "The Beatles treated the album as a journey from one place to another," Tim Riley observes. "They built cornerstones into their records by positioning their songs in relation to one another: beginnings and endings of sides can sum up, contradict, qualify, or cast a shadow over the songs they introduce or follow" (29–30). For this reason, one can hardly imagine hearing the final a cappella chords of "Because" without anticipating "You Never Give Me Your Money" and the bittersweet nostalgia of the symphonic suite that punctuates the end of the band's career on *Abbey Road*. Similarly, the manner in which "Drive My Car" and "Taxman" introduce *Rubber Soul* (1965) and *Revolver* (1966), respectively, not only signals us about the musical direction of various stages of the band's development, but also becomes inextricably bound up in our successive "listenings" (or readings) of those recordings. In short, the positioning of the Beatles' songs on their albums underscores the ways in which the band intended for us to receive—indeed, to interpret—their artistic output. Who could conceive, for example, of listening to the beginning of the *White Album* (*The Beatles*; 1968) and not hearing the soaring jet engines that announce the familiar opening strains of "Back in the U.S.S.R."?

Perhaps the band's abiding self-consciousness about the overall production, design, and presentation of their art invites us to read (and reread) the Beatles in the first place. From their heyday as recording artists from 1962 through 1969, the Beatles enjoyed a staggering musical and lyrical leap that takes them from their first album *Please Please Me* (1963), which they recorded in a mere sixteen hours, to *Sgt. Pepper's Lonely Hearts Club Band* (1967), the *White Album*, and *Abbey Road*, which took literally hundreds of hours to complete. Paul McCartney astutely recognized the artistic integrity of their musical oeuvre when he recently spoke of their albums as a singular and sacrosanct "body of work." When considered in this fashion, the Beatles' corpus reveals itself to be a collection of musical and lyrical impressions evolving toward an aesthetic unity that appears to reach its artistic heights during the late 1960s and the band's studio years. Numerous music critics echo McCartney's sentiments, including Ian MacDonald, who notes that "so obviously dazzling was the Beatles' achievement that few have questioned it." Their recordings, he adds, comprise "not only an outstanding repository of popular art but a cultural document of permanent significance" (1, 33). Riley similarly describes their canon as a "very intricate art. . . . The Beatles are our first recording *artists*," he writes, "and they remain our best" (9, 26; emphasis added). The chapters herein, with their emphasis on the literary, musicological, and ideological components of the band's phenomenal success, tell us why.

Divided into three parts, *Reading the Beatles* traces the sociocultural impact of the Beatles via their music's interdisciplinary connections with various modes of literary, musicological, and cultural criticism. The chapters in part one, titled "'Speaking words of wisdom': The Beatles' Poetics," examine the literary and musicological qualities of selected Beatles songs in relation to their social and cultural ramifications. In "'I am he as you are he as you are me and we are all together': Bakhtin and the Beatles," Ian Marshall draws on Mikhail M. Bakhtin's wide-ranging theories of dialogism in a reading of the formal structures inherent in the Beatles' poetics. In addition to applying Bakhtinian concepts such as novelization, chronotope, carnival, and genre blending to the Beatles' musical corpus, Marshall discusses the qualities of open-endedness and irresolution, in Bakhtin's phraseology, that characterize the band's evolving artistic legacy. In "From 'Craft' to 'Art': Formal Structure in the Music of the Beatles," John Covach demonstrates the ways in which early John Lennon–Paul McCartney compositions are closely dependent on models drawn from American music of the 1950s and early 1960s. Using models such as "From Me to You" and "I Want to Hold Your Hand," Covach chronicles the Beatles' musical development from "craft" to "rock" and sug-gests that such analysis forces us to rethink conventional accounts of rock style and its development—a point that extends well beyond the music of the Bea-tles in specific and rock music of the 1960s in general. Sheila Whiteley's "'Love, love, love': Representations of Gender and Sexuality in Selected Songs by the Beatles" explores the ways in which sex plays an integral role in the fanatic adoration of the Beatles by young, predominantly white girls caught up in the throes of Beatlemania. Drawing on recent insights in cultural sub-jectivity, sexuality, and gender, Whiteley investigates the relationship among musical, narrative, and lyrical focuses in representative songs throughout the Beatles' career. In "Painting Their Room in a Colorful Way: The Beatles' Exploration of Timbre," Walter Everett argues that the Beatles' recordings provide their listeners with vivid means for encountering both the inner and outer worlds of the human imagination. Everett highlights the band's use of tonal color, or timbre, as the mechanism via which the Beatles revivified the brilliant sensory world of their lyrics in their music.

The contributions in part two, "'A splendid time is guaranteed for all': Theorizing the Beatles," trace the development of the Beatles' artistry from their filmic efforts through classic works such as *Revolver*, *Sgt. Pepper*, and the *White Album*. Kenneth Womack and Todd F. Davis's "Mythology, Remythol-ogy, and Demythology: The Beatles on Film" examines the manner in which the band appropriated the power of Beatlemania and self-consciously estab-lished a cultural mythology to ensure their commercial and popular dominion. Womack and Davis discuss the infancy, maturity, and ultimate disillusionment the band experienced during the production of their four feature films—*A Hard Day's Night* (1964), *Help!* (1965), *Yellow Submarine* (1968), and *Let It Be* (1970)—as well as their television movie, *Magical Mystery Tour* (1967). In "*Vacio Luminoso:* 'Tomorrow Never Knows' and the Coherence of the Impos-sible," Russell Reising argues that *Revolver's* final track, the psychedelic

"Tomorrow Never Knows," affords the album with a sense of musical coherence by incorporating all of the album's major themes in a single song. Reising contends that the album's wide-ranging musical styles come together in a truly revolutionary fashion through the oscillating rhythms and themes inherent in "Tomorrow Never Knows." In "The Spectacle of Alienation: Death, Loss, and the Crowd in *Sgt. Pepper's Lonely Hearts Club Band*," William M. Northcutt discusses the Beatles' vastly influential album in terms of its overarching themes of sociocultural detachment and alienation. Northcutt devotes particular attention to the work's inherent "political unconscious," especially in terms of the ways in which *Sgt. Pepper* impinges on salient issues regarding class consciousness and class conflict. Jeffrey Roessner's "We All Want to Change the World: Postmodern Politics and the Beatles' *White Album*" illustrates the manner in which the album's radical eclecticism and self-reflexivity function as the band's attempt to adorn their work with a scathing political commentary. Roessner argues that the Beatles employed postmodern notions of pastiche and parody on the *White Album* in an effort to challenge the commodification of popular music and our larger assumptions about what constitutes political relevance during the late 1960s and beyond.

The chapters in part three, "We can work it out': The Beatles and Culture," explore the ways in which the band functions as a cultural, historical, and economic product that both adheres to and challenges established ideological norms. Paul Gleed's "'The rest of you, if you'll just rattle your jewelry': The Beatles and Questions of Mass and High Culture" investigates the many ways in which the Beatles' musical accomplishments blur existing distinctions between what constitute high and low forms of culture. In addition to demonstrating that the Beatles—through a process of "double-coding"—self-consciously merged divergent genres of musical expression such as classical and Eastern music, Gleed contends that this inventive and original approach to their art resulted in the band's virtual remapping of prevailing cultural value systems. In "A Universal Childhood: Tourism, Pilgrimage, and the Beatles," Kevin McCarron discusses the Fab Four's vaunted place in contemporary British tourism, especially in terms of the manner in which it serves to maintain their iconoclastic image and the myths associated with the story of Beatlemania. McCarron devotes particular attention to the quasi-religious dimensions of the band's legacy, as well as to England's Beatles shrines and the Beatles "pilgrims" who annually visit them. James M. Decker's "'Baby You're a Rich Man': The Beatles, Ideology, and the Cultural Moment" dissects the ideological and economic imperatives behind the band's dramatic resurgence in popularity during the late 1990s and the early years of the new century. In addition to investigating McCartney's considerable role in engineering the Beatles' revival, Decker highlights the ways in which McCartney, Ono, Harrison, and Starr marketed the band's artistic output for consumption by new generations of fans. In "Spinning the Historical Record: Lennon, McCartney, and Museum Politics," John Kimsey examines the recent museum exhibition, "Lennon: His Life and Work," along with McCartney's contemporaneous public activities in the light of an ongoing struggle over the meaning of, and the power to configure, the Beatles' historical legacy. Kimsey argues that the Lennon exhibition can be seen as working officially to confirm Lennon's status as cultural icon and martyr—to canonize him, in effect, as a pop-culture saint—while rewriting the popular narrative that depicts Lennon's Beatles work as the finest of his career and by reframing McCartney not as Lennon's greatest collaborator/rival, but as a relatively marginal figure in his artistic life. Finally, Jane Tompkins's Afterword, "I Want to Hold Your Hand," offers a poignant autobiographical account about the ways in which the Beatles afforded her with the self-actualizing means to become less alienated from popular culture, gender expectations, and herself during the early 1960s.

Part I

"Speaking words of wisdom"

The Beatles' Poetics

Chapter 1

"I am he as you are he as you are me and we are all together"

Bakhtin and the Beatles

IAN MARSHALL

AT FIRST, my favorite Beatle was Ringo, a fact that surprises me now. I was young, and I had watched the Beatles on the *Ed Sullivan Show*, and I think (now) that maybe Ringo was the first to make an individual impression. I mean, the concept of Beatles meant long hair, electric guitar, and Liverpool accent. John, Paul, and George ran together in my young mind (they are common names), but Ringo stood out—the name, the rings, the only one playing something other than guitar. Obviously, I was not alone in being quick to identify a favorite Beatle. Everyone did. Is it too much to say that your favorite Beatle was a teen and preteen version of a Rorschach test? It spoke volumes about who we were.

My Ringo phase did not last long. The appeal must have been his goofiness, and his grin, which were all a nine-year-old could hope to aspire to in terms of being cool. For a while after that it was John and Paul together—after all, they wrote the songs. That lasted through my first purchase of an album, *Sgt. Pepper*. After that it was George, and by that time it was becoming clearer to me what the appeal was. George was the unrecognized talent, the lead guitarist who was not the leader, writing great songs (by then) that nobody seemed to recognize as great songs, the one who was dealing with the really important stuff, such as the state of one's soul. He was like Superman springing from

Clark Kent, another "quiet one," and that was me, too, in my mind, a quiet one concerning myself with the spiritual essence of life, whose genius nobody yet recognized. In college, on my way to becoming an English major (and becoming interested in changing the world and finding out about the milder forms of mind alteration), my allegiances shifted to John. I admired his way with words, his intelligence, his social conscience, and his passion.

I imagine neither that my shifting identifications are universal, nor that my reasons for the identifications are unique, but I am struck, in the wake of George Harrison's death, by the numerous media references to George as the "quiet Beatle," the "spiritual one," or the mystical or soulful Beatle. John, of course, was the intellectual, the wordsmith, the activist. Paul was the cute one, the source of mellow melody to accompany John's hard-hitting rhythms and words, playing the role of heart to John's mind and George's soul. Ringo was the genial goofball with the easygoing, tolerant, accepting nature. A clear tendency exists to see the Beatles as distinct personality types or as different aspects of the self. Maybe a fully integrated self, or a functioning society, contains all of these, or allows for the interplay of these aspects. And perhaps it is that sort of interplay that accounts for some of the enduring appeal of Beatlemusic—and Beatlelyrics, too.

☜☞

Literary theorist Mikhail M. Bakhtin suggested that the magic of the novel derives from what he calls "dialogics." His claim is that the novel, above all other literary forms, is more open to various sorts of dialogue than other literary forms.

I must interrupt myself here: I have the Beatles playing in the background. My plan is to play all of their records (*Please Please Me* through *Abbey Road*) from start to finish as I write, so that I, too, engage in a kind of dialogue with the Beatles. "Chains," they are singing now, "my baby's got me locked up in chains." Bakhtin sees poetry as a literary form bound in chains. It is an inherently limited form notable for its lack of dialogue. What we generally get in poetry, says Bakhtin (and this would hold true for song lyrics as well) is the poet/songwriter's monologic voice—his worldview, his distinctive character, his thoughts expressed in his own voice. In the novel, by way of contrast, the author allows in other voices and language styles, the voices and language styles of the narrator and of all the other characters, each with their own worldviews implicit in their speech. But Bakhtin is not speaking of actual dialogue where characters speak within quotation marks. He shows that the narrator's voice takes on the inflections of other characters as the narrator moves in and out of different "character zones." In the novel, we have this constant interplay of voices and worldviews interacting with other voices and worldviews, as well as an openness to that sort of interplay.

A few literary critics have demonstrated that Bakhtin's generalizations about poetry's tendency toward the monologic voice are open to challenge. David B. Morris, for instance, in "Burns and Heteroglossia," has shown that Robert Burns blends the language styles of both Scots vernacular speech and the formal diction of the English poetic tradition. And Patrick Murphy, in "Reclaiming the Power: Robinson Jeffers's Verse Novels," contends that verse narratives, such as those by Robinson Jeffers, often take on novelistic and dialogic qualities.

My claim is that the Beatles also give voice to dialogic impulses, and that constitutes part of the appeal of their songs.

⊙╪☉

What I am not talking about is the fact that Lennon and McCartney cowrote many of the Beatles songs. As we now know, and as was in fact quite clear at the time, the later songs were not cowritten at all: they were Lennon songs and McCartney songs. And when John and Paul were actually writing together, in the early days, the result was the most insipid—and least dialogic—of their songs. It is a stretch even to call those early songs *mono*logic since lyrically not much of a distinctive voice at all lies behind the utterances. There is an "I" who pines after a "you," with the characters identified only by pronouns and little to distinguish the speaker from every other pining lover of pop rock, then and now.

But even as I write, I hear hints of more interesting ideas:

> There's a place where I can go
> When I feel low, when I feel blue
> And it's my mind, and there's no time
> When I'm alone.

The lyrics of "There's a Place" anticipate some of the later introspection of John, an investigation into personal pain and emptiness. So a dialogue is at work here: this voice out of the desert place of the soul meets the pop tradition's stock celebration of love:

> In my mind there's no sorrow,
> Don't you know that it's so,
> There'll be no sad tomorrow
> Don't you know that it's so.

In a few songs, conversations move beyond the uttered plea of the lover to the beloved. In "She Loves You," a third party serves as mediator in the relationship, convincing the lover that his case is not hopeless. It is a slightly more complex situation than is typical of the pop tradition, and a new voice, that of the helpfully interceding friend. Perhaps this song echoes some of the shared confidences of the Beatles during the Hamburg days, when their friendships were as tight as they would ever be.

But for the most part in these early songs, lyrically at least, we have just the monologic voice of the pop tradition's preoccupation with the idea of love, the idea, that is, and not a real love at all because neither the lover nor the beloved is distinguished by any hint of a developed character, nor is the romantic relationship distinguished by any particulars. I am also struck by the frequent use of the imperative in these early songs as well: "Please Please Me," "Love Me Do," "Don't Bother Me," and "Hold Me Tight." Such commands seem the essence of the monologic as the speaker seeks to assert the primacy of his wishes—and his worldview—through the agency of the compliant addressee.

So lyrically not much evidence of the possibilities of dialogism is seen in the early Beatles. But the music is another story. Think of the understated and tasteful restraint of George's lead guitar or Ringo's drums. I once heard folksinger Mike Cross talk about the purposes of different kinds of music. The purpose of bluegrass, he said, is to play everything as fast as you can ("A good bluegrass picker can take a three-minute song and get it over with in about fifteen seconds"). Jazz is about justifying your mistakes: you keep returning to the discordant notes as if you meant to put them there. And rock 'n' roll, says Cross, is all about finding excuses for totally irrelevant guitar solos and totally irrelevant drum solos. That is all too true of all too many rock 'n' roll bands, but not of the Beatles. We find no guitar and drum solos (not until "The End," at least)—nothing that is not integrated into the song. The lead guitar riffs are never allowed to go on long enough to take over the song or to dominate it. Nor are the drums just keeping the beat. Interesting things are often happening on the offbeat in Beatles songs. Nor does Paul's bass simply keep beat. It is a very melodic bass, which Paul once attributed to the light weight of his violin-shaped Höfner bass, which he said had a "liberating effect . . . because it's so light you treat it more like a guitar. I found I became more melodic on bass than other bass-players because I could do lots of high stuff on the twelfth fret. Being melodic in my writing, it was good not always to have to play the root notes" (*Anthology* 80).

In addition to the guitars and drums, of course, we hear the distinctive voices of John and Paul. Musically, then, even in the early Beatles, instruments and voices with recognizable personalities blend in a kind of conversation, none of them dominating. But the lyrics were not yet very distinctive—or dialogic.

❧

Help! and (even more so) *Rubber Soul* marked the beginnings of the most striking Beatles innovations, and many of those can be understood in terms of Bakhtin's dialogics. Specific Bakhtinian ideas evident in the songs of the Beatles from *Help!* forward are genre blending, novelization, intertextuality, open-endedness, carnival, the chronotope, and character zones. Let us consider these Bakhtinian concepts one at a time.

GENRE BLENDING

Bakhtin's admiration for the dialogics of the novel is based in large part on its elasticity in absorbing or incorporating other literary genres. The Beatles did something similar with the popular song. Of course, rock 'n' roll has always had some genre blending, growing, as it has, out of the rhythm-and-blues tradition. But the Beatles did more than anyone before (or since) to blend other traditions with rock 'n' roll.

Perhaps this is the most striking element of Beatles dialogics: their openness to musical genres and the language styles associated with those genres. Although the Beatles' first few albums were solidly in the context of the pop tradition, later albums are marked by a wide range of explorations into other musical genres, as well as a massive incorporation of them into rock 'n' roll. On songs such as "You've Got to Hide Your Love Away"—the acoustic guitar, the tone of a line such as "Gather round all you clowns"—we can hear the influence of Bob Dylan. Perhaps we also hear Dylan's influence in John's early expressions of soul searching and personal pain in "I'm a Loser" and "Help!" It was revolutionary in the mid-1960s for rock music to look inward so searchingly, to express emotions such as self-doubt, self-loathing, ennui—to express anything beyond love, yearning, recrimination, or misery. Of course, this may seem anything but dialogic (more like the height of monologism to deal with ego as John does), but he is bringing this self-searching into contact with the rock tradition. There is the dialogue—confessional poetry meets rock 'n' roll. One of John's early ventures in this vein, "Nowhere Man," can in fact be read (or heard) as a complaint about the constraints of the monologic. The Nowhere Man, kin to one of Thoreau's "mass of men [who] lead lives of quiet desperation," according to John's critique of conformity, "Just sees what he wants to see," or worse, "Doesn't have a point of view." John's songwriting voice would become increasingly expressive of a particular point of view, and increasingly it would attempt to encompass seeing things from other viewpoints. "Nowhere Man, please listen," sings John. "You don't know what you're missing." What he is missing is the sound of other voices, an awareness of other points of view.

In acknowledging Dylan's influence on "You've Got to Hide Your Love Away," John said it "was written in my Dylan days for the film *Help!* I am like a chameleon, influenced by everything that's going [on]" (qtd. in Giuliano 1999, 56). George says something similar about all the Beatles songwriters (meaning himself and Paul as well as John). Referring to the days circa *Sgt. Pepper*, George said, "We were all opening our minds to different areas, and then we'd come together and share it all with each other. It was exciting, because there was a lot of cross-fertilization" (*Anthology* 241).

George's intellectual exploration, of course, led him to the East. In John's "Norwegian Wood (This Bird Has Flown)" *(Rubber Soul)*, we have an introduction to Indian music and a blending of that music with Western traditions, an intergenre dialogue that would continue in greater depth on later albums. Here, George plays the sitar as if it were a lead guitar, using the Western chromatic scale, but it is certainly a new voice being brought into conversation with pop music. On later albums, the dialogue with the Indian musical tradition would deepen with George's acquaintance with that tradition. On "Lucy in the Sky with Diamonds" *(Sgt. Pepper)*, George has said that he was imitating "an instrument called a sarangi, which sounds like the human voice." George wanted to incorporate the practice of the sarangi playing in unison with the vocalist, "but because I'm not a sarangi player I played it on the guitar. In the middle eight of the song you can hear the guitar playing along with John's voice. I was trying to copy Indian classical music" (*Anthology* 243). In "Within You Without You," George and musicians from the Eastern Music Circle of London do play Indian instruments—tambouras, tabla, bowed dilruba, sitar—and they share acoustic space with violins and cellos. The raga meets Western classical music—on a rock 'n' roll record.

Obviously, plenty of other Beatle songs incorporated Indian instruments and techniques, but the influence was more than just musical. A whole worldview associated with transcendental meditation, and a language associated with it as well, became an integral component of Beatles music. Consider the reference to maya (the illusion of what we take to be reality) in these lines from "Within You Without You":

> We were talking about the space between us all
> And the people who hide themselves behind a wall of illusion,
> Never glimpse the truth.

But the dialogue continued even beyond the songs incorporating Indian sounds and techniques. After bringing Eastern ideas and values into contact with the musical (and cultural) traditions of the West, a time came when the Beatles, or at least John, challenged those ideas and values. And so we have the harsh rejection of Maharishi Mahesh Yogi in "Sexy Sadie," a scornful and angry response to what John saw as the Maharishi's hypocrisy. During their extended stay with the Maharishi, while he preached otherworldliness and the life of spirit during the day, he was hitting on the women traveling with the

Beatles at night. So we see a range of response to the worldview of transcendental meditation, from listening to it and engaging with it, to talking back to it—and telling off the Maharishi.

As several critics have pointed out (Whitley, Schaffner, Kozinn), the *White Album* marks the high point of the Beatles' borrowings from a variety of genres—the calypso sound of "Ob-La-Di, Ob-La-Da" (or as Stewart Copeland from the Police terms it, "one of the first examples of white reggae" [Giuliano 124]); a lullaby in "Good Night"; a quasi-children's song in "The Continuing Story of Bungalow Bill"; country and western in "Rocky Raccoon"; the blues in "Yer Blues"; the 1920's music hall sound of "Honey Pie" (the latter complete with scratches as on an old 78 rpm recording); the Baroque-sounding "Martha My Dear," or as John termed those songs, Paul's "fucking Cole Porter routine" (qtd. in Giuliano 1999, 125); the Beach Boys sound (with a nod to Chuck Berry's "Back in the U.S.A.") in "Back in the U.S.S.R." Ed Whitley terms the harpsichord on George's "Piggies" "pseudo-Baroque" and points out that "Blackbird" and "Mother Nature's Son" imitate "the folk sound" of Dylan and Joan Baez (112). John claimed that the three stanzas of "Happiness Is a Warm Gun"—which his notes label "Dirty old man," "the junkie," and "the gunman"—manage "to run through all the different kinds of rock music" (*Anthology* 307, 306). All of which gives the album an "irreducible plurality" that adds up to what Whitley calls "bricolage," a term that, in Jean-François Lyotard's usage, refers to "the multiple quotation of elements taken from earlier styles or periods" (110, 108). The avant-garde *musique concrète* of "Revolution 9," with the blended loops of people screaming, bits of classical music, and other things that John found in the studio archives, is itself pure bricolage (albeit a not always musical one), mirroring the form of the album as a whole.

Whitley argues convincingly that the extensive use of bricolage makes the *White Album* a postmodern work, with the Beatles using fragmentation and blended genres to deliberately evade the possibility of unity and monolithic meaning, and to offer instead multiple meanings and a space for the listener's reflection on just what constitutes rock 'n' roll. It denies the apparent unity of, say, *Sgt. Pepper*. The postmodernity of the *White Album* is entirely compatible with Bakhtinian dialogics; the *White Album* offers multiple voices and world-views in place of a single privileged voice.

Notice what underlies such commentaries on the album as a work of art: it assumes that the album, not the song or the live performance of selected songs or a film that features the songs, is the work of art. The advent of *Rubber Soul*—and, pointedly, once the Beatles had stopped touring and the films *A Hard Day's Night* and *Help!* were in the can—was the impetus for the band to convene to record the new songs that they had written. And we should remember that this was a new phenomenon in pop music. Previously, the single was the primary means of packaging and selling songs. Although the

Beatles still released singles, we came to recognize their albums as their principal form, as the ultimate goal for their artistic output. Among other things, their songs, other than the released singles, garnered widespread recognition for the first time and could no longer be considered throwaways; some of their finest music was the "other stuff" on the album. This is an important step for the artistry of the Beatles, and it, too, opened up a space for the introduction of the dialogic element. The individual song may make a statement, but an album can constitute a whole speech or a drama or a story. The song may present a vignette; the album can piece those vignettes together to make a novelistic collage. This is not to say that the albums after *Rubber Soul* were conceived of as unified works. John claimed that even the unifying threads of *Sgt. Pepper* and *Magical Mystery Tour* were, at best, pretty thin. But the album was the occasion for the making of music; it became the performance. And the people buying the albums conceived of them as the artistic work, as we still do today, so we see reviews of new albums and CDs, not (usually) individual songs. Our assumption is that together the songs make a statement, even if that statement is that the multiple voices and views presented therein do not add up to a single assertion. In a sense, the *White Album*'s refusal to issue a unified view contributes to a dialogue on the medium itself. *Sgt. Pepper*, hailed as the first concept album, suggests that the songs of an album add up to a unified and coherent whole. The *White Album* offers a rebuttal.

INTERTEXTUALITY

Related to the idea of genre blending is the concept of intertextuality, whereby one text makes reference to another, responding to it, engaging it in dialogue. In a sense, all texts are in dialogue with all other texts; a Beatles song, for instance, can be seen as engaging in dialogue with a Shakespearean sonnet because the Beatles, in writing the song, are writing in a poetic climate touched by the sonnet, even if they had not read the sonnet. Looked at another way, we can read the song in the context of the sonnet, even if only to point out how unsonnetlike a song may be. But most texts engage in more immediate sorts of dialogue, referencing the works that the writers are consciously influenced by or are responding to, and that is the case with the Beatles. For the Beatles many of the texts that they engaged in dialogue with were other songs, often their own, and many were literary texts. And again this was revolutionary in rock 'n' roll. As of the early and mid-1960s, the folk movement could comfortably situate itself in a literary context, but that context had not yet been introduced to rock 'n' roll.

The literary reference points of the Beatles are many, and again, the references become more apparent post–*Rubber Soul*. In many cases the intertextuality is more outright borrowing or incorporation than mere reference. "Tomorrow Never Knows" *(Revolver)*, where John encourages the listener to "Turn off your mind, / Relax, and float downstream," is taken from the drug-use instructions in Timothy Leary's *The Psychedelic Experience*, itself a response to or an interpretation of the *Tibetan Book of the Dead*'s guide to spiritual bliss. John's "Julia" (on the *White Album*) is taken from Kahlil Gibran, Paul's "Golden Slumbers" *(Abbey Road)* from a poem by Thomas Dekker. And "Being for the Benefit of Mr. Kite" *(Sgt. Pepper)* comes from an old circus poster. Said John, "I hardly made up a word, just connecting the lists together. Word for word, really" *(Anthology* 243). One of the things Bakhtin admired about novels is the remarkable freedom and flexibility evident in that sort of incorporation of other texts, and the Beatles brought the same freedom to the popular song. In the hands and voices of the Beatles, rock music became an expansive enough medium to become a container for ideas encountered elsewhere and a gathering place for phrases from offbeat corners of the culture.

Usually the literary references are fleeting or subtle. George has said that "While My Guitar Gently Weeps" emerged from his reading of the *I Ching*'s "Book of Changes":

> In the West we think of coincidence as something that just happens—it just happens that I am sitting here and the wind is blowing in my hair, and so on. But the Eastern concept is that whatever happens is all meant to be, and that there's no such thing as coincidence—every little item that's going down has a purpose.
>
> "While My Guitar Gently Weeps" was a simple study based on that theory. I decided to write a song based on the first thing I saw upon opening any book—as it would be relative to that moment, at that time. I picked up a book at random, opened it, saw "gently weeps," then laid the book down again and started the song. *(Anthology* 306)

Several of John's songs reveal the influence of Lewis Carroll—no surprise to anyone who has encountered the mad wordplay of John's prose in *In His Own Write* and *A Spaniard in the Works*. John said the images in "Lucy in the Sky with Diamonds" come from *Alice in Wonderland*: "It was Alice in the boat. She is buying an egg and it turns into Humpty Dumpty. The woman serving in the shop turns into a sheep and I was visualizing that" (qtd. in Giuliano 90). So, too, does "I Am the Walrus" come from *Alice*, specifically from "The Walrus and the Carpenter." These sorts of allusions often suggest a deeper level of dialogue between the texts, and in this case, as Walter Everett points out, the reference to *Alice* is thematically pertinent. John's statement that "I am he as you are he as you are me and we are all together" is reminiscent of Alice's identity crisis in *Adventures through the Looking-Glass*, when she asks, "*Was* I the same when I got up this morning? . . . I'm sure I'm not Ada . . . and I'm sure

I can't be Mabel. . . . Besides, *she's* she, and *I'm* I. . . . Who am I, then?" (qtd. in Everett 135). John's answer suggests that Alice *is* Mabel *and* Ada, that self and identity are relational, and so dialogue with others, textual or not, is a means of self-exploration. The Alice books are also evoked in John's statement, "I am the eggman," which suggests Humpty-Dumpty, and of course the song is full of Humpty-Dumpty-like riddles and inspired nonsense.

Often the literary incorporations of the Beatles are not heard directly in the lyrics but in the background soundtrack that sets the milieu for the lyrics. In "I Am the Walrus," snippets of a BBC radio broadcast of Shakespeare's *King Lear* play in the background. The excerpt is of Oswald's death, "a serviceable villain," says Edgar, "As duteous to the vices of thy mistress / As badness would desire" (IV.vi.255–57). And of course we find villains serviceable enough vilified in the song, among them the "expert textperts" (that would be us literary critics) who are guilty of "kicking Edgar Allan Poe." Everett points out that in the play this excerpt is preceded by Edgar's comment on Lear's speech as consisting of "matter and impertinency mixed! Reason in madness!"—a fair indication of John's lyrical strategy in the song (135). John typically scoffed at those who found deeper meanings in his lyrics, pretending that the words were simply impertinent (if delightful) nonsense. But clearly we find much reason amid the song's madness. The Alice and Lear allusions reinforce the song's themes and give literary precedent for the seemingly nonsensical style.

Most often the Beatles engaged in dialogue with their reading from periodicals and newspapers. The title of "Happiness Is a Warm Gun" came from a magazine cover, but in the song the warm gun becomes the stuff of a sexual pun rather than a tool of violence. Paul's "Lovely Rita" came from a newspaper story about a retiring meter maid. If John deflates an image of violence with sexual wordplay in "Happiness Is a Warm Gun," Paul deflates officialdom with a similar strategy in "Lovely Rita." In a comment on the song's origin, Paul gives it a salacious twist: "to me a 'maid' was always a little sexy thing: 'Meter maid. Hey, come and check my meter, baby'" (*Anthology* 247).

Of course the Beatles' most famous newspaper borrowing came in "A Day in the Life," inspired by items in the London *Daily Mail*, which John says was "propped in front of me on the piano. I had it open at their News in Brief, or Far and Near, whatever they call it. I noticed two stories. One was about the Guinness heir who killed himself in a car. That was the main headline story. He died in London in a car crash. . . . On the next page was a story about 4,000 potholes in the streets of Blackburn, Lancashire" (*Anthology* 247). Dialogue enters in because a voice and a life exist in encountering these bits of news. The opening line, "I read the news today," ends with an "oh, boy," and that "oh, boy" suggests a response to the news of the death—a response combining elements of sympathy and despair. It's a solemn "oh, boy," as in "what a world," or a quiet, detached "oh, no." And of course there's the bridge where we see the everyday activities of a narrator, waking up, combing his hair, catching a bus, smoking a cigarette, dreaming of a sexual encounter. This is our life, inside and out. The juxtaposition of the news of the day with the life of the narrator, and his suggested response to the news, brings to my mind two poems: Edwin Arlington Robinson's "Richard Cory," which has the same sort of ironic envy of a rich man's life, and W. H. Auden's "Musée des Beaux Artes," about how everyday lives go on amid extraordinarily tragic events. Neither poem is explicitly invoked by the song, of course, but the comparisons do suggest something of the richness of the poetic situations of the best of the Beatles, in this case because of the situated voice responding to the events and the printed source that inspired the song.

Of course, the Beatles also engaged in dialogue with nonliterary sources, and often those came from music. The Beach Boy harmonies of "Back in the U.S.S.R." bring a quintessentially American sound into dialogue with a worldview and political system that is usually deemed counter to all that is American. The celebration of national landscapes ("Show me round your snow-peaked mountains way down south"), the rural life ("Take me to your daddy's farm"), traditional folkways ("Let me hear your balalaikas ringing out"), and womanly resources ("That Georgia's always on my mind"—and notice the punning reference to the shared geography of a Georgia in both the United States and the U.S.S.R.)—all these could be right out of an all-American songbook. It's a way of saying that there's a lot of the United States in the U.S.S.R. ("Back in the U.S., back in the U.S., back in the U.S.S.R.") and of suggesting that there should be more dialogue between the two countries.

"Yer Blues" makes reference to another of the Beatles' influences when John sings that he's feeling "just like Dylan's Mr. Jones—I'm lonely, want to die." The reference is to "Ballad of a Thin Man," where Dylan says, "There's something happening here, and you don't know what it is, / Do you, Mr. Jones?" His Mr. Jones is an uncomprehending soul, unable to make sense of the bizarreness around him. At one point he cries out, "Oh my God, am I here all alone?" Again, the borrowing is pertinent, suggesting a source of John's blues. At the same time, John responds on behalf of the Mr. Joneses of the world. Dylan seems to be attacking Jones, mocking his inability to make sense of the world's craziness. Lennon sings "Yer Blues" for the Joneses, giving voice to their anguish and bewilderment.

The Beatles' most frequent musical references are to their own works, exemplified in "Glass Onion," which includes allusions to five other Beatles songs ("Strawberry Fields Forever," "I Am the Walrus," "Lady Madonna," "Fixing a Hole," and "The Fool on the Hill"). To some extent, the song is a put-on, a joke at the expense of those who insist on seeking deeper meanings in Beatles lyrics. But the image of an onion is arresting: it consists of layer within layer. Peel all the layers back and there's nothing at the center. The onion consists of the layers themselves. And, of course, it is a "glass" onion, presumably transparent. So the message, perhaps, is that the message is not hidden inside the songs—the message is the songs themselves. And "Glass Onion" is itself another layer, added to the previous layer, just as is every dialogic utterance.

NOVELIZATION

Bakhtin claimed that the novel was so important a genre that its techniques would inevitably find their way into other genres, a process he called *novelization*. And part of the interest of Beatles lyrics is their success in bringing storytelling tactics to the popular song. These techniques begin to appear as early as 1965 in *Rubber Soul*. If there were still some conventional songs such as "You Won't See Me," "Drive My Car," and "Run for Your Life," where again the characterization goes no further than pronouns, songs with more particularized visions of romance were also included. In "Michelle," in many ways a conventional pop love song ("I love you, I love you, I love you"), the object of affection is now particularized with an actual name and with a particularized background that calls for a new mode of address: in French. New situations are entering the tradition, and we perceive a sense that new voices are needed to address those situations.

Novelistic particularization is evident in the vignettes that begin to enter Beatles songs around this time, little slices of life that are the essence of the novel. In "Norwegian Wood" we get details—quickly sketched, but details nonetheless—of character, setting, and a plot of sorts. The scene is a woman's apartment, unfurnished. She tells the narrator to "sit anywhere," but he notices, "there wasn't a chair." His motives are clear when he says he sits on her rug, "drinking her wine, biding my time." They talk "until two, and then she said, 'It's time for bed.'" For a moment, it seems his seduction will be a success, but then we learn otherwise:

> She told me she worked in the morning and started to laugh,
> I told her I didn't and crawled off to sleep in the bath.

This is a strange little love story, and that is part of the point. We can think of this as part of a dialogue with the pop-romance tradition, deflating the conventions and reworking them with wry realism. This, of course, has traditionally been the novel's function: to address the excesses of romance with some of the deflations of realism. Even the first line of "Norwegian Wood" indicates a shift from the normative pop romance: "I once had a girl, or should I say she once had me?" Note the wordplay here, the "having" suggesting both sexual conquest (of lover as possession, the sort of love spoken of in "Run for Your Life" and most pop romances) and, as it turns out, also "having someone on" or playing a trick on them. In this case, he who would "have" the girl is had. But he was a bit of a cad anyway, not the pop romance's usual idealized lover. And the beloved has such realistic characteristics as a bare apartment and a job she has to get to in the morning. Their little affair also ends with a deflation of expectations. The love, unidealized and sexualized as it is, is not necessarily consummated. In the pop romance, unachieved love can only be cause for anguish. But here, the would-be lover seems to accept his banishment from bed to bathtub with something akin to aplomb:

> And when I awoke I was alone, this bird had flown.
> So I lit a fire, isn't it good, Norwegian Wood.

In its particularization of character and setting, its details seemingly drawn from real life, and real lives, in its deflation of the conventions of romance: in all these ways the song has something in common with the novel.

John's renderings of novelistic vignettes continued to appear in later Beatles albums. On *Revolver*'s "She Said She Said," he builds a song around a snippet of conversation from a party. The key line, "I know what it's like to be dead," was apparently lifted from a hallucinogen-inspired dialogue with Peter Fonda. John's response at the time was, "Who put all that shit in your head?" On *Sgt. Pepper*, of course, we get John's most famous vignette in song, "A Day in the Life," with its novelistic fascination for some of the gory details of a car accident.

Although John was the actual writer of the group (the pun-filled *In His Own Write* and *A Spaniard in the Works*), Paul was the more consciously novelistic in his approach to songwriting, evident in his adoption of the "Paperback Writer" persona. On *Revolver*'s "Eleanor Rigby," he offers novelistic character sketches of both Eleanor Rigby, picks "up rice in a church where a wedding has been," and Father McKenzie, "darning his socks in the night when there's nobody there." Their stories merge in the final verse, with Father McKenzie "wiping the dirt from his hands as he walks from [her] grave." Without the closely observed particularity of the images that sketch these characters, the song's theme ("Ah, look at all the lonely people") might have been trite and unconvincing.

Paul's "dime-store fiction approach to songs," as Giuliano calls it, "whose characters included meter maids, mailmen, and secretaries," is consistently evident on *Sgt. Pepper*, most notably in the persons of Lovely Rita, bandleader Billy Shears, and the unnamed protagonist of "She's Leaving Home" (93).[1] In fact Paul, in describing the concept of *Sgt. Pepper*, said it was "like writing your novel" (Martin, "Making of *Sgt. Pepper*"). Mainly he was referring to the adoption of "an alter-ego band," a group persona: "We would be Sgt. Pepper's band, and for the whole of the album we'd pretend to be someone else. So, when John walked up to the microphone to sing, it wouldn't be the new John

Lennon vocal, it would be whoever he was in this new group, his fantasy character. It liberated you—you could do anything when you got to the mike or on
your guitar, because it wasn't *you*" (*Anthology* 241). This is not far from
Bakhtin's conception of the novel as the literary form that, above all others,
makes space for narrators and characters to speak for themselves and that
requires the author to relinquish his voice to allow narrators and characters
their space and their voice.

Consider the mininovel "She's Leaving Home," a song that, musically,
always struck me as too sentimental.[2] But lyrically it offers a fascinating and
complex interplay of voices and narratives. In the first verse, Paul sings in the
third person about the girl leaving home, leaving a note "that she hoped would
say more," tiptoeing downstairs in the early morning "clutching her handkerchief," turning her key in the door. Like a fiction writer, he selects telling
moments and details to propel the story. The second verse shifts to a narrative
description of the parents' reaction: while the father snores, mother discovers
the note as she stands "alone, at the top of the stairs." Although this is ostensibly in the third person, the "alone" gives us a flash of the mother's perspective; Bakhtin would say the narrative voice slips into her "character zone." In
the next line, "she breaks down," and the "down" follows from her precarious
position at "the top of the stairs," as if she has taken a fall, which metaphori-
cally, if not physically, she has. Much of the language here, although not spoken directly by the mother, reflects her perspective. Similarly, the final comment at the end of the first verse enters into the character zone of the girl:
"Stepping outside she is free." The third verse reverts to the perspective of the
girl, "meeting a man from the motor trade," apparently running away with
him, and now, for the first time, "she's having fun."

Whereas Paul advances the plot in the third-person narrative of the
verses, a perspective maintained in the background of each chorus as he sings,
"She's leaving home," John sings a series of choruses that present the view-
point of the parents in first-person plural: "We gave her most of our lives, sac-
rificed most of our lives." And so we have contrapuntal narratives—the girl's,
the parents'.

What is really interesting (and characteristically novelistic) is that both
narrative voices, both perspectives, may be unreliable. The directly reported
dialogue of the mother on finding the note exposes the selfishness of their
perspective: "Why would she treat us so thoughtlessly," she asks, "How could
she do this to me?" The mother's self-orientation is telling, as if running away
is something the girl has done *to* her parents and not *for* herself. In the first-
person plural utterances of the choruses we find that the parents, in their
attempt to comprehend, focus mainly on their self-sacrifice and expenditures
("We struggled hard all our lives to get by"; "We gave her everything money
could buy"). Thus, they are revealed as self-centered and materialistic. At the
same time, we have reason to question the third-person narration's apparent

celebration of the girl's newfound freedom and fun because between the freedom of leaving home and the fun of meeting her man, we have the touching scene of the parents feeling the pain of their loss. Although we may perceive their faults even more clearly than they do, we most likely sympathize with them when, after asking, "What did we do that was wrong," their defense is understandable: "We didn't know it was wrong." But then the parents come around to recognition: "Fun is the one thing that money can't buy."

The effect of the dual (and, to some extent, dueling) narratives here is that we are able to sympathize with both the girl and the parents and to judge each party negatively. Sympathy versus judgment at odds with one another: this has traditionally been the novel's classic tension.

OPEN-ENDEDNESS

When Bakhtin speaks of the novelization of other genres, he stresses that the most important element of that novelization is the presence of "indeterminacy, a certain semantic open-endedness" ("Epic" 7). This concept is sometimes translated as "inconclusiveness" or "unfinalizability," referring to a kind of irresolution or lack of closure that reflects the unfinished nature of real life and suggests that the dialogue the text initiated can and should continue. The author's last word in the text is not the final word regarding the topic. Even early on, and even more so later on, Beatles songs typically remain openended. In "I Don't Want to Spoil the Party," the narrator announces his intention to leave a party where the object of his attention has failed to show. We never learn why (the background story behind the narrator's apparent rejection and sense of dejection remains forever obscured in the song's margins), and we never learn the outcome. Although he says, "If she turns up while I'm gone, please let me know," we do not know whether she turns up. Or think of the story in "Norwegian Wood"; full of particularized images instead of abstractions as it is, the story has no resolution. Is this love? Will they be together? Was the affair consummated? None of this is clear. That lack of resolution is one of the things that Bakhtin identifies as the mark of dialogism, requiring the reader to enter into the text to wonder about and fill the gaps in the narrative.

The classic instance of irresolution in a Beatles song is perhaps best exemplified by "Revolution," where John sings, "But if you talk about destruction, don't you know that you can count me out," but following the "out," like an inverse echo, comes the word "in." John says, "I put in both because I wasn't sure" (*Anthology* 298). The listener, hoping to be told how to proceed to enact the revolution in question, is left equally unsure, or at least no direction is spelled out for us; we must decide for ourselves whether we are out or in on the question of violence as a means to bring about revolution.

Beatles songs are full of such spaces where the reader must enter to provide answers or, often, sense. John has spoken disparagingly of his nonsensical, imagistic lyrics in songs such as "I Am the Walrus": "In those days I was writing obscurely, à la Dylan, never saying what you mean but giving the *impression* of something, where more *or* less can be read into it. It's a good game" (*Anthology* 273). John may belittle his songwriting practice, but his description of it suggests exactly the attraction of those Dylanesque, image-laden songs. To say exactly what you mean would be monologic; to give the impression of something means that the writer will use the sort of language that makes an impression—concrete, sensory, imagistic language—and the reliance on impression rather than direct statement requires the reader to sort out the significance of the image, to read something into it, more or less. It is indeed a good game: "You just stick a few images together, thread them together, and you call it poetry" (273). Precisely. And if the images are interesting enough, fresh enough, it is poetry, which shares (or exceeds) the novel's tendency to rely on language gaps that require the reader's involvement to complete the making of sense from language.

But, of course, the novel plays with open-endedness not simply in terms of playful language but in unresolved situations, where competing worldviews speak and neither (or none of many) emerges as the dominant voice. In his study of "The Postmodern *White Album*," Whitley points out that the *White Album* relies on "plural perspectives, based on multiple narratives," which "generate discourse between the reader and the text, because when a text does not explicitly spell out its meaning, a place develops for the reader to contribute to the production of meaning" (106). And so "Dear Prudence" can be read as either "a call to spiritual awakening" or "a sexual proposition" (118). "I'm So Tired" could be "the yearning of the disenchanted transcendentalist" or "the complaining of a forlorn lover" (119). "Helter Skelter," "rebellious rock and roll," judging by the shrieking voices and guitars, or "a children's song," with lyrics about riding a slide (119–20). "Happiness Is a Warm Gun" is both an "anti-gun tract" and a sexual come-on (120). And so on. Even the blank cover of the *White Album*, notes Whitley, serves as "a *tabula rasa* that shifts the center of meaning from the text itself and onto the readers" (108). Whitley is pointing out that the *White Album* honors the postmodern view of the world in which meaning is constantly deferred, but the point is similar to the irresolution of which Bakhtin speaks.

Of course, the strategy is not limited to the *White Album*. To offer just one other example: on *Sgt. Pepper*'s "A Day in the Life" we are told neither what to make of the images taken from the news of the day, nor how we should respond to them. Keep going on with our daily routines, dragging combs across our heads and having smokes on the bus? Escape into dreams? Give up in despair? A Beatles song offers not the pontificating of a sermon, but the open-endedness of dialogue where the next word is the reader's.

The irresolution of the lyrics is often reinforced by the music. Ken Womack, in conversation, has pointed out to me that many Beatles songs work by creating a musical dilemma; they establish a problem and try to "work it out." In the *White Album*'s "Sexy Sadie," for instance, the lead guitar and piano work together musically, making upward steps toward a key change but never seeming to arrive at the next logical note—they tease us with that note, the progression being repeated but unresolved when the guitar takes us close to that note, arriving there only at the end of the song. And yet, there is still no final resolution because that note becomes the opening note of the next song, "Helter Skelter." And then "Helter Skelter" resists closure by seeming to come to an end three times, first reaching a concluding note before continuing, then fading to silence and coming back again, finally ending only with Ringo crying out, "I got blisters on my fingers!" It is not, it seems, the internal dynamics of the song that lead to an ending, or some sort of organic structure inherent in the music that requires a certain ending, but simply the musicians running out of gas or solid flesh. Open-endedness is reinforced, too, in songs that continue past their apparent ending. Think of the extended coda to "Hey Jude," or the forty-five-second sustaining chord at the end of "A Day in the Life," or the repeating run-out groove afterward, so that, on a manual turntable at least, the record is never over until you say it is over and lift the stylus. On *Abbey Road*, "I Want You (She's So Heavy)" ends abruptly in mid-bar, concluding side one of the album. The effect is, as Everett puts it, that "we don't really know *where* the song ends, as we don't feel we've heard an ending" (*Revolver* 256). On side two, too, the songs do not end tidily because we have the medley of songs from "You Never Give Me Your Money" through "The End," and, of course, "The End" does not come at the end. "Her Majesty" does, but the final chord of the song is chopped off from the end, and it actually appears buried under the opening chord of "Polythene Pam." Both lyrically and musically, then, Beatles songs resist closure.

CARNIVAL

Because the novel, according to Bakhtin in "Forms of Time and of the Chronotope in the Novel," allows for the interplay of many voices and worldviews, it often takes on a carnival atmosphere. Often the incorporation of carnival elements is quite explicit, involving festival scenes. Of course, the carnival element is often metaphoric as well, and the spirit of carnival is represented, or included, via carnival-like or festival-like events. Carnival emerged from the harvest celebration, and it is a celebration of abundance, indulgence, and license—even licentiousness, indecency, and insolence. It is a celebration of the spirit and life of the people, a time of mischief and good humor, unpredictability, with a touch of madness to it all. Carnival is not

something to be viewed from the outside; no spectator sport, it involves participation from within. Often there is a putting-on of masks, perhaps an
attempt to absolve one's "real" self from the unbridled play and tricksterism
and licentiousness of one's actions during carnival. But carnival also engages
serious themes, frequently involving the recognition of the reality of death and
our fear of death in the midst of a celebration of life and the spirit of renewal
and the possibility (or the certainty, even) of revival. There can be a merging
of the self with the natural world or with cosmic and universal forces.

Carnival also has a political element. It arises from the people, as opposed
to being put on by the state or sanctioned by the state. In fact, carnival is an
opportunity to challenge established authority. It is subversive and antiestablishment, breaking down codes of class and privilege. Carnival admits the
voices of the lower class and allows them to talk back to officialdom.

It is difficult to find an element of carnival that is not part of the Beatles'
whole shtick, and it all became rock 'n' roll's. These tendencies in rock 'n' roll
cannot be attributed exclusively to the Beatles' influence, but clearly they had
a huge impact in making rock music the literature of the masses and in promoting its ethos of talking back to authority and celebrating release from constraining cultural norms. What is surprising is not the extent to which the
Beatles adopted or expressed carnival's spirit of license and its antiestablishment stance, but the extent to which they consciously incorporated carnival as
a motif in their albums after they stopped performing live. When they were
performing in concert, of course, there was Beatlemania, the quintessence of
carnival arising from the people, shrieking fans who were out of control, seemingly out of their minds, some reportedly screaming and squirming themselves to orgasm while they watched. And then, gasp, growing their hair long,
experimenting with drugs, speaking out against war, celebrating free love—all
in the face of scowling authority.

The antiestablishment tone had become prominent by *Revolver*, released
in 1966 right around the time of their final concert performances. "Tomorrow
Never Knows" reflects the influence of LSD, and the lack of a rhyme scheme
suggests its breaking from societal strictures. "Doctor Robert" contains even
more overt drug references. "I'm Only Sleeping" complains about the bustle of
contemporary society, whereas "Eleanor Rigby" exposes the sad emptiness of
ordinary lives in our culture. Even "Taxman," featuring a wealthy man complaining about high taxes, passes itself off as an antiestablishment song, skew-
ering the government. From *Revolver* on, examples could be endless. The
Beatles celebrate love and peace and freedom, the pursuit of spiritual fulfill-
ment, self-expression, and sex, drugs and rock 'n' roll, and decry war and violence, materialism, conformity, hierarchy, and authority. One would be hard
put to find a song that is not consistent with these values, and of course they
were adopted as the values of the 1960s, and of a large portion of the generation who came of age during that era.

Almost instinctively, the Beatles drew on carnival motifs as a means of expressing these values. The carnival atmosphere of their live performances was reinvigorated and reimagined in their next two records, *Sgt. Pepper* and *Magical Mystery Tour*. *Sgt. Pepper* is framed by the carnival scene of Sgt. Pepper's Lonely Hearts Club Band playing before a crowd. The album begins with the crowd's murmurings, and we hear their cheers following the opening song. John's "Being for the Benefit of Mr. Kite" also consciously invokes a carnival scene with the lyrics promoting a variety of circus acts taken almost verbatim from a poster John saw. The carnival scene cannot truly be said to surface throughout the album, but when it is not, the Beatles speak for those outside of officialdom, the lonely hearts such as Lovely Rita, the girl running away from home, the guy reading the back of a cereal box, and the guy reading the newspaper and riding the bus. Even "Within You Without You" is about the little guy wondering about his place in a large world, troubled by "the space between us all," realizing "life goes on within you and without you." If the photos on the much-heralded album cover have a common theme, perhaps it is that these are all people who in one way or another have talked back to authority, among them the Beatles themselves, old and new, Bob Dylan, Aleister Crowley, Mae West, Lenny Bruce, W. C. Fields, Dylan Thomas, William Burroughs, Karl Marx, Laurel and Hardy, Aldous Huxley, Edgar Allan Poe, Marlon Brando, Oscar Wilde, Sonny Liston, and Albert Einstein.

In *Magical Mystery Tour*, of course, the carnival element is the mystery tour itself, an occasion for ordinary people to band together and let loose with the invitation to come along issued by the title song. On both *Sgt. Pepper* and *Magical Mystery Tour* we see the Beatles donning masks, which Bakhtin says permits carnivalesque eruption into licentiousness and boundary-testing play. "I Am the Walrus" is full of references to the wearing of masks: walrus, egg man, joker. In fact, the song's strange chain of images, which John insisted was simply a bunch of nonsense, perhaps can be read as pictures from a carnival, a place populated by jokers and clowns, a dead dog with "yellow-matter custard" dripping from his eye, a mob kicking Edgar Allan Poe. The inscrutable lyrics demonstrate John's conscious adoption of carnival's crucial role, that of the fool, he who speaks sense in nonsense. Bakhtin's description of the fool's role seems especially pertinent. Fools, he says, claim:

> the right to confuse, to tease, to hyperbolize life; the right to parody others while talking, the right to not be taken literally, not "to be oneself"; . . . the right to act life as a comedy and to treat others as actors, the right to rip off masks, the right to rage at others with a primeval (almost cultic) rage—and finally, the right to betray to the public a personal life, down to its most private and prurient little secrets. ("Forms" 163)

The obscure and mocking lyrics of songs such as "Walrus" certainly suggest John's claiming of "the right to confuse" and "to not be taken literally." The story goes that a teacher in Lennon's old school was using Beatles lyrics in a literature class. Savoring the irony because he had been something less than a model student at Quarry Bank, Lennon devised "Walrus" as a big put-on, deliberately impenetrable to tweak those (like us!) who would take his witticisms for wisdom. He talks back to authority by offering us comic "literature" that features lines drawn from children's street ditties. The mask-wearing of *Magical Mystery Tour* and *Sgt. Pepper* demonstrates the refusal "to be oneself." His exposure of the personal and private is evident in "Strawberry Fields Forever," which John called "psychoanalysis set to music" (*Anthology* 231). Of course, John plays the fool on other albums as well. The fool's rage is evident in the scorn of the *White Album*'s "Sexy Sadie," the prurience evident in the sexual openness, or raunchiness, of songs such as *Abbey Road*'s "Come Together."

Paul, of course, also adopts the guise of the fool in the contrary utterances of "Hello Goodbye," and even more explicitly in "The Fool on the Hill." His fool on the hill is someone detached from society, and ignored and scorned by that society: "Nobody wants to know him" or hear him. Interestingly, he is a very heteroglossic fool, a "man of a thousand voices." No monologism for this fool. Although he is "talking perfectly loud . . . nobody ever hears him, or the sound he appears to make." This is the voice of the people; it speaks with many voices about another way of life (one of stillness as opposed to peace), its utterances remain open-ended ("he never gives an answer"), and the powers-that-be do not listen or hear.

On the *White Album* we find the challenge to authority of George's "Piggies" and the licentiousness of Paul's "Why Don't We Do It in the Road?" But the spirit of carnival surfaces even more on *Let It Be*, where the sessions were originally to be edited into a television documentary directed by Michael Lindsay-Hogg, who had directed (shades of carnival) the *Rock 'n' Roll Circus* show, and the rehearsals culminated in the rooftop concert that tweaked the authorities enough that London businessmen looked upward askance, and the police were summoned to force the Beatles to turn down the music.

CHRONOTOPE

By his term *chronotope*, Bakhtin refers to the intersection, the interrelationship really, of time and space in a literary work. Bakhtin speaks not of a single chronotope in literature but of varieties of chronotopes. For example, a romance may make use of "adventure time" with a story of separated lovers spanning decades, but that passage of time has no real effect on the characters or their situation. They remain devoted to one another even as they are separated, and although the plot is working itself out to eventually bring them together, they experience no real change in the interim. Similarly, the geography they range over may be extensive, but it is basically irrelevant to the story, rendered so abstractly that the story could just as well take place somewhere else. Opposed to this sort of chronotope is folkloric time, intimately connected with a particular landscape and the seasonal cycles of that landscape.

Bakhtin identifies other chronotopic patterns, but he does not claim universality for any of them. Individual novels may establish their own space-time relationships, their own chronotopes, that may or may not approach the folkloric time and space that Bakhtin seems to admire.

And the Beatles? Theirs is a chronotope of the day, a world of circadian rhythms. Their time frames rarely invoke annual cycles, but they return repeatedly to daily life with the emphasis on the day-to-dayness of our lives. Joy is conveyed via "Good Day Sunshine." Love everlasting is offered "Eight Days a Week." Exhaustion follows "A Hard Day's Night." The past is "Yesterday." The blank expanse of the future is expressed as "Tomorrow Never Knows."

The preoccupation with daily existence culminates in "A Day in the Life," a song built around the internal chronotope of day. It opens with a morning routine with the speaker reading about a death reported in the morning paper (the *Daily Mail*), then heading out on the daily commute. The song leads eventually, if not in the form of a direct narrative then by suggestion and impressions derived from the daily news, through the potholed streets of Blackburn, Lancashire, to a scene from an evening out (the holes in Albert Hall). As the title suggests, the song offers a view of a day in the life of our time; it is one of many Beatles songs that does so—from the upbeat bustle of "Penny Lane" to the grim ennui of "Good Morning Good Morning"—or even the disjointed cacophony of "Revolution 9," built from random snippets of tape from our culture at large. The geography, too, is that of daily life, typically urban, from Liverpool's Penny Lane and Strawberry Field (an orphanage) to London's bustling Abbey Road.

The Beatles' preoccupation with daily life may seem a long way from the folkloric time Bakhtin admires. But perhaps it is just as much the time frame and geography of the middle and lower classes. The sad truth is that seasonal cycles no longer govern the lives of urban and suburban folk, and daily cycles do. For the Beatles, the preoccupation with daily life is often offered as critique, as in "A Day in the Life." Our daily routines seem purposeless, and the news is usually bad—and not new. Our lives are not epic in terms of geographic scale, and we do not see our lives spread out across time as some grand narrative. We live day-to-day, if not in terms of sustenance, at least in terms of spirit, and Beatles songs capture the chronological and geographical constrictions of our lives.

At the same time the focus on the details of daily life have made the Beatles and their songs markers of time and place. Mention the Beatles to anyone of a certain age or older, and you are bound to hear how their songs bring back very powerful memories of a certain time and place. The idea that the Beatles provided the soundtrack for a generation is not new, but it is not just the sound that makes their songs such profound triggers of time and place; it is the details of that cultural moment invoked in the songs. The Beatles were able to articulate the values and concerns of the people of that time and place. In commenting on their role as generational spokesmen, John once denied that the Beatles were leading a generation through the 1960s; rather, they were simply good observers:

> We were all on this ship in the Sixties. Our generation—a ship going to discover the New World. And the Beatles were in the crow's-nest of that ship. We were part of it and contributed what we contributed; I can't designate what we did and didn't do. It depends on how each individual was impressed by the Beatles, or how shock waves went to different people. We were going through the changes, and all we were saying was, "It's raining up here!" or "There's land!" or "There's sun!" or "We can see a seagull!" We were just reporting what was happening to us. (*Anthology* 201)

In the course of their reporting, the Beatles told us that ours was a time of coldness, conformity, constraint, materialism, and violence and that what we needed was more love, peace, soul, and individual freedom.

CHARACTER ZONE

Bakhtin points out that even when a novel, or novelized genres, has a single narrative voice, that voice takes on the inflections, language styles, and world-views of characters in the text as it moves into their "character zones." This makes possible the "multivoicedness" or polyphony of a text, the essence of its dialogic nature. And perhaps this "multivoicedness" has the most pertinence to the lyrical dialogics of the Beatles.

After the first couple of albums, the voices of John and Paul become much more recognizable. I am speaking literally here, that is, musically, referring to the sound of the actual voices. About the same time the separate narrative styles of the lyrics become obvious. John's distinctive voice becomes apparent in songs such as "I'm a Loser," "In My Life," and "Help!" These are all very personal songs, managing to look inward while at the same time crying out. Often making use of the first person, John's songs admit pain and tell truths. In later songs, John is much more forthright than the others about sexuality, drug use, and social protest. John offers a raw edge, both in the voice itself and in the lyrical content of his songs, although he also specialized in dreamy songs. Paul, of course, was more the crooner, more prone to sentimentality, but less likely to delve deeply inward or to deal with emotional discord. He was certainly capable of rocking out on occasion ("Helter Skelter,"

"Birthday"), but his musical forte lay in his melodic gifts. Lyrically, he did not have John's way with wordplay or daring with images, but he could offer telling slices of sympathetically observed lives of ordinary people. George explored the human condition, not so much his own inner self, or mind, consciousness, and soul, but the human self, the idea of consciousness. If the voice was somewhat less expressive than those of John and Paul were, his guitar lines were even more so. Then we have Ringo, steady on the drumbeat, offering interesting fills on the offbeat and singing the upbeat material.

This is just to say that the Beatles had different lyrical styles and different voices that reflected their different personalities, which is not to say much in the way of Bakhtinian dialogics. But it is the melding of those personalities into a whole that is of interest. It is not so much that the Beatles offered something for everyone as that they spoke to different parts of us and brought those different parts into harmony. In Bakhtinian terms, we had a narrator called *Beatles* who entered the character zones of John, Paul, George, and Ringo, and thereby expressed different worldviews—or rather, accommodated the expression of different worldviews. And, of course, there was cross-fertilization: the sentimentality we associate with Paul shows up in songs such as John's "Julia" or "Because," or George's "Something"—the coarseness of John is evident in Paul's "Why Don't We Do It in the Road?" or George's "Piggies"—and George's spiritual questing is evident in John's "Tomorrow Never Knows" or in Paul's "The Fool on the Hill." They reflected each other's worldviews, borrowed inflections from each other's voices, in short, listened to one another. Learned from one another. And sang with one another.

It is a balancing act, however, to find a place for the individual voice amid the group song. In fact, this is the tension that Bakhtin sees as the essential theme of carnival: the struggle to assert the individual self within the context of a community. Early on, the Beatles' individual selves were subsumed by their community, that community consisting of the band itself and the massive culture of Beatlemania that threatened to devour them whole. Pre–*Rubber Soul*, the Beatles' songs did not really make room for the distinctively individual voice. The blend began with *Rubber Soul* and hit its high point, perhaps, on the *White Album*. Consider these opposing views of the work on that album: Ringo says, "While we were recording the *White Album* we ended up being more of a band again, and that's what I always love. I love being in a band" (*Anthology* 311). John says, "Every track is an individual track; there isn't any Beatles music on it. It's like if you took each track off it and made it all mine and all George's. It was just me and a backing group, Paul and a backing group" (qtd. in Giuliano 124). These seem like irreconcilable views, and yet it may be that both John and Ringo are right. As George put it, the *White Album* "felt more like a band recording together. There were a lot of tracks where we just played live, and then there were a lot of tracks that we'd recorded and that would need finishing together. There was also a lot more individual stuff and, for the first time, people were accepting that it *was* individual" (*Anthology* 305). The band playing together, the individual voice having its say: these things can go together, and the result can be harmonious. Perhaps we respond so strongly to the Beatles because in their music we hear something of the balance we yearn to achieve: to be a member of a community, or a society, and at the same time to have an individual voice.

We need to consider one more voice in the music of the Beatles: the voice of technology. The Beatles were the first band to foreground the technology by which they were making their music. In "I Feel Fine" we have the first use of feedback. The machine speaks. Before long (from *Revolver* onward), the Beatles would be integrating into their music a variety of the machine's language styles, as tapes of guitars, drums, and voices would be played backward, or sped up, or slowed down. Technology became an active part of the music rather than serving simply to amplify the music. Technology also made possible a recording process that quite literally makes use of dialogue. In their use of four-track taping, the Beatles were recording tracks at different times, so what was laid down on a second or third or fourth track was, in essence, part of a dialogue with the previous utterances of the song. And from the listener's perspective, stereo technology meant different sounds would be coming out of the two speakers, so that different elements of the song, different instruments, engage in dialogue with one another. For some later bands, the voice of technology would take over, drowning out the human voices. So just as we might find cultural lessons in the way the Beatles opened up space for the individual voice within the construct of a band, so, too, we might admire their relationship with technology, admitting its voice, giving it a place, and engaging in dialogue with it while not allowing it to dominate.

But, lord, these sorts of harmonies are difficult to maintain. Consider the debacle of *Let It Be*.

⚙

MONOLOGUES BEFORE THE END

> PAUL: On "Hey Jude" when we first sat down and I sang "Hey Jude . . . ,"
> George went "nanu nanu" on his guitar. I continued, "Don't make it
> bad . . ." and he replied "nanu nanu." He was answering every line—and
> I said, "Whoa! Wait a minute now. I don't think we want that. Maybe
> you'd come in with answering lines later. For now I think I should start it
> simply first." He was going, "Oh yeah, OK, fine, fine." But it was getting
> a bit like that. He wasn't into what I was saying. In a group it's democratic and he didn't have to listen to me, so I think he got pissed off with me
> coming on with ideas all the time. I think to his mind it was probably me
> trying to dominate. (*Anthology* 316)

GEORGE: Personally, I'd found that for the last couple of albums—probably since we stopped touring—the freedom to be able to play as a musician was being curtailed, mainly by Paul. There used to be a situation where we'd go in (as we did when we were kids), pick up our guitars, all learn the tune and chords and start talking about arrangements. But there came a time, possibly around the time of *Sgt. Pepper* (which was maybe why I didn't enjoy that so much), where Paul had fixed an idea in his brain as to how to record one of his songs. He wasn't open to anybody else's suggestions. John was always much more open when it came to how to record one of his songs. (*Anthology* 316)

RINGO: George was writing more. He wanted things to go his way. When we first started, they basically went John and Paul's way, because they were the writers. But George was finding his independence and he wouldn't be dominated as much by Paul—because in the end Paul wanted to point out the solo to George, who would say, "Look, I'm a guitarist. I'll play the solo." And he always did; he always played fine solos. It got a bit like, "I wrote the song and I want it this way," whereas before it was, "I wrote the song—give me what you can." (*Anthology* 316)

JOHN: By the time the Beatles were at their peak we were cutting each other down to size. We were limiting our capacity to write and perform by having to fit it into some kind of format, and that's why it caused trouble. (*Anthology* 317)

GEORGE: "I Me Mine" is the ego problem. There are two "I"s: the little "i" when people say, "I am this," and the big "I"—i.e., Om, the complete, whole, universal consciousness that is void of duality and ego. There is nothing that isn't part of the complete whole. When the little "i" merges into the big "I" then you are really smiling! After having LSD, I looked around and everything I could see was relative to my ego—like, "That's *my* piece of paper," and, "That's *my* flannel," or, "Give it to *me*," or, "*I* am." It drove me crackers; I hated everything about my ego—it was a flash of everything false and impermanent which I disliked. But later I learnt from it: to realize that there *is* somebody else in here apart from old blabbermouth (that's what I felt like—I hadn't seen or heard or done anything in my life, and yet I hadn't stopped talking). "Who am I?" became the order of the day. (*Anthology* 319)

THE END

During the painful personality conflicts of the *Let It Be* sessions, the group's individual selves no longer seemed willing to make accommodations to the constraints of the group—or the group was no longer commodious or flexible enough to accommodate the talents and needs of such strong and remarkable personalities. There was no more dialogue, and no more harmony, at least in the metaphoric sense. As if sensing, however, that the bitterness of those sessions was no way to end things, the Beatles returned to the studio to make *Abbey Road*. And it all came together again. "The End" can serve as a summing up of Beatle dialogics. Paul's wonderful lyric—"And in the end, the love you take / Is equal to the love you make"—manages to convey something of the worldview of each of the Beatles: an expression of Paul's utopian optimism that could just as well be George singing the law of karma, Ringo offering a simple and sincere sentiment, or John pushing social change or exploring personal growth. And it is a song that accommodates a solo by each of the Beatles. Ringo does his only drum solo as a member of the Beatles, the greatest drum solo of rock 'n' roll history, in my opinion, because rather than going off on its own and then returning to the song proper, it manages to remain part of the track throughout. On guitars, John, Paul, and George trade licks, John's distorted, driving, and direct—Paul's rocking, energetic, and precise—George's pure, sweet, clean, and soaring. The individual lines bespeak the character of the player, but the musical dialogue fits within—or better yet, creates—the space of the song.

True, it's a short song. It was all too short, and for most of us, the Beatles ended way too soon. Not surprisingly, all four went on, post-Beatles, to make some remarkable music, and perhaps all of that music can be seen as continued dialogue with the others—sometimes very directly, as when John, Paul, and George wrote songs of mutual recrimination about their financial squabbles and interpersonal dissension (Paul's "Too Many People" and "Dear Boy"; John's "How Do You Sleep?"; George's "Sue Me, Sue You Blues") or when Paul effects a dead-on imitation of John in "Let Me Roll It." They clearly still had things to say to each other. In terms of listening to each other, however, and giving to one another what they had to offer musically, well, all things must pass. But not all. We still have a record of their musical dialogues, lots of records.

Listen:

NOTES

1. John was less admiring of Paul's novelistic tendencies: "He makes them up like a novelist. You hear many McCartney-influenced songs on the radio—these stories about boring people doing boring things: being postmen and secretaries and writing home. I'm not interested in writing third-party songs. I like to write about me, because I *know* me" (*Anthology* 247).

2. Perhaps the song's saccharine quality—as well as its seeming incongruousness with the rest of the album—can be attributed to the string arrangements of Mike Leander, whom McCartney commissioned for "She's Leaving Home" when Martin was unavailable because he was overseeing another recording session. As McCartney recalls, "He [Martin] was busy, and I was itching to get on with it; I was inspired. I think George had a lot of difficulty forgiving me for that. It hurt him. I didn't mean to" (qtd. in Dowlding 171).

CHAPTER 2

From "Craft" to "Art"

Formal Structure in the Music of the Beatles

JOHN COVACH

MOST HISTORIES OF ROCK MUSIC cite early February 1964 as an important date in American popular music; the appearance of the Beatles on the *Ed Sullivan Show* on two consecutive Sunday evenings ignited a craze for British-invasion pop that had a dramatic effect on the development of rock music, catching the American music business entirely by surprise. Reading from most accounts, one might easily conclude that early Beatles' music was very different from the American pop that it so effectively displaced.[1] Musical analysis reveals, however, that the music of the Beatles engages in a much more complicated relationship with the American pop that preceded it than most writers have thus far detected. John Lennon and Paul McCartney were serious students of both American songwriting and performance traditions. The band covered dozens of American pop tunes during their early years, including many by the Brill Building songwriters of the late 1950s and early 1960s.[2] The BBC sessions reveal that most of the time the Beatles performed approximate versions of the tunes that they covered, working to get the vocal inflections, the accompaniment, and even the guitar solos as close to those on the records as possible.[3]

This chapter focuses on formal design and argues that as songwriters Lennon and McCartney were greatly influenced by American pop and that early Beatles music as a result uses 1950's and early 1960's American pop as its model, sometimes following its standard organizational practices closely and at other times innovating within its constraints.[4] In the course of the Beatles' tremendous U.S. success in 1964, Lennon and McCartney began to show signs of finding their own voices as songwriters; each began trying out new ideas that would gradually lead them away from standard songwriting practices; how these changes occur is the focus of this chapter. In the first interviews of 1963–1964, both Beatles composers seem to stress the fact that they consider themselves primarily songwriters; in response to questions with how they see their careers in music unfolding, McCartney states quite plainly that he and Lennon will most likely continue as songwriters long after the Beatles are no longer a top act.[5] Importantly, initially almost everybody, including the band members themselves, saw the Beatles as a fad—a quirky pop group that would rise and fall quickly, nothing more than the latest flavor of the week. Although the group greatly admired the original rock 'n' rollers of the 1950s, and Elvis Presley especially, they also admired Brill Building songwriters such as Gerry Goffin and Carole King, Jerry Leiber and Mike Stoller, and Phil Spector. And even among the first wave of rock 'n' rollers, Chuck Berry and Buddy Holly were especially important to Lennon and McCartney as performers who wrote their own songs. The connection to the Brill Building songwriters is particularly important with regard to early Beatles music, and in many ways their development after the initial splash of early to mid-1964 can be measured music-analytically by how closely each song models Brill Building practices.

Lennon and McCartney begin their careers aspiring to be songwriters in the American pop tradition, and, accordingly, they view themselves as craftspeople, using formal designs and arrangement schemes that are common to much of early 1960's pop. Most readers know where things ended up in just a few short years for the Beatles, as *Sgt. Pepper's Lonely Hearts Club Band* (1967) made its mark as *the* album that—in the now-famous words of Wilfrid Mellers—elevates rock music from simple dance fare to serious listening music.[6] From *Sgt. Pepper* forward, rock takes itself very seriously—at times too seriously, we should acknowledge. Rock musicians no longer aspire so much to be professionals and craftspeople; rather, they aspire to be artists, adopting and adapting notions of inspiration, genius, and complexity that derive directly from nineteenth-century European high culture. And not only were musicians' attitudes changing, but listeners after 1967 also began to think of rock music as an aesthetic experience that might, at times, rise above mere pop culture.

Hence, the space between 1964 and 1967 is an important time in pop music's developing sense of aspiration in general. Such stylistic and aesthetic changes almost never happen overnight, and the change from pop songwriters to songwriting artists occurs gradually in the Lennon-McCartney songs from that three-year period. To track this change, two general ideas will be employed to organize the discussion. As the term has already been used here, *craftsperson* refers to an approach that privileges repeatable structures; songs are written according to patterns that are in common use. When innovation occurs within this approach, there is no difficulty with the idea of duplicating this innovation in subsequent songs. Opposed in a loose way to the craftsperson approach is the *artist* approach. Here, the emphasis is on the nonrepeatability of innovations; the worst criticism that can be leveled against a creative individual according to this approach is that he or she is "rewriting the same song over and over." One can see quite readily how such criticism aligns squarely with modernist notions of artistic integrity, while making almost no sense in regard to Brill Building songwriting practices; indeed, evaluating songwriters such as Goffin and King according to the artist model is unfair— or at least aesthetically misguided. The argument here is that Lennon and McCartney move from the craftsperson model to the artist model increasingly and gradually from 1964 until 1968. When the group decides to return to their roots in the wake of the failed *Magical Mystery Tour* project, both Lennon and McCartney strike a balance between these two seemingly contradictory aesthetic and poetic approaches.

To support this interpretation, this chapter depends primarily on an account of formal design and its development, although one could also track this evolution by considering aspects of harmonic, melodic, and text-music relationships. The principal claim is that the Beatles' debt to the American pop tradition can be seen clearly in the group's repeated use of a limited number of typical formal designs and arrangements in their early music. As Lennon and McCartney begin to move away from the craftsperson model, this tendency can be detected in singular innovations within this context that eventually begin to occur so frequently that they obscure the original stylistic context, and perhaps even transform it.

Because this chapter depends on formal analysis, introducing a number of formal types and labels for them may prove helpful.[7] In most rock music up to the 1970s, four formal patterns occur (see accompanying list). The *AABA* form is clearly inherited from the thirty-two-bar *AABA* structure common to Tin Pan Alley pop of the first half of the twentieth century in which each section tends to be eight bars in length. Tunes such as "Over the Rainbow" or "Misty" are good examples of a frequently used formal pattern.[8] Even in the years before rock 'n' roll, the *AABA* pattern had begun to exceed the thirty-two-bar template. Sections can be found that are twelve or sixteen bars in length, rather than the standard eight, making for designs that exceed thirty-two bars but retain the *AABA* pattern. Playing once through the *AABA* pattern usually does not result in enough music for most situations, and so the question arises regarding how much of the music needs to be repeated to fill out a given arrangement. If the entire *AABA* form is repeated, this is termed a *full reprise*; when only part of the *AABA* form returns, this is called an *abbreviated reprise*.

TABLE 2.1
Formal Patterns in Rock in the 1950s and 1960s

1. *AABA:* thirty-two-bar and more, full or abbreviated reprises
2. Simple verse-chorus (harmonic pattern does not contrast between sections)
3. Contrasting verse-chorus (harmonic pattern does contrast)
4. Simple verse (verses only, no chorus)

Standing in stark contrast with the *AABA* formal type are the two kinds of verse-chorus forms. The focus of an *AABA* is always on the verses (or *A* sections), with the bridge (*B* section or middle eight) offering contrast to prepare listeners for the return of the verses. In a verse-chorus song, the focus is usually on the chorus with the verses being used to separate chorus statements. When the verse and chorus employ the same harmonic pattern, the result is a *simple verse-chorus* form; when the harmonic pattern between these sections is different, a *contrasting verse-chorus* results. When no chorus at all occurs—only a repeated verse—this is called a *simple verse* form. For representative *AABA* forms drawn from 1950's rock 'n' roll, consider Jerry Lee Lewis's "Great Balls of Fire," Fats Domino's "Blueberry Hill," and the Everly Brothers' "All I Have to Do Is Dream." Good examples of simple verse-chorus structures include "Rock Around the Clock," "Shake, Rattle, and Roll," and "Johnny B. Goode." Contrasting verse-chorus patterns can be found in Berry's "Rock and Roll Music" and in Holly's "That'll Be the Day." Simple verse forms can be found in Elvis's "Hound Dog," and "Heartbreak Hotel," and in Berry's "School Day."

As a general rule, professional songwriters tend to use *AABA* forms, and simple verse and simple verse-chorus structures tend to derive from rhythm-and-blues (and even folk) practice. In the period before the mid-1960s, contrasting verse-chorus patterns are in the minority, although not rare. In the period after the mid-1960s or so, contrasting verse-chorus forms become the norm and *AABA* forms tend to disappear from rock. To generalize somewhat loosely, we find a constant presence of simple verse and simple verse-chorus tunes in rock throughout the 1950s, 1960s, and 1970s owing to its clear association with electric blues. We find, however, a marked move from *AABA* type forms to contrasting verse chorus structures that occur in the mid-1960s. If the *AABA* form is marked as the preferred form of the professional songwriter—the Brill Building craftsperson—then the move away from that formal design at precisely the time in which musicians were drifting toward an image of themselves as artists makes a good deal of sense. In this context, the argument for the Beatles' development is approximately representative of a more general practice (and we will defer for current purposes the question of whether the Beatles' songwriting aesthetic is a principal cause of this change).[9]

TABLE 2.2
"From Me to You," Thirty-Two-Bar *AABA* with Abbreviated Reprise
(Recorded March 5, 1963)

Introduction	4 mm.
A-verse	8 mm.
A-verse	8 mm.
B-bridge	8 mm.
A-verse	8 mm.
A-verse	8 mm., 4 mm. instrumental + 4 mm. vocal
B-bridge	8 mm.
A-verse with tag	12 mm.

TABLE 2.3
"I Want to Hold Your Hand," Forty-Seven-Bar *AABA*
with Abbreviated Reprise, *AAB* Phrase Structure in Verse
(Recorded October 17, 1963)

Introduction	(4 mm. prolongation of G: V drawn from *d*)
A-verse	12 mm., 4*a* + 4*a* + 4*b*
A-verse	12 mm.
B-bridge	11 mm., 4*c* + 7*d*
A-verse	12 mm.
B-bridge	11 mm.
A-verse with tag	15 mm., 4*a* + 4*a* + 7*e*

Let us now turn to some early Beatles music. Table 2.2 provides a formal diagram for the Beatles' "From Me to You." Here, similarities with earlier American songwriting are clear: after a four-bar introduction, the song follows the standard thirty-two-bar template. An abbreviated reprise brings back an instrumental version of *A*, followed by the bridge and verse. A brief tag concludes the song. Table 2.3 shows another instance of the *AABA* form, but with "I Want to Hold Your Hand," the standard eight-bar verses are expanded to twelve measures (denoted as "mm." in Tables 2.2 and 2.3), while the bridge expands from eight to eleven measures, making a forty-seven-bar structure. Again, the song begins with a brief introduction and ends with a tag. The abbreviated reprise brings back only the bridge and the last verse. "A Hard Day's Night" (not shown) is another example of the twelve-bar verse scheme as found in "I Want to Hold Your Hand." In this

TABLE 2.4
"Eight Days a Week," Fifty-Six-Bar *AABA* with
Abbreviated Reprise, *aaba* Phrase Structure
(Recorded October 6 and 18, 1964)

Introduction	4 mm.
A-verse	16 mm., 4*a* + 4*a* + 4*b* + 4*a*
A-verse	16 mm.
B-bridge	8 mm.
A-verse	16 mm.
B-bridge	8 mm.
A-verse with tag	20 mm.
Codetta	4 mm.

TABLE 2.5
"She Loves You," Contrasting Verse-Chorus with Modified Chorus Introduction
(Recorded July 1, 1963)

Introduction	8 mm.
Verse 1	16 mm., 4 + 4, 4 + 4
Verse 2	16 mm.
Chorus	8 mm.
Verse 3	16 mm.
Chorus with long tag	21 mm.

case, the bridge is the standard eight bars, making a forty-four-bar *AABA* structure. The formal layout of "A Hard Day's Night" employs an abbreviated reprise of the *ABA*.

Note that Table 2.3 indicates that each verse can be heard in three phrases, each of four measures. A common pattern in Beatles verses is an *AAB* phrase scheme in which the first four-bar phrase is repeated (often with new lyrics), and this second four-bar phrase is followed by a contrasting phrase. This last phrase often contains the melodic "hook" that is repeated with each new verse; such a hook is often called a "refrain." Both "I Want to Hold Your Hand" and "A Hard Day's Night" employ the *AAB* phrase pattern, and in "I Want to Hold Your Hand," the *B* phrase functions as a refrain. Table 2.4 illustrates another phrase pattern that often occurs in Beatles verses. "Eight Days a Week" uses sixteen-bar verses that break down into four four-bar phrases. These phrases are arranged in an *AABA* pattern. When this phrase structure is used in the context of an *AABA* form, an intriguing structural replication arises between the phrase and sectional levels. Note as well that in "Eight

Days a Week" the use of these longer verse sections expands the structure to encompass fifty-six measures. An abbreviated reprise brings back the bridge and final verse with a tag and codetta ends the arrangement.

Tables 2.2, 2.3, and 2.4 provide a representative sample of the variations one can find in early Beatles music among songs employing the *AABA* form. Contrasting verse-chorus forms can also be found, and "She Loves You" is perhaps the best-known early example. Table 2.5 shows that the song begins with an eight-measure introduction based on the chorus, followed by two sixteen-bar verses and the eight-bar chorus proper. The song closes with the third verse and a chorus employing a long tag. Given that so much of the Beatles' early music used the *AABA* design, Lennon and McCartney may have initially thought of the song as an *AABA* form akin to that found in the later song "Eight Days a Week." The problem in that case would have been that the bridge was not a bridge at all, but rather a chorus—and a rather catchy one at that. So the faulty bridge was moved to the front of the song, creating in the process one of the most striking opening moments in Beatles music. In the process, they created two versions of the chorus, hardly a standard practice in contrasting verse-chorus forms and a formal design that we might call the *Beatles verse-chorus*. Subsequent songs to employ the Beatles verse-chorus design are "Can't Buy Me Love," "I'm a Loser," and "Help!" which all begin with an altered version of the chorus. While trying to read an *AABA* source into "She Loves You" may seem to be forcing things somewhat, it is nevertheless clear that in 1963 and 1964 the Beatles employed *AABA* thinking as a kind of default mode in issues of form and arrangement. Also important to note is that Lennon and McCartney seemed to have no qualms about reusing the Beatles verse-chorus form after the success of "She Loves You," which further underscores their adherence to the craftsperson model during this time.[10]

As much as one can glimpse certain formal types clearly in use across much early Beatles music, interesting innovations begin to emerge in Beatles songs during 1965 and 1966 that show them innovating within the formal conventions of standard pop songwriting. The Beatles verse-chorus is already an innovation, but one can also identify a form based on the *AABA* structure that we might usefully describe as a "broken *AABA*" pattern. Thus far we have been thinking about the *AABA* as a form that could include either a full or an abbreviated reprise of material. How much of the full *AABA* that returns in each case is often determined by how closely a tune can be made to fit into the length of about two minutes, the standard duration of a single played on AM radio in the first half of the 1960s. After going through a single iteration of the *AABA* structure, there would only be one reprise of that material, whether full or abbreviated. In the broken *AABA* forms that begin to appear in 1965 and 1966, the initial statement of the *AABA* portion of the form is followed by more than one repetition of some combination of *A* and *B* sections, creating a design that is much less predictable.

"Nowhere Man," written mostly by Lennon, provides a clear instance of this formal innovation. After a relatively clear statement of the *AAB* portion of the form, the *A* that would complete the form includes a guitar solo, a feature previously reserved for the reprise. This is followed by alternating *A* and *B* sections that do not conform to either the *AABA* pattern or to the usual kinds of abbreviated reprises found in earlier songs. "Michelle," written mostly by McCartney, employs a broken *AABA* scheme with slightly different results. After a four-measure introduction, two six-bar verses are presented, and these verses are followed by a ten-measure bridge (the last four bars of the bridge are used as the introduction and coda for the song). So far, then, the *AAB* components are present; what follows, however, is a succession of verses and bridges that breaks the *AABA* pattern much as in "Nowhere Man." Interestingly, the harmonic structure of McCartney's verses paints him into a bit of a corner with regard to providing a satisfactory closing for the song: in technical terms, each verse ends on the dominant, which compels the artist to continue the song ad infinitum. Rather than altering the end of the last verse to arrive on tonic harmony, McCartney opts for a fade out, leaving the song to loop verses and bridges into infinity as the music fades away.

"Nowhere Man" and "Michelle" provide instances of the artist approach briefly emerging within an overall context of the craftsperson approach. Admittedly, this phenomenon occurs in small ways in these two tunes, and making too much of these details may seem to be stretching things. Bear in mind, however, that the argument is that the artist approach emerges gradually; as we move forward in the Beatles' music, the dialectic between standard practice and innovation becomes increasingly pronounced. What emerges most clearly from broken *AABA* forms is that the venerable *AABA* pattern serves as a basis for formal designs that may not look much like that form after it has been modified. Table 2.6 shows the formal design of Lennon's "Norwegian Wood," which also has its roots in the *AABA* form, although this might not be clear outside of the context of the other, more conventional songs that precede it. Note that the song has no real chorus, but verse and bridge sections of eight bars' duration. This suggests that the form is, in fact, a modified *AABA* structure—an *AABA* pattern missing one of the usual *A* sections—that can be viewed as a twenty-four-bar *ABA* form with full reprise. Here, one can clearly note a formal innovation that works for this song but that is not repeated directly in subsequent ones. Unconventional formal designs found in a few earlier Beatles tunes (such as "Ask Me Why," "It Won't Be Long," and "I'll Be Back") and repeatable formal innovations employing the Beatles verse-chorus and broken *AABA* forms, but the design of "Norwegian Wood" is an important transitional step away from the craftsperson approach and toward the artist one.[11]

When the Beatles were exploring new approaches to the *AABA* model in 1965 and 1966, they had also begun increasingly to employ the standard contrasting verse-chorus form (as opposed to the Beatles verse-chorus form) with

TABLE 2.6
"Norwegian Wood (This Bird has Flown),"
Twenty-Four-Bar *ABA* Form with Modal Shifts
(Recorded October 12 and 21, 1965)

[Measures counted in 6/8, all numbers doubled in 3/4]

Introduction	4 + 4 mm. (E Mixolydian)
A-verse	8 mm. (E Mixolydian)
B-bridge	8 mm. (E Dorian with Ionian cadence)
A-verse	8 mm. (E Mixolydian)
A-verse	8 mm., instrumental
B-bridge	8 mm.
A-verse	8 mm.
Codetta	4 mm.

greater regularity. Perhaps the most conspicuous use of the standard contrasting verse-chorus form can be found in Lennon's "You've Got to Hide Your Love Away" (recorded in February 1965), although McCartney's "Every Little Thing" (recorded in late September 1964) is also an early example. By the fall of 1965, the Beatles' music included an amalgamation of traditional *AABA*, contrasting verse-chorus, and broken *AABA* forms. *Rubber Soul* (released in early December 1965) blends the broken *AABA* forms of "Nowhere Man" and "Michelle" and the *AABA*-derived "Norwegian Wood" with the traditional *AABA* design of "I'm Looking through You" and the divergent verse chorus of "Drive My Car" and "The Word." By contrast, the album's tracks and singles throughout the summer of 1965 consists primarily of traditional *AABA* designs, the exceptions being Beatles verse-chorus tunes and a few scattered instances of singular designs.

After *Rubber Soul*, the band continued to blend this variety of forms and developed a series of one-time formal designs that most clearly underscore their increasingly artistic aspirations. Perhaps the use of E Mixolydian tonality in "Norwegian Wood" inspired the static C Mixolydian of "Tomorrow Never Knows" (see Table 2.7). In any case, the much-remarked-on use of tape loops on this track clearly indicate that the Beatles were heading into new territory in several domains. The harmonic stasis of the C Mixolydian tonality is matched by a kind of formal stasis because a succession of verses with no chorus or bridge create a simple verse form that appropriately reflects Lennon's call—fashioned after the *Tibetan Book of the Dead*—to "turn off your mind, relax, and float downstream." Very few simple verse forms are found in the Beatles' music ("I'm Down" offers another example), and this one seems motivated entirely by the song itself. Here, the Beatles appear to leave the Brill Building—and the idea of using the standard *AABA* form—far behind.

TABLE 2.7
"Tomorrow Never Knows," Simple Verse Form
(Recorded April 6, 7, and 22, 1966)

Introduction	4 mm.
Verse 1	8 mm.
Verse 2	8 mm.
Verse 3	8 mm.
Interlude	16 mm.
Verse 4	8 mm.
Verse 5	8 mm.
Verse 6	8 mm.
Verse 7 with tag	20 mm.

TABLE 2.8
"Penny Lane," Contrasting Verse-Chorus Form
(Recorded December 1966–January 1967)

Verse 1	8 mm., in B
Verse 2	8 mm.
Chorus	8 mm., in A
Verse 3	8 mm.
Verse (instrumental)	8 mm.
Chorus	8 mm.
Verse 4	8 mm.
Verse 5	8 mm.
Chorus	8 mm.
Chorus	9 mm., 8 mm. in B (with 1 m. added at end)

One often hears that whereas Lennon was a word person, McCartney was a music person; and whereas Lennon was interested in pushing the envelope with avant-garde ideas, McCartney was happy to write yet another charming tune. We should remember, however, that the tape loops on "Tomorrow Never Knows" were recorded at Paul's suggestion, and while Lennon was at home most nights with his wife and son, Paul lived a bachelor's existence, attending concerts and art exhibitions around swinging London. Many of the Beatles' most expansive conceptual ideas stemmed from McCartney; the *Sgt. Pepper* concept, the *Magical Mystery Tour* project, the aborted *Let It Be* film, and the medley on the second side of *Abbey Road* were all Paul's ideas. A revealing example of McCartney hitting on an innovative one-time solution can be found in "Penny Lane." The song features a con-

TABLE 2.9
"Sgt. Pepper's Lonely Hearts Club Band"/"With a Little Help from My Friends"
(Recorded February–March 1967)

Introduction	8 mm.
Verse 1	16 mm.
Bridge	10 mm. (brass band)
Chorus	24 mm.
Bridge	10 mm. (sung)
Verse 2	16 mm.
Transition	6 mm. (introduces "Billy Shears")
A-verse 1 with refrain	16 mm. (8 + 8)
A-verse 2 with refrain	16 mm.
B-bridge	8 mm.
A-verse 3 with refrain	16 mm.
B-bridge	8 mm.
A-refrain only	11 mm. (with extension)

trasting verse-chorus form as shown in Table 2.8, and although the verses are in B-major, the choruses are in A-major. Harmonically, each chorus has a change of key back to B built into its final bars, and McCartney uses this structure to modulate to B for the last statement of the chorus, a move that reconciles the conflict that might have been created by ending the song in A, rather than in the key of B in which it began.

The Beatles began to experiment with the idea of creating a medley of songs with the *Sgt. Pepper* album in early 1967. Often cited as the first concept album, the record began as a series of songs about growing up in Liverpool, but after "Penny Lane" and "Strawberry Fields Forever" were released as a double-A-sided single, that idea had to be abandoned. The Beatles then came up with the idea of an album that would act out a live concert hosted by a fictitious band and present the songs in as smooth a succession as possible, much as an in-person performance might. The group gave up this idea after the first two tracks, although the reprise of the title track before the last song on the second side continues the "concept." These first two tracks, "Sgt. Pepper's Lonely Hearts Club Band" and "With a Little Help from My Friends," are placed together in an uninterrupted musical flow, creating a one-time formal design with some interesting features. The first track, "Sgt. Pepper," is not a complete song, but rather a fragment. As Table 2.9 shows, the song seems to be based on the contrasting verse-chorus model that is broken off before the second appearance of the chorus. What makes the form peculiar is the presence of a bridge section after the first verse (where Sgt. Pepper's brass band is featured) and the repetition of this same material (now with singing)

TABLE 2.10
"A Day in the Life," Compound *ABA*
(Recorded January–February 1967)

A	Introduction	8 mm., entire section in G
	Verse 1	8 mm.
	Verse 2	12 mm.
	Verse 3	8 mm.
	Verse 4	12 mm.
	Verse 5	8 mm.
	Verse 6	11 mm.
	Interlude	23 mm., orchestral build-up
B	Introduction	4 mm., entire section in E
	Verse 1	9 mm.
	Verse 2	9 mm.
	Bridge	20 mm.
A	Verse 7	8 mm., entire section in G
	Verse 8	11 mm.

Interlude conclusion: 24 mm., as before; 1 m. with fermata at end on E

after the chorus. The form thus emerges as a kind of hybrid of contrasting verse-chorus and *AABA* forms. After the transition, "With a Little Help from My Friends" unfolds as an *AABA* form with abbreviated reprise. Although ending each verse of an *AABA* with a catchy refrain is common, in this case the refrain is just as long as the other verse material that precedes it, tempting one to view the refrain as a chorus. After the bridge is heard the second time, the song ends with an *A* section that omits the first eight measures of the verse but includes the eight measures of the refrain, extended by three measures to create a sense of closure. The medley of these two tracks creates the most complicated Beatles formal structure that the band had attempted up to that point, although in this case this complexity clearly arises largely from the segue that unites the two tracks.

"A Day in the Life" is perhaps one of the most important single tracks in the history of rock music; clocking in at only four minutes and forty-five seconds, it must surely be among the shortest epic pieces in rock. Table 2.10 shows that this track is in a compound *ABA* form. This composite form is the result of putting a Lennon song (section *A*) together with a McCartney fragment (section *B*). In contrast with the first two tracks on the album, these two songs are not combined to form a smooth link between two tracks, but rather they are merged together to form a single piece. Section *A* is a simple verse form, similar to "Tomorrow Never Knows." The *B* sec-

TABLE 2.11
"Lady Madonna," Broken *AABA*
(Recorded February 3, 1968)

Introduction	4 mm.
A-verse	4 mm.
A-verse	4 mm.
B-bridge	8 mm.
A-verse	4 mm.
A-verse	4 mm. (horns)
B-bridge	8 mm. (sax solo)
A-verse	4 mm.
A-verse	4 mm. (horns)
B-bridge	8 mm.
A-verse	4 mm.
Coda	4 mm.

tion starts out like an *AABA* pattern, but breaks off after the bridge to return to the *A* section. The twenty-three-bar orchestral build-up that connects the *A* section to the *B* section returns to end the track, the final chord of which is a heavily compressed E-major played on three grand pianos.[12] Although we might be able to spot traces of earlier tunes and practices, the "Sgt. Pepper's Lonely Hearts Club Band"/"With a Little Help from My Friends" medley and "A Day in the Life" represent unmistakable steps away from the craftsperson model. The specific formal details cannot be repeated, and any attempt by the Beatles (or even Oasis) to do so is bound to ring hollow.

The Beatles' music after the disappointing reception of *Magical Mystery Tour*—or at least the next two successful McCartney-penned singles—returns to the *AABA* and broken *AABA* forms that had delivered so many hits for the band in their prepsychedelic years. As Table 2.11 shows, "Lady Madonna" uses a broken *AABA* form. "Hey Jude" employs an *AABA* form with an abbreviated reprise *(BA)* to which a long coda is attached. Lennon's contributions to the *White Album*, on the other hand, include some of his most formally complex songs, including "Happiness Is a Warm Gun" and "Glass Onion." McCartney generally tended to work from standard formal models during this time much more than Lennon did. McCartney, however, took the lead in designing and arranging the medley that comprises most of the second side of *Abbey Road*, an impressive extension of the formal experimentation that he and Lennon had begun with the "Sgt. Pepper" medley and "A Day in the Life."[13] Lennon also worked with standard formal models during this time; his "Sexy Sadie" is an *AABA* form, whereas "Revolution" is a contrasting verse-chorus form. In

TABLE 2.12
"Here Comes the Sun," Compound *AABA* Form
(Recorded July–August 1969)

	Introduction	8 mm.
	Chorus	7 mm.
A	Verse 1	8 mm.
	Chorus	9 mm.
A	Verse 2	8 mm.
	Chorus	9 mm.
B	Bridge	37 mm. (7 + 7 + 7 + 7 + 9 with changing meter)
A	Verse 3	8 mm.
	Chorus	7 mm.
	Chorus	13 mm. (with extension and changing meter)

1968 and 1969, then, Lennon and McCartney each found a balance between conventional pop formal patterns and novel formal solutions suited to a specific song.

Thus far discussion has focused on the songs of Lennon and McCartney, but a survey of George Harrison's songwriting for the band shows that it partially aligns with the tendencies of John and Paul's work. Early songs such as "Don't Bother Me" (1963), "I Need You" (1965), and "If I Needed Someone" (1965) employ the *AABA* form, whereas "Taxman" (1966) and "Within You Without You" (1967) use simple verse form, and "Blue Jay Way" (1967) uses contrasting verse-chorus patterns. "While My Guitar Gently Weeps" (1968) employs an *ABA* form derived from the *AABA* model, much as "Norwegian Wood" had done earlier. Of Harrison's two contributions to *Abbey Road*, "Something" uses *AABA* form, whereas "Here Comes the Sun" employs a form that became standard in 1970's rock. As Table 2.12 shows, an introduction and chorus begin the song, which then descends into a compound *AABA* pattern, with each *A* section comprising a verse and a chorus, and a bridge made up of five statements of a phrase employing changing meter. The verse and chorus here could be viewed as a verse with a refrain as in "With a Little Help from My Friends," although in "Here Comes the Sun" the focus on the chorus/refrain in the beginning of the song, combined with its repetition at the end, probably tips the balance toward hearing the "Here comes the sun" phrase as a chorus. The articulation of an *AABA* structure without reprise makes that aspect of the overall form clear in this instance. Later rockers would further clarify this compound *AABA* structure, allowing for little ambiguity regarding the chorus.

That most Beatles experts will accept the notion that by the time of *Sgt. Pepper*, the band's music tended to break with the conventions of previous rock and pop music, or even that it was composed according to the artist approach articulated here, is probably safe to assert. The principal aim in this chapter has been to show a kind of gradual movement in that direction between 1963 and 1967, that in the next few years a kind of balance is struck between increasingly innovative formal designs and the use of a range of standard pop-song forms, and that musical analysis reveals some of the specific ways in which this change in compositional approach occurs in the domain of formal design. The Beatles' willingness to modify or even discard the formal templates that they inherited from the U.S. pop tradition (without generating new templates, no less) may be attributed to an adherence to the artist approach to music. And what goes for the Beatles across the 1960s can be found also in the music of other groups such as the Byrds or the Beach Boys. Dan Harrison, for instance, has shown how Brian Wilson's approach was increasingly motivated by a search for novel solutions to musical problems that he set for himself.[14] Although speculating about whether the Beatles led this drive in artistic aspiration in pop music or were rather swept up in a kind of pop-culture Zeitgeist that they both rode and fueled is tempting, the mid-1960s clearly saw a general shift away from the formulaic and toward the experimental.

NOTES

This chapter benefited greatly from my many discussions on this topic with Paul Harris during an independent study at the University of North Carolina at Chapel Hill.

1. Mikal Gilmore elegantly represents the idea expressed by many writers over the years that the Beatles' *Ed Sullivan Show* performances marked an important moment of change in the history of popular music: "Virtually overnight, the Beatles' arrival in the American consciousness announced not only that the music and times were changing, but also that *we* were changing. Everything about the band—its look, sound, style, and abandon—made it plain we were entering a different age, that young people were free to redefine themselves in completely new terms" (68). See Gilmore's chapter entitled "The Sixties" in *Rolling Stone: The Decades of Rock and Roll*.

2. For a discussion of the Beatles' cover repertory, see Walter Everett's *The Beatles as Musicians: The Quarry Men through* Rubber Soul (141). See also Michael Brocken's "Some Other Guys! Theories about Signification: Beatles Cover Versions."

3. The Beatles' *Live at the BBC* (1994) provides only a sampling of the many sessions that the band performed for the BBC, but even on that two-CD set one can hear how much American pop the Beatles covered, as well as note how carefully they imitated it.

4. Ironically—and perhaps to the consternation of those who insist on the novelty of this repertory—one can almost claim that most British-invasion music of 1964–1966, including that of the more blues-influenced Rolling Stones, is essentially American music. I will stop short of making that claim, and instead focus on the role that American pop played in the development of Lennon and McCartney as songwriters during the 1960s.

5. These interviews appear in the television documentary *The Beatles Anthology* (1995).

6. See Wilfred Mellers's *Twilight of the Gods: The Music of the Beatles* (86).

7. For a more detailed discussion of this topic, see my chapter entitled "Form in Rock Music: A Primer" in *Music Theory in Practice*.

8. For a detailed overview of formal schemes in popular music among America's foremost songwriters of the first half of the twentieth century, see Allen Forte's *The American Popular Ballad of the Golden Era, 1924–1950*, especially chap. 6.

9. Timothy E. Scheurer's "The Beatles, the Brill Building, and the Persistence of Tin Pan Alley in the Age of Rock" and Jon Fitzgerald's "Lennon-McCartney and the 'Middle Eight'" explore the Beatles' use of the *AABA* form. Although both Scheurer and Fitzgerald offer much helpful music-analytical insight into the band's use of the *AABA* form, neither focuses on how the use or avoidance of the form figures into the songwriters' development.

10. With regard to the Beatles verse-chorus form discussed here, Martin has remarked that when the Beatles brought "Can't Buy Me Love" into the studio it did not begin with a version of the chorus, but rather with the verse. See Martin with Jeremy Hornsby, *All You Need Is Ears* (133). It may be that Martin is remembering "She Loves You" and not "Can't Buy Me Love." The latter of these is closely modeled on the former, not only in terms of form, but also in terms of the opening chords and melody. A melodic ascent to G supported by an E-minor harmony is common to both, and although "She Loves You" continues with an A-major chord, "Can't Buy Me Love" follows with an A-minor chord. Admittedly, the tunes are in different keys thereafter, but the opening similarities and the common formal design strongly suggest that the later song was directly modeled on the earlier one.

11. Although it is not an aspect of the argument concerning form being developed here, it is nonetheless interesting that the topic of the song is uncertainty (will our protagonist sleep with the woman or not?), and to that end the modal shifting—from Mixolydian to Dorian and Ionian—in both the verse and chorus sections captures this attitude. The verse is primarily Mixolydian and the bridge shifts to Dorian while using an Ionian ii–V to return to the verse in both cases, which is marked in Table 2.6.

12. Compression is an electronic process whereby the volume of a sound is increased to offset its natural decay. By compressing the sound of the three pianos, the

recording engineer is able to make the pianos sustain far longer than they ever could naturally.

13. For a detailed analysis of the medley, see Everett's "The Beatles as Composers: The Genesis of *Abbey Road*, Side Two."

14. See Daniel Harrison's "After Sundown: The Beach Boys' Experimental Music."

CHAPTER 3

"Love, love, love"

Representations of Gender and Sexuality in Selected Songs by the Beatles

SHEILA WHITELEY

THE STORY OF THE BEATLES has been told countless times, and today the group is recognized as the most successful and accomplished band in the history of pop music. Beatles albums—in particular *Revolver* (1966)[1] and *Sgt. Pepper's Lonely Hearts Club Band* (1967)—regularly top the Best 100 charts, and their compositional output has influenced diverse musicians, including the so-called Brit-pop bands of the 1990s (and, in particular, Oasis[2]). Tribute bands, such as those in Japan,[3] have venerated both the Beatles' image and their music, and stories about the four "lads from Liverpool" continue to exert a strong pull on popular sentiment. The deaths of John Lennon and, more recently, George Harrison have led not only to the band's recognition as cultural heroes, but also equally to memorials in their home city, with the Liverpool airport being named after Lennon, as well as the creation of a garden of remembrance for Harrison. Today, not just girls idolize the Beatles. Rather, their broad-based appeal and eclectic musicianship have led to their universal enunciation as towering figures within the annals of popular music. From our twenty-first-century vantage point, it is worth considering whether their appeal shifted across the seven years when they were together or after their creative dissolution. More significantly, what in the nature of their musical address attracted the adoration of so many young girls in the early years of Beatlemania? As Barbara Ehrenreich, Elizabeth Hess, and Gloria Jacobs observe, "Beatlemania was the first mass outburst of the Sixties to feature . . . girls, who would not reach full adulthood until the Seventies. . . . In its intensity, as well as its scale, Beatlemania surpassed all previous outbreaks of star-centered hysteria" (85, 86). The fanatic adoration of the Beatles by young, predominantly white girls is well documented, and for those "who participated in Beatlemania, sex was an obvious part of the excitement," Ehrenreich, Hess, and Jacobs write. "The Beatles were sexy; the girls were the ones who perceived them as sexy" (90). In short, *the girls* were the pursuers. Interpretations of the Beatles' sexual appeal focused on a particular vision of sexuality, one that "mocked gender distinctions" and offered a "sexuality that was guileless, ebullient, and fun" (102).

Building on my previous research into subjectivity, sexuality, and gender,[4] this chapter addresses whether the Beatles' representations of gender and sexuality mediate preexisting notions of femininity or whether they help to construct them. This chapter involves an investigation into the relationship between musical focus (tune, vocal/instrumental gesture), narrative focus (verbal message), and lyrical focus (tensions between verbal meaning and vocal/instrumental) in representative songs from 1962 to 1969 and the relationship between the songs and subjectivity/identity. This chapter devotes particular attention to addressing whether they provided a common-sense framing of femininity that was both conservative and oppressive or one that was revolutionary. Specifically, I want to explore how and why female fans could recognize themselves in the modes of address ("I need somebody, not just anybody"—that is, who is that "somebody"?) and whether the Beatles' representations of femininity and, hence, their mode(s) of address, shifted across the years. Richard Middleton defines this phenomenon as the "variability of pertinence," which asks, in Middleton's words, "*what* is pertinent (that is, in the text) and *to what, for whom,* and *in what way*" is it pertinent in terms of "the contexts, needs, and place of the listening subject"? (240).

The Beatles first came to national attention with their debut single, "Love Me Do," and their subsequent appearance on British television's *Thank Your Lucky Stars* on February 13, 1963. This appearance allowed the band to debut their new single, "Please Please Me," before some six million viewers, and it marked a pivotal moment in their career. Successive hits, including "From Me to You" and "She Loves You"—especially the song's catchy chorus, "Yeah, yeah, yeah"—ensured that they became household names as their catch phrase was echoed in newspaper headlines and television alike. By 1964, after an appearance on the *Ed Sullivan Show*, their popularity in the United States overshadowed their preeminence in Great Britain. By April, they held an unprecedented top five spots on the *Billboard* Hot 100, and in Canada they boasted nine records in the Top Ten. They quickly spearheaded a new direction in popular music, one that extended peripherally into fashion and the arts and, more specifically, ousted the solo singer in favor of an irrepressible flow of Merseybeat talent that focused on group dynamics.

Unlike the first generation of rockers (such as Elvis Presley, Little Richard, and Buddy Holly) who were already established performing musicians, the second generation of British pop idols had been chosen primarily for their looks and their ability to copy the rock 'n' roll gestures—pouting lips, gyrating hips, surly gaze—that had characterized Presley's performances. These new artists were also given appropriately evocative names—Adam Faith, Tommy Steele, Marty Wilde—and thus drew on Presley's two most notable contributions to the language of rock 'n' roll: the assimilation of romantic lyricism and "boogification," where the basic vocal rhythms are triplets and an off-beat quaver is often given an unexpected accent, producing cross-rhythms and syncopation and a sexy, jittery effect (Middleton 18–19). The result was to commercialize what was originally a largely improvised and undemandingly simple musical format[5] and to bring to the fore the manufactured pop idol, single, boyish, white, good-looking, and replaceable, so allowing for swings in fashion both in terms of music and image. To a certain extent, the Beatles reflected this emphasis on personality. Despite their earlier promotion as the four Mop Tops (an allusion to their hairstyle, designed by Stu Sutcliffe's German girlfriend, Astrid Kirchherr), they had four unique personalities, thereby allowing for identification by a diverse fan base: Paul, the boyish figure with the big spaniel eyes; John, the sexy one; George, the quiet one; and Ringo, the lovable (if undistinguished) drummer.

As with the many other young bands of the period,[6] the Beatles' early repertoire consisted largely of cover versions of songs by Chuck Berry, Buddy Holly, Carl Perkins, and Little Richard. Additional material came from the likes of Bacharach and David, Leiber and Stoller, and Goffin and King, so providing influences that spanned rock 'n' roll, uptown rhythm and blues,[7] and the more lyrical ballads of Tin Pan Alley. Touring and residencies at clubs in Hamburg (including the Kaiserkeller, Bruno Koschminder's Indra Club, the Top Ten Club, and the Star Club) and Liverpool's Cavern had afforded them with valuable performance experience, as well as the opportunity to hone their repertoire and resilience—six-hour sets were common in German clubs at the time. The band had also engaged Brian Epstein as manager and attracted the attention of EMI producer George Martin, who signed them to a contract with Parlophone in June 1962. By autumn of that year, the Beatles broke through the British charts with "Love Me Do" and the rest, as they say, is history.

Although a thorough analysis of the Beatles' love songs would provide a more rigorous investigation into gender and mode of address, a study of selected songs from each of their major periods of composition provides some indication of representative shifts in their lyrics and appeal between 1962 and 1969. As discussed previously, the early 1960s were characterized by copy-cat rock 'n' roll (Adam Faith, "Poor Me") and skiffle (Lonnie Donegan, "My Ole Man's a Dustman"), and included artists such as Elvis Presley ("Are You Lonesome Tonight?"), the Everly Brothers ("Walk Right Back"), as well as British groups and vocalists such as the Shadows ("Kon Tiki"), Cliff Richard ("The Young Ones"), Helen Shapiro ("You Don't Know Me"), and the Temperance Seven ("You're Driving Me Crazy").[8] By 1963 chart toppers included Cliff Richard and the Shadows ("The Next Time"/"Bachelor Boy"), Gerry and the Pacemakers ("How Do You Do It?"), and Frank Ifield ("Wayward Wind"). Each month heralded a new hit (albeit from a limited stable), and these songs were largely formulaic and aimed at a young audience. Also evident is that the principal point of interest was the lead singer with the exception of instrumental bands such as the Temperance Seven and the Shadows. As such, the launch of the Beatles was significant in attracting attention to the group as a collective musical fusion emphasized by the band's distinctive vocal harmonies, acute sensitivity to color and textual detail, and the almost incantatory effect of repetitive rhythmic motives. As Martin recalls in *With a Little Help from My Friends: The Making of Sgt. Pepper* (1994):

> Paul was warbling away and John was backing him with that peculiarly distinctive, nasal, almost flat second harmony that was to become a trademark of their early sound. And it suddenly hit me, right between the eyes. This was a group I was listening to. I should take them as a group, and make them as a group. That distinctive harmony, that unique blend of sound—that was the selling point. It was something that I had dimly remembered from the demo lacquers. . . . There were echoes here of the Everly Brothers and the old blues heroes, of Elvis Presley and Chuck Berry, but there was also something entirely new, something English, something that was Liverpool, something Beatles. (31–32)

In short, what really made the Beatles' early hits memorable was not so much the instrumental style, although it, too, included some distinctive licks, but the vocals. Interestingly, the Beatles favored perfect fourths and fifths in their vocal harmonies (thereby distinguishing them from rockabilly) and independent melodic lines, again, setting them apart from the more usual close harmonies of the doo-wop groups. Significantly, they sounded like "scousers" (that is, from Liverpool) and their particular use of language was colloquial, thus distinguishing them from the mid-Atlantic drawl that characterized so many British songs of the period.

   "Love Me Do" is, as Charles Gower Price observes, "a pleasantly scruffy version of the Everly Brothers harmonies," and although not the most dynamic of the early Beatles songs, it is characterized by a bouncy feel, a highly memorable and climactic "So plea-yee-yee-yee-se," and a "colloquial turn of phrase at the end of the title refrain—'love me do,' an imperative call to physicality as opposed to mere talk" (183). The intensity of the song is largely attributable to the build at the end of the first section. As Stephen Valdez explains:

> the singing ("love, love me do") begins with an open fifth that converges briefly on a third and then immediately opens to a fifth again. As the song builds, the harmony on "plea-yee-yee-yee-ase" blends on a consonant minor third, the upper third of the tonic chord. While McCartney remains on the same pitch in the upper part, Lennon descends to a fourth and fifth before ending the anguished "please" with the minor third. . . . The anxiety felt in the harmony is ended with a brief rest followed by McCartney singing solo the words "love me do" an octave lower than the preceding phrase; after harmonizing throughout the verse, the hook is presented as the solo line. ("Vocal Harmony" 246).

The originality of the vocal harmonies provides an indication of why the Beatles sounded so fresh and different at the time and why Martin singled out such hallmark sound gestures as a unique selling point:

Clearly, for some of the early audiences, Lennon's harmonica playing was also something new. Although we find influences, most notably in the harmonica introduction and fills between vocal phrases, that echo Bruce Channel's "Hey Baby," Lennon nevertheless provides a memorable feel to the song (always important in an introduction that can be later whistled or hummed by the fan, so effecting recall), as well as setting the rhythmic mood for what is clearly a danceable track. Arguably, such concerns were determining factors in influencing Martin's choice of the song for the band's debut single. Also probable is that the passing resemblance to Carl Perkins's "I'm Sure to Fall" probably contributed to, rather than detracted from, its popularity. Familiarity (or, to be more precise, the notion of being similar but different) is an important feature of popular music. It ensures that an audience interacts with the track and intuitively recognizes the mood of the song while tuning into its distinctive features.

This sense of interaction is also important in terms of their second single and first number-one hit, "Please Please Me." By the time of its release, "Love Me Do" had edged its way into the Top Twenty in at least one London trade paper and the Beatles had appeared on *Thank Your Lucky Stars*. Their energetic performance style and hallmark vocals (not least of which included the clever use of the words "please please me," which drew on the evocative regionalism of the vowel sounds "plea-yee-yee-yee-ase" inherent in "Love Me Do") were thus recognizable, thereby engaging with the expectations of a growing community of fans. Again, the song is eclectic, having evolved from Roy Orbison's "Only the Lonely," but with a more upbeat, rock feel. Lennon again sets the mood with his harmonica (double-tracked here for the first time and drawn from the opening of the verse) and sings the vocals with McCartney droning a high E backing vocal reminiscent of the Everly Brothers' "Cathy's Clown." This time, the lyrics are more sexually explicit and, in Price's words, "the tight two-voice vocal responses of the Isley Brothers' inspired 'come on (come on),' which climaxes on the falsetto jump in the lead on the second 'please' of the title refrain" (184), suggests the reciprocal "please please me (oh yeah) like I please you."

"Love Me Do" and "Please Please Me" both appeared on the Beatles' first album, *Please Please Me* (released March 22, 1963). It also contained "I Saw Her Standing There," an R&B inspired song, again characterized by falsetto (an "ooh" at bars eleven and twelve). Harmonized a tenth below and coinciding with an IV–bVI progression that was to become a Beatles trademark, this use of a minor third root progression was without precedent in the popular R&B songs of the time. Three bars earlier, the change in bass guitar from eighth-note arpeggios to repeated crotchets had signaled a sense of expectation. When the progression finally arrives, its effect is heightened by the shock value of the falsetto "ooh" and the boldness of the perfect intervals in the vocal harmonies (O'Grady 29). The effect creates memorability and excitement, a characteristic also engendered by Harrison's lead guitar solo, which "is introduced," Terence O'Grady writes, "by the kind of ecstatic screams first encountered in the Beatles' recording of 'Twist and Shout'" (30) and the song's boisterous introduction. The Beatles' fourth single, "She Loves You," heralded the advance of Beatlemania in spectacular fashion. The high range of the unison melody, with its many dissonances against the underlying harmonies and the added sixth chord that concludes the opening section, provides a memorable "hook," which is picked up in the refrain, again introduced by ecstatic falsetto "oohs." It was, however, the repeated "yeah, yeah, yeah" that contributed most to the song's success. The words quickly became synonymous with the Beatles and, as a trademark sound gesture, is unparalleled in the early Beatles' repertoire.

Even more significantly, "She Loves You" is a song that adheres to the advice formula of girl-group songs, a genre that presented an explicitly female perspective (girl talk) and a variety of female viewpoints that were often based on "real" or quasi-real situations. This genre drew on teen argot and an often-dramatic interchange between two, often first- and second-person characters ("Then He Kissed Me," "Will You Still Love Me Tomorrow?"). Familiarity with the genre is evidenced in the Beatles' first two albums where five girl-group songs are covered ("Baby It's You" and "Boys," by the Shirelles; "Chains," by the Cookies; "Please Mr. Postman," by the Marvelletes; and

"Devil in Her Heart," originally titled "Devil in His Heart," by the Donays).
In essence, girl-group songs are characterized by a sharing of knowledge, and
in "She Loves You," McCartney "takes a friend aside," writes Jacqueline Warwick, "and passes on the gossip about the state of his (the friend's) romance,
dutifully repeating the message the girl entrusted to him" (165):[9]

> You think you've lost your love
> Well, I saw her yesterday-yi-yay
> It's you she's thinking of
> And she told me what to say-yi-yay

Harmonies (in this instance, the use of parallel harmonies in the second part
of the verse) provide a softening effect and the central focus on the nature of
"love" now becomes crucial to the Beatles' lyrics, first as the subject matter of
their songs and, as the 1960s progressed, through to the angst of "Yesterday"
(*Help!*, 1965), "Eleanor Rigby" (*Revolver*, 1966), "She's Leaving Home" (*Sgt.
Pepper*, 1967), and beyond to the more universal "All You Need Is Love."

The early Beatles songs discussed thus far can be classified by their ebullient and catchy qualities, and although we see a certain movement from the
imperative of "Love Me Do" and the underlying sexuality of "Please Please
Me" to the discursive nature of "She Loves You," their songs maintain a certain naïveté that renders them unthreatening. As McCartney recalled during
an interview with Mark Lewisohn in *Recording Sessions*:

> We knew that if we wrote a song called "Thank You Girl" that a lot of the
> girls who wrote us fan letters would take it as a genuine thank you. So a lot
> of our songs—"From Me to You" is another—were directly addressed to the
> fans. I remember one of my daughters, when she was very little, seeing
> Donny Osmond sing "The Twelfth of Never," and she said "he loves me"
> because he sang it right at her off the telly. We were aware that that hap-
> pened when you sang to an audience. (9)

Here, of course, they differ from the more nihilistic image of the Rolling Stones
who, along with the Beatles, established the rock/pop binary and its associated
images of being rebellious and dangerous in contrast with the conforming, boy-
next-door profile that marked their early repertoire. The Beatles were never
characterized as "cock rock," that raucous genre in which "all men are attractive
and potent and have endless opportunities to prove it," in the words of Simon
Frith and Angela McRobbie, and where the world they inhabit is "an ideal
world without physical or emotional difficulties" (382). Rather, the Beatles come
across as being "acceptable," as ideal boyfriends who are sexy but tuned into a
girl's perspective, thus allowing them both to enjoy and to explore their own sexuality through association with their respective idols.

The Beatles' vocal style is significant to our understanding of the connection that they shared with their massive female audience. In *Where the Girls Are: Growing Up Female with the Mass Media*, Susan Douglas suggests that the Beatles' magnetism was due at least in part to the fact that John, Paul, George, and Ringo sang in voices high enough for girls to sing along, thus affording Beatlemaniacs with the opportunity to participate in the music while they listened. Warwick explores this notion further and contends that the band's adoption of girl-group techniques meant that they seemed to speak from a girl's point of view. As Warwick notes, even as early as the band's Hamburg days, female audience members giggled and screamed, seeming to relish the fact that the Beatles were musically enacting the subject position of a girl. Whether this is empirically justified is uncertain, but what is apparent is that "many solo girl singers, girl bands, and girl groups produced songs responding to the Beatles," Warwick writes, "songs with titles like 'Ringo Boy' (Dori Peyton), 'Last Train to Liverpool' (the Plummons), 'I'll Let You Hold My Hand' (the Bootles), and 'Ringo, I Love You' (by Bonnie Jo Mason, an occasional *nom de plume* for Cher)" (163–64). The most commercially successful of these songs was the Angels' "Little Beatle Boy," possibly a tribute to George Harrison. Not insignificantly, the singer evinces little interest in wanting a "real" relationship with her Beatle boy; she is content to imagine that he is singing only to her and remains quite cheerful about the fact that he is going back to England:

> Little Beatle boy
> In my heart you'll always stay
> Even though you're far away
> I'll be true
> To only you
> My little Beatle boy.

Although the lyrics might denote a certain passivity on the part of the girl (and the solo singer is joined by her fellow Angels for the fourth line of each verse, thus implying support from her girlfriends), they do suggest that the Beatles' young fans were involved in an "imaginary" relationship of sorts with the Beatles, rather than pursuing the more active role of "groupie" associated with the Rolling Stones at the time. Despite the obvious hysterical responses at their concerts, the Beatles seemed to provide their fans with one particular route to adult sexuality. To be loved, their songs suggest, you have to please your man and he, suitably advised by his friends, will stand by you and try to understand. Moreover, all four Beatles seemed uniformly committed to this somewhat romanticized view of love. After all, they shared the same hairstyle and wore matching outfits.

By 1964 the Beatles had achieved the status of superstars, playing at a Sunday night concert at the London Palladium and a Royal Variety Performance at the Prince of Wales Theatre in London. Their second album, *With the Beatles* (1963), had attracted advance orders of 250,000 copies and immediately rose to the number-one position on the *Melody Maker* charts, remaining there for twenty-two weeks. By 1968 more than one million copies had been sold, making it the best-selling British album at the time. In 1966 the Beatles performed their final concerts on a world tour that brought them to Germany, Japan, the Philippines, and the United States. Girl-group cover songs became increasingly rare by this period in their career, although *Help!* includes the Lennon-McCartney original, "You're Going to Lose That Girl," which once again demonstrates the band's distinctive girl-group mannerisms in its vocal relationships and subject matter. What happens, however, to the Beatles' mode of address as the group becomes more immersed in studio recordings and, in effect, further removed from their original fan base?

Clearly, *Help!* and *Rubber Soul* reveal a more pronounced individuality and are dominated by Lennon and McCartney songs. As with their fans, the Beatles had become both older and wiser, and although this aspect is reflected in their more adventurous compositional techniques, their developing interest in alienation resonated with the mood of the times. Economic difficulties, humiliating defeats in foreign policy (not least, the rejection of Great Britain's application to join the Common Market [1963]), an increasing subordination to U.S. interests, scandal (the Profumo affair), and the prevalence of satire (especially underscored by the broadcast of television's *Private Eye* and the radio program *That Was the Week That Was*) had rapidly eroded the somewhat naïve sense of optimism that had characterized the late 1950s. Also apparent was that the end of the class war—promised initially by the British Labor party on the concept of reformed capitalism and appropriated by a reformed Conservative Government under the slogan "capitalism for the people"—was unlikely. The Conservatives bowed out, but the promise of renewed growth by Harold Wilson's newly elected Labor Government (1966) proved little more than Tweedledum to the Tories' Tweedledee. A wage freeze, cuts in public expenditure, a seaman's strike, and a move to more coercive and punitive measures in the sphere of industrial relations led increasingly toward a harsh and pervasive "control" culture. This phenomenon, in turn, was accompanied by a series of measures directed against the rising tide of permissiveness characterized, partly, by an emerging drug culture and an increase in sexual promiscuity. This shift in the prevailing mood in Great Britain is both reflected and constructed by the Beatles' songs between 1965 and 1969, and whereas their repertoire continues to engage with the concept of "love" (thus suggesting a continuing appeal to their female fans), we see a distinct change in emphasis.

"Ticket To Ride" *(Help!)*, for example, curiously resembles the verse melody of "She Loves You," both in contour (the use of the fourth degree of the scale) and the bridge with its exclusive reliance on the IVb7 and V7 chords. The mood, however, is different. This is largely achieved by the verse remaining on the tonic chord for six bars before a change in harmony against a repeated triadic riff, so effecting a stark, austere effect heightened by an emphasis on the root and fifth of the tonic chord by the rhythm guitar and bass. The words are equally bleak: "I think I'm gonna be sad, / I think it's today, yeah." The underlying sense of despair is heightened by the second half of the verse that begins (almost predictably) with a relative minor chord and an underlying dissonance to effect a sense of vulnerability because "she's got a ticket to ride." The ecstatic "yeahs" are also gone. In this instance, the vocal chorusing is both reflective and stark in the realization that:

she said that li-ving with me   is bring-ing her dow - - - n - yeah

This lack of self-assurance is also evident in "Help!" a song that reflects Bob Dylan's influence in the lyrics' highly personalized commentary:[10]

> When I was younger, so much younger than today,
> I never needed anybody's help in any way

McCartney's "Another Girl" also reflects an underlying cynicism as he ponders a new love interest who's "sweeter than all the girls and I've met quite a few," as well as the problems that plague his current relationship: "you're making me say that I've got nobody but you." The mood is inflected by another Beatle trademark, the use of chromatic mediant relationships between individual chords and bridge sections that begin on the submediant or subdominant without any real sense of modulation, thus evoking a feeling of being "stuck," both in terms of the music and the song's narrative. This quality is equally evident in Lennon's "You're Going to Lose That Girl," where a three-part harmonized vocal is assumed (against a continuing call and response vocal interaction) and a temporary modulation to the flat mediant is made via the reharmonization of a note common to both keys (O'Grady 73), as in McCartney's song:

a - noth - er girl   -   who will love   -   me till the end

During this period, Harrison appears equally disillusioned with romance and girls, and his song "If I Needed Someone" is similarly distinguished by a sense of cynicism—"carve your number on my wall and maybe you will get a call from me"—although it is the evocative "Yesterday" that most effectively sums up the band's prevailing mood of growing older, growing wiser.[11] Commercial pop music had long used string arrangements, but we find no evidence here of the lushness that is generally associated with the genre. Rather, the string quartet in "Yesterday" is restrained, adding subtle touches to the song, most specifically the sustained, inverted pedal note on first violin that effects a moody dissonance with the vocal line. Although the song is equally notable for McCartney's sweetly naïve vocal delivery and the sensitivity of the lyrics, it is also indicative of the Beatles' move toward a more extensive instrumental and stylistic experimentation. Lennon's "Norwegian Wood (This Bird Has Flown)" uses a North Indian sitar, courtesy of Harrison, and its ballad style and narrative-driven lyrics leave it far removed from Lennon's more usual rock style. McCartney's "Michelle" draws on the popular French chanson, and its tempo and general mood of restraint make it an unlikely candidate for the dance floor. Accompanied by "a mellow electric guitar and soft, pattering percussion," O'Grady writes, it is well removed from "the energetic, biting guitar and percussion combination found in so many Beatles' songs" (83). As O'Grady argues, *Rubber Soul* represents a new departure in the Beatles' career, situating their music in a context unrelated to the social dance function previously considered germane to rock and, indeed, to their own fan base. This phenomenon is also reflected in the overall dynamic of the album, where the emphasis shifts from the ear-catching sound gestures and rock rhythms of their earlier songs toward a more understated style and an emphasis on musical detail. In retrospect, this shift can be seen as a consolidation of pop/rock into a hybrid form, rather than pop inflected with the rock or folk conventions or both that had characterized their earlier compositions. It also suggests the cultivation of a more adult audience, one attracted to listening rather than dancing.[12]

As the Beatles so tellingly sing in "We Can Work It Out," "try to see it my way," a statement that is arguably at odds with the ebullience associated with their earlier songs and, perhaps, more in tune with older fans who had, themselves, experienced failing relationships and whose expectations about enduring love were somewhat jaded. Even more significantly, these songs are narrated, in contrast with their earlier work, from a masculine point of view. The woman in the singer's life has either failed him or she fails to listen, so precipitating a flight to a new, and one hopes more understanding, lover. The sense of celebration and lament that had earlier characterized the Beatles' repertoire thus becomes increasingly replaced by a new seriousness and cynicism, and although conventional love songs do not disappear from the band's musical horizon, we see a growing interest in psychedelia and hallucinatory experience reflected both in *Revolver* and in *Sgt. Pepper*. Significantly, we no longer find any particular ingredients that could be identified as constituting the Beatles' sound. Rather, the later albums, as Ray Connolly remarks, "came like multi-sorted variety shows offering a little of very many different kinds of music" (1). This was also true of their image. No longer the nice young men with their look-alike Mop Tops, they had moved increasingly toward individuality, albeit circumscribed by the beards and long hair favored by the mid-1960s counter-culture. This shift in emphasis is also reflected in their portrayals of women: Lennon's sarcastic wit emerges in "And Your Bird Can Sing," whereas Harrison reveals a growing interest in Eastern mysticism in "Love You To." McCartney, the only unmarried Beatle at the time, retains his romanticism in "Here, There, and Everywhere," although his sunny optimism is tempered by the reality of the morning after in "For No One."

By 1967 women seem to fall into radically different categories for the Beatles: those who hurt, those who nurture, those who exist as potential new love interests, and those who offer the possibility of one-night stands. We also find those women who are etherealized, including lost mothers ("Julia" and Paul's "mother Mary" in "Let It Be") and lost sons ("Hey Jude"), thus effecting a realization that the Beatles have indeed grown older and that some have children of their own. In consequence, this interest in the complicated ties that bind appears to shift the lyrical emphasis of their songs toward an increasingly masculine point of view. Because I have already written extensively on the Beatles' use of subjectivity and representation in *Revolver*[13] and *Sgt. Pepper*,[14] respectively, here I simply summarize some key points regarding how these issues relate to the band's changing modes of address within the context of a shifting fan base.

Songs such as "Julia" and "Hey Jude," among others, are notable for the ways in which they inscribe women within an idealized frame of reference. They draw on traditional definitions of femininity, where such associations as "gentleness, modesty, humility, supportiveness, empathy, compassion, tenderness, nurturance, intuitiveness, sensitivity, [and] unselfishness" (3), in the words of Rosemarie Tong, provide a commonplace yet fiercely patriarchal basis for constructing appropriate codes of behavior. "To be feminine, according to an ordinary definition," Susan Sontag writes, "is to be attractive, or to do one's best in being attractive and to attract" (118). To be fulfilled, according to patriarchy, is to marry, to have children, and to remain faithful, that is, to be a good, reliable mother and wife. This simple equation provides the necessary distinction between the unfulfilled spinster as inscribed in "Eleanor Rigby" and the maternal figure in "Hey Jude," where the mother is portrayed as comforter: "Let her into your heart," McCartney tells us, and "then you can start to make it better." In "Julia," Lennon's late mother is magically transformed via her "floating hair and seashell eyes" to the rank of goddess. Where "Eleanor Rigby" is marked by the anonymity of her existence, her unfulfilled status as a woman, and her nameless grave, the others have succeeded in fulfilling their feminine destinies.

"Lucy in the Sky with Diamonds" (1967) is equally a fantasy figure, albeit one inscribed within hallucinogenic culture. The image of the "girl with the sun in her eyes" both reflects and constructs the preferred face of the late 1960s—the "kaleidoscope" eyes and the waiflike figure epitomized by the omnipresent Julie Driscoll/Twiggy/Marianne Faithful genre. As Annette Kuhn observes, the idealization of the image is subtle in effect and plays on the "desire of the spectator in a particularly pristine way: beauty or sexuality is desirable to the extent that it is idealized and unattainable" (12). In effect, the woman is enhanced through illusion, detached from reality, and defined by the male as a fantasy escape from reality. The significance of this representation can be seen in the ways in which the idealized image was displaced onto the style of the period. The long hair, the emphasis on the eyes, and the use of body makeup reaffirmed the "made-up-ness" of the image of the woman herself, as one composed of surfaces, defined by appearance.

In contrast, songs such as "Lovely Rita" (1967) are generally considered mere "novelties" within the Beatles' repertoire, although the falling vocal "oohs" in thirds are reminiscent of early hits such as "Thank You Girl" (1963). Here, however, the earlier emphasis on love is replaced by the song's sexually driven coda, again demonstrating a shift in emphasis from romantic naïveté to the more knowing sexuality associated with the late 1960s. Even so, some songs suggest an underlying cynicism. "Lady Madonna" (1968) arguably represents the archetypal Earth Mother with her "children at her feet" and "wonder how you manage to make ends meet," whereas "Sexy Sadie" (also from 1968) is not so much about a woman but the Maharishi Mahesh Yogi with whom the Beatles had undertaken a three-month transcendental meditation course in February 1968. "Martha My Dear" is also misleading, given that the song was written about McCartney's sheepdog with the implication that those who are named are not necessarily female. "Sexy Sadie" and "Martha My Dear" include, respectively, stereotypic images such as Lennon's "you'll get yours yet" (presumably Sadie's comeuppance for appearing sexy yet not delivering the goods) and McCartney's mildly insulting "silly girl" putdown—"look what you've done!" Meanwhile, Lennon's "Dear Prudence" (1968) continues to endorse the childlike qualities the patriarchy values in stark contrast to his 1969 track, "I Want You (She's So Heavy)," where heavy metal inscribes an earthy sexuality to Yoko Ono and where the directness of expression and intensity of love evinced in the lyrics leave little room for sentimentality. We find, then, a suggestion that Lennon was already more interested in his personal life than in the group as a whole, and this is equally evidenced in the direction the other Beatles took. By the *White Album* (1968), it was becoming increasingly evident that they were disintegrating as a group and that they were more interested in their individual lives.

But were the Beatles any different at the beginning of their careers? Surely, their early compositions equally inscribe women within the patriarchy, moving them safely from family-of-origin to family-of-destiny without the problems associated with real-life sexual encounters. Later, whereas the emphasis shifts somewhat, we see a similar conservatism, albeit tempered by the occasional cynicism. What is evident is that the sentiments expressed in Beatles songs are countered by their skills as composers. Repressive attitudes are masked by an initial ebullience, later by a mastery of compositional style and diversity in instrumentation (including studio technology). The shift in emphasis is equally matched by a shift in their fan base from that of young females to a more broad-based appeal. On a personal note, I recognized myself in the songs of 1966 and beyond. They exerted a fascination and an image to which I subscribed. At that time, I was in my midtwenties and well into psychedelic rock and the more universalizing definitions of love that are encapsulated in the Beatles' 1967 hit, "All You Need Is Love," a song in which the faint echo of the refrain of "She Loves You" suggests a parody of both the "love generation" itself and the Beatles' own earlier apostolic roles. Perhaps this sense of self-mockery accounts most for the band's continuing appeal.

NOTES

1. For a thorough discussion of *Revolver*, see Russell Reising's anthology "Every Sound There Is": *The Beatles' Revolver and the Transformation of Rock and Roll* (2002).

2. See Derek Scott's "What's the Copy?: The Beatles and Oasis" for additional discussion of the Beatles' abiding influence in popular music.

3. See my "No Fixed Agenda: The Position of the Beatles within Popular/Rock Music."

4. See my books, *Sexing the Groove: Popular Music and Gender* and *Women and Popular Music: Sexuality, Identity, and Subjectivity*.

5. Huge violin sections, for example, replaced the guitar, sawing away at songs that were intended to represent rock 'n' roll.

6. McCartney joined John Lennon's skiffle band, the Quarry Men, in 1957. They were joined a year later by George Harrison and in January 1960 by Stu Sutcliffe. After a brief spell as Johnny and the Moondogs, they rechristened themselves as the Silver Beetles. Soon thereafter, they had become the Beatles and had recruited drummer Pete Best. Sutcliffe left the group later in 1960 and died in 1962 of a brain hemorrhage. Ringo Starr replaced Best in August 1962.

7. The phrase *uptown rhythm and blues* refers to a mostly black repertoire influenced by the blues but with a greater harmonic variety than is usually associated with the blues tradition. Gerry Goffin and Carole King often composed in an "uptown" style. Other performers included Chuck Jackson and Ben E. King (both cited by Lennon and McCartney as favorite singers and whose song "Chains" was included on the Beatles' first album in 1963), Smokey Robinson and the Miracles (whose song "You Really Got a Hold on Me" the Beatles recorded in 1964), as well as the girl group the Shirelles (whose song "Baby It's You" the Beatles also covered).

8. See "Number One Hits (1961–1962)" in *Guinness British Hit Singles*, compiled by Tim Rice, Paul Gambaccini, and Mike Read.

9. See also Matthew Bannister's "Ladies and Gentlemen, the Beatelles!: The Influence of Sixties Girl Groups on the Beatles."

10. The Beatles had become intrigued by Dylan and all attended his 1964 London concert, where they met with him afterward. Although his influence is not immediately evident, the Beatles' new thoughtfulness and use of imagery during this period are significant.

11. In "Yesterday," the track's use of a string quartet and acoustic guitar chords also marks it as an unlikely song for live performance by the band. Any substitution for the instrumentation would have changed the mood of the song and, as such, it represents the first critical step toward "studio rock," that is, music that is too complex or requires extensive technology, thus inhibiting live performance.

12. The Beatles stated that one of the reasons for no longer touring was that the endless screaming meant that their music could not be heard. This seems to indicate that they felt their music was sufficiently serious to merit a listening context and their increasing use of technology and unusual instrumentation equally made live performance by a four-piece band problematic.

13. See my chapter, "'Love is all and love is everyone': A Discussion of Four Musical Portraits," in "*Every Sound There Is*": *The Beatles' Revolver and the Transformation of Rock and Roll*.

14. See the chapters on "*Sgt. Pepper's Lonely Hearts Club Band*" and "1967 and Psychedelic Rock" in my book, *The Space between the Notes: Rock and the Counter-Culture*.

CHAPTER 4

<hr>

Painting Their Room
in a Colorful Way

The Beatles' Exploration
of Timbre

WALTER EVERETT

"TANGERINE TREES and marmalade skies," . . . "Cool cherry cream and a nice apple tart," . . . "The man of a thousand voices talking perfectly loud," . . . "The touch of the velvet hand like a lizard on a window-pane," . . . "Swaying daisies sing a lazy song beneath the sun," . . . the invocation of vividly represented sensations is often at the core of the Beatles' message. Particularly in their psychedelic years, these poets asked us to attend and consider in new ways scores of sights, sounds, tastes, and feelings. Paradoxically, at this same time, the group also proclaimed the Vedic and Taoist belief that worldly sensations distract the seeker from finding true knowledge in lines such as, "The more I learn, the less I know" and "See all without look-ing."[1] Listeners were advised to explore both inner and outer worlds as deeply and imaginatively as possible, each search adding insight to the other. This call to the imagination was placed by musical elements just as much as it was by words. But whereas values such as melody, counterpoint, harmony, rhythm, and formal construction are sometimes crucial in such expression, the Beatles most directly paralleled the acutely detailed sensory world of their lyrics in music in the realm of tone color—timbre.[2]

One can think of elements such as form and harmony as analogous to the structural foundation and the columns that block in a building's rooms, whereas the choices of instrumentation and vocal qualities are more like the paint that add color to the surface. The Beatles' imaginative play with timbre peaked in the records produced in the group's final years, 1966–1969, but their curiosity in this area had been aroused early in their recording career, only to find creative application in ever-increasing frequency, until by 1965 certain songs ("Yesterday," "Norwegian Wood [This Bird Has Flown]") were discussed chiefly for their instrumentation and by 1966, with *Revolver*, timbre seemed not so much an afterthought as an elemental part of composition. This chapter traces some of the many developments the Beatles made in the realms of instrumentation, voice colorings, and the electronic manipulation of same from their first buds through full flowering in their most imaginative recordings. We note both the contrasts and the blendings of the familiar with the unique in a domain in which the group always consciously sought innovation.

A LIMITED ROLE FOR TONE COLOR THROUGH 1964

In their early days as a successful live performance band, c. 1960–1962, the Beatles seem to have given little thought to instrumental tone color. Driving rhythm, striking harmony, unity of ensemble, and formal contrasts were of far greater importance to them, and generally remained so through the composition and recording of their first four albums. At this time, the group sometimes added harmonica to their regular stage lineup of two electric guitars, bass, and drums; in the studio, acoustic guitars, keyboards, handclaps, and assorted percussion also made occasional appearances. The core instruments themselves were not chosen for tonal qualities as much as for playability and visual style, although Harrison's Gretsch Duo-Jet (acquired in the summer of 1961) allowed far more variety of effects than did Lennon's dull-sounding Rickenbacker Capri (purchased in November 1960) or McCartney's Höfner bass (spring 1961). The sounds of all, however, were more or less equally marred by poor amplification equipment through mid-1962.[3] In their early recordings, producer George Martin would occasionally add piano, as in "Money," "Slow Down," "Matchbox," "Rock and Roll Music," and "Kansas City" (as did Paul himself in "Little Child"), or Hammond organ, as in "I Wanna Be Your Man." But in these cases, all rock 'n' roll "ravers," the keyboard seems to have been added to the group's prior arrangement simply to fill any possible textural gap or to amplify a rhythm and not in any demonstration of an interest in timbre per se. Conversely, Martin's addition of piano to "Misery" (with its odd tremolo in the introduction and the double-speed octaves in the bridge), celesta to "Baby It's You" (beefing up George's guitar solo), and a Steinway line to "Not a Second Time" are noticed for the timbral contrast they provide. The solo for "Not a Second Time," standing in for absent guitar, is articulated so sensitively, the notes placed so delicately, that the baritone piano part seems to speak for the fragile singer.

If the Beatles' early instrumental backing was not rich with timbral variety, their vocals were usually crafted with this goal in mind. This is particularly appreciable in the many arrangements in which John sings a main vocal line that is adorned by an upper harmony part, a descant line sung by Paul. Their suburban-Liverpudlian voices could blend as closely as would those of the brother pairs on which they modeled their early duet style: Phil and Don Everly and Carl and Jay Perkins. In duet, John and Paul would generally create contrasting colors not through variation of vocal technique, but by changing contrapuntal relationships within song sections (alternating parallel, contrary, and oblique voicings with unison passages; see the verses of "There's a Place" and "Thank You Girl") or among repeated sections (see the addition of a descant part to a previously single-line passage in the verses of "All My Loving" and the bridges of "From Me to You"). Rarely, other pairings would provide a differently colored duet, as do John and George in "You Really Got a Hold On Me" and Paul and George in "Don't Ever Change," and sometimes a three-part vocal arrangement would oppose some sections against others involving a single voice (as with the sustained backing vocals of the bridge in "Anna" or the three-part harmonies in the verses of "Chains"). When singing solo, however, John Lennon produced his own especially broad array of contrasting vocal colors, as with falsetto (see the Roy Orbison–like leaps in "Ask Me Why" or the "mi-een" climax in "I Saw Her Standing There") or various sorts of ornamentation (as with the sobbing "oh-oh-oh-oh-oh-oh" repercussions in the "Anna" retransition, the mordents in "There's a Place," the multiphonics in "Twist and Shout" and "Mr. Moonlight," and the emotive modulation of colors in "Baby It's You," as at 1:27–1:40).[4] The electronic manipulation of vocals was generally confined in these years to balancing them against the instrumental mass and the provision of occasional reverb and echo (see particularly "Rock and Roll Music" and "Everybody's Trying to Be My Baby").

Otherwise, color at this time (and indeed as the Beatles' compositional skills grew through 1964) was largely an aspect of harmony, in the variety of secondary chord choices and mode mixture, of intonational idiosyncrasies (Ringo's unorthodox temperament is particularly interesting and charmingly attractive), of nonchord tones added in the decoration of a final sonority (as with the sixths that decorate the final chords in "Matchbox," "She Loves You," and "No Reply," the lowered seventh ending of "Everybody's Trying to Be My Baby," or the ninth of "Devil in Her Heart"), or even of novel chord configurations, such as the simultaneous combination of E-minor and A[7] fingerings in the "She Loves You" coda (at 2:11–2:13), pointing ahead to more highly developed dissonances such as that which opens and has motivic value throughout "A Hard Day's Night." Such a handful of effects aside, each of the first four albums has a largely homogenous texture with little timbral contrast. This point established, we review the small details by which color might distinguish one song from another and might evidence slow but steady growth during this period; first we examine all work through 1963 and then trace the innovations in both 1964 albums.

The Beatles' most vivid instrumental colorings early on were sometimes tied to rhythmic effects. Most vividly, the Beatles often recreated stylized Latin rhythms, consciously seeking "the next big beat" in the cha-cha wood-block of "P.S. I Love You" and the maracas of "Devil in Her Heart" (giving the guitar thirds there the quality of a substitute for Mariachi trumpets!).[5] In the cases of both "Till There Was You" and "And I Love Her," the Beatles rejected attempted arrangements with electric guitars and full drum sets, moving instead to a much more sensitive Latinized color with George's Spanish classical nylon-string Ramírez guitar and Ringo's bongos. Other colorful rhythmic effects not tied to particular styles include the "stop time" by which Paul's nervous vocal gets the solo spotlight in "Love Me Do" or the way Ringo's around-the-kit drum fills direct the listener from refrain to bridge in "Please Please Me" and the repeated rhythmic pattern that highlights a syncopated hi-hat in "All I've Got to Do" just as it did in "Anna." And Ringo's contrasting rhythmic effects usually perform a form-defining function in the early recordings: note the way sticks are tapped together only in the bridge in "Do You Want to Know a Secret" and how different treatments of the ride cymbal color the contrasting sections of "She Loves You."

George's adoption of the softer nylon-string guitar points to one of the factors that can be most closely tied to timbral innovations: the increasing independence of instrumental parts, a trend that began very slowly but gathered momentum in 1965. Prior to that, Harrison can be seen as the group's sole color commentator; he was the fastest to develop an interest in tone color, most likely because as lead guitarist his instrumental contribution usually stood apart from that of the rest of the quartet, even if only in short melodic bent-note bursts that provided suffixes to phrases (see "From Me to You" and "She Loves You"), filling in the corners of the band's arrangements. One little-recognized technique by which George repeatedly marked his "sound" in the 1962–1963 singles was to double his lead riffs in double-stopped octaves, such as in the introductions to "Please Please Me" and "From Me to You" (the instrumental break of which tripled and quadrupled the line in further registers in harmonica and bass), and the coda of "This Boy." This octave doubling is a direct precursor to Harrison's adoption of the electric twelve-string guitar in 1964, and it even can be seen as an initial attempt to get the complex wave-shape maximized only much later with the sitar.

George's first recorded composition, "Don't Bother Me" (1963), marks an important watershed moment in the early tone-color history; it is here that a guitar's tone is first manipulated electronically. EMI engineers treat the signal from the lead guitar (in this case, actually the Rickenbacker John played) to heavy compression, which squeezes flat the strings' color and dynamic ranges, removing all traces of attack and decay, as if in imitation of an electronic organ. In the same track, George's own guitar is given heavy amp tremolo not heard in any previous Beatle recording, and the part's distinctive chiming of each chord change in the bridge (a texture also present but more buried in the bridge of "Hold Me Tight") further differentiates its role from that of Lennon's instrument. The highly contrasted guitar timbres stand out from these albums' typical homogeneity of sound and suggest an aim that becomes a bit more prevalent in the 1964 albums.

Just as it represents a culmination of early-style traits in all other musical domains, the late 1963 single "I Want to Hold Your Hand" summarizes the early Beatles approaches to tone color taken in the group's pre-Sullivan Show ascendancy. Vocally, we note that Lennon provides a falsetto retransition and McCartney adds a descant line to the second bridge, which initially Lennon sang alone. Harrison's guitar work includes bent-note suffixes and a slow chiming effect in the bridge. Lennon plays an organlike Rickenbacker compressed just as it had been in "Don't Bother Me." McCartney provides unusual double-stops in the bass in the bridge, as he had in the dark and stable verses of "All I've Got to Do" and as he would only in rare spots thereafter. Moreover, Harrison adds a chromatic bass overdub underneath his bent-note suffixes, increasing the drive to the cadence on the ambivalent mediant chord. Handclaps complete the early Beatles references.

The most dramatic timbral shift in *A Hard Day's Night* is due to a happy accident: the unanticipated presentation of a new electric Rickenbacker twelve-string guitar to George by its manufacturer in February 1964. Instead of six strings, the instrument possessed six courses, the four lowest of which were tuned in octaves and the two higher, at the unison. As opposed to the normal acoustic twelve-string arrangement, Rickenbacker paired the octave courses so that in normal play, the higher register would sound before the lower, adding to its brightness. The resulting timbre and its full resonance, heard on many tracks of the new album, was not unlike that produced by an unmuted Baroque harpsichord with a four-foot stop coupling the regular eight-foot register. The acoustic twelve-string guitar had long been used by folk acts with multiple singers and a single guitarist, who could achieve a very bright and chorally rich sound by strumming anywhere on the string (whereas a six-string could approximate this brightness only by overexciting the upper partials through plucking near the bridge). Whether the Rickenbacker designers had folklike strumming in mind when they created the electric version is unknown, but Harrison used it chiefly for melodic lead lines with occasional chording adding variety. Its remarkable difference from Lennon's rhythm work on his own Rickenbacker gave *A Hard Day's Night* a new stratification of guitar timbres that would characterize nearly all of the Beatles' remaining work together. Still, the album has a largely uniform sonority, with the nylon-string "And I Love Her" providing a sort of "vertical" textural break the way that "Till There Was You" did for *With the Beatles*. At the same time,

"I'll Be Back" looks ahead to the 1965 albums with its stratification of acoustic guitars: Harrison plays solo lines on the Ramírez, Lennon strums his Gibson J–160, and Harrison overdubs his own J–160 part.

Harrison's distinctive twelve-string soloing is most characteristic in the break of "I Should Have Known Better" (as played against Lennon's strumming of the Gibson electric-acoustic), in the introduction and nicely figurated solo of "I Call Your Name," and in the opening ostinato of "You Can't Do That" (where George's and John's Rickenbackers achieve strong contrast). His new guitar is doubled for greater depth by Martin's piano in the solos of "A Hard Day's Night" and "Any Time at All." His chiming, also demonstrated on the Country Gent in the verse of "Things We Said Today" and on the Ramírez in the "And I Love Her" bridge, takes on the new twelve-string sheen in the "Should Have Known" bridge and in the introduction to "If I Fell." In the latter, Harrison announces the exotic chord changes that are continuously rearticulated by Lennon's Gibson—an excellent example of the album's stratification of guitar timbres. Elsewhere in "If I Fell," Harrison overdubs his twelve-string guitar over the verse's first ending (at 0:39–0:40) to emphasize in high register the poignancy of the "sad" color of the minor-mode mixture, an operatic—and perhaps a first—example of color used for text-painting purposes.

Except for two portentous electronic effects, later 1964 recordings (for the fall single and album, *Beatles for Sale*) introduced only subtly new instrumental sounds. True, Harrison brought a new Gretsch to the sessions, and the Tennessean produced a pronounced nasal—bright, full treble, and twangy—quality to songs such as "I'm a Loser" and "I Don't Want to Spoil the Party" that had not been heard before, but this was a relatively small change from the sound of the Country Gentleman.[6] Other new guitars make for even less of a change of color, but point in new directions: McCartney strums an acoustic in "I'll Follow the Sun" (this initial adoption of the guitar will soon lead to much more radical playing on his part) and in "Honey Don't," Lennon plays a Framus acoustic twelve-string guitar (later responsible for new sounds on the *Help!* and *Rubber Soul* LPs). But the two new electronic effects—the feedback for the opening of "I Feel Fine" and the silvery articulation in the lead guitar for "Baby's in Black," both involving a novel sort of partnership (Lennon using McCartney's amplified bass tone to set his midrange-enhanced Gibson vibrating and feeding back in "I Feel Fine," and Lennon continuously turning the volume knob of Harrison's Gretsch to mask the attacks and create swells in a "Baby's in Black" guitar line whose last notes are also altered in pitch by the changing tension applied by the Bigsby vibrato)—represent a collective second deliberate step (after "Don't Bother Me") toward the electronic manipulation of timbre that will mark the Beatles' most colorful work. (Lennon takes the opening feedback gesture to a new level in 1967 when he ferociously applies the whammy bar in a nod to Hendrix in opening Harrison's "It's All Too Much.")

Otherwise, guitar combinations represent a continued effort at stratification (the electric twelve-string guitar sounding the opening and coda of "Eight Days a Week," as in "If I Fell," as opposed to the Country Gent heard elsewhere there), new ensemble sonorities from careful unison doublings (John and George each playing an electric twelve-string guitar in "Words of Love"), and something in between (in "What You're Doing," Lennon and Harrison play different electric twelve-string parts).[7] The Gretsch solo doubled at the unison in "She's a Woman" (including all ornamental hammer-ons, pull-offs, and portamento slides) shows how double-tracking could alter the tonal qualities of a guitar solo.

Another subtle aspect of arrangement exists in the way that all guitars and drums change their rhythm in the last verse of "Baby's in Black," a feature that becomes far more celebrated when redone at the same spot in "Help!" New drums also produce a bit of variety in the use of a pitch-bending African drum in "Mr. Moonlight" and a single timpani in "Every Little Thing." A very brief but prominent innovation is the bass drum/tom-tom figure leading to the repeated-note bass solo in "What You're Doing," calling unusual attention to a rhythm section that will become much more soloistic by late 1965 and 1966. McCartney takes his keyboard work to a new level in his overdubbed Steinway line in "She's a Woman," which substitutes for lead guitar in the second verse. (In addition to his newly highlighted bass and piano work, McCartney steps out vocally in the retransition of "What You're Doing," in the suddenly confident melismatic line "it's me-ee-ee-ee-ee-ee-ee!" presaging a similar retransitional effect to be created in "Yesterday.") Elsewhere, the piano fills a registral role in the bass of "Every Little Thing," much as it had in "Not a Second Time."

The low register is also home to some new tones from Lennon's voice in "Words of Love" and "I'm a Loser," one of several indications that the Beatles were working from an expanding vocal palette as well as an instrumental one. An unusual new emphasis on open perfect intervals (as opposed to the sweeter parallel thirds and sixths favored throughout earlier recordings) brings a new, edgy kind of vocal counterpoint to "No Reply" (in the en*light*ening sustained fourths at 0:17–0:18 ff., recalling the power of the sustained chromatic "green" third of "You Can't Do That"), "Mr. Moonlight" (in the weirdly awesome repeated fourths at 0:25–0:29), "Eight Days a Week" (in the hollow alternating pairs of parallel fifths and parallel fourths, replete with nonharmonic tones at 1:03–1:14), and "Words of Love" (in the mesmerizing sustained fifth at 0:20–0:21 ff.), a type of sonority hinted at previously only in the octave doubling in the introductory motto of "I'll Get You."

Despite the large number of details counted in the past few pages, the Beatles' recordings through 1964 were in nearly every case made with similarly combined voices, electric guitars, bass, and drums with minor modifications and additions to the basic formula. Even when some of the more noticeable changes were made, as in the adoptions of the electric twelve-string guitar and then the Tennessean, entire albums often had a more or less continuous texture, sometimes relieved by an all-acoustic number or an occasionally conspicuous appearance of soloistic color. But the overall sound of each new album in 1964, however homogenous in isolation, was different from that of all preceding efforts. And in the year to come, this regular but slow color change was to refract into different layers, each of which would change at different tempos, and be replaced by a mindset through which every song might be recorded with a new and singularly appropriate combination of instruments.

CONTINUED TRENDS AND NEW SOUNDS IN 1965

In the two album projects of 1965, *Help!* and *Rubber Soul*, the Beatles made incremental although significant advances in approaches to instrumentation, while adding further contrast to the stratification of guitars that had opened up in 1964. One scheduling-related circumstance can partly account for the increasing variety of sound: with more time devoted to each album, overdubs might be done on different days than those on which basic tracks were laid, and it was less common for several titles to be recorded from start to finish in the same session. This fact carries with it the corollary that amplification/microphone setups, and even which particular instruments might be out of the cases at any given time, might now be more routinely different from recording to recording, promoting conscious decisions—as opposed to convenience and happenstance—in determining color. In addition, George Harrison admits to choosing his guitars for the first time this year for their sonority: "It was funny, because all these American bands kept coming over to England, saying, 'How did you get that guitar sound?' And the more I listened to it, the more I decided I didn't like the guitar sound I had. . . . But anyway, I decided I'd get a Strat, and John decided he'd get one too."[8] In addition to these Fender Stratocasters (heard first in "You're Going to Lose That Girl"), Paul bought an Epiphone Casino and added a hot new color (the open hollow body resonating almost to the point of feedback) as well as new technique to the Beatles' lead-guitar arsenal in "Another Girl" and the "Ticket to Ride" retransition and coda. Both John and George were to acquire their own Casinos, and John's was eventually to become his favorite guitar. Also important to the early-1965 sound is the new Hohner Pianet, an electric piano that amplified vibrating reeds, which John and Paul played alternatively in "The Night Before," "Tell Me What You See" (once again, Mariachi trumpets are suggested by triplets in parallel lines), and many other songs recorded through the rest of the group's career.[9] In the introduction to "You Like Me Too Much," Lennon turns a knob to saturate the keyboard with maximum tremolo (perhaps to complement the hand tremolo of the parallel sixths in Martin's Steinway part, and in contrast against the new sort of guitar/piano dialogue heard in the instrumental break).

Whereas Harrison had once needed Lennon's help to mask the envelope of his guitar signal in "Baby's in Black," he used a new device in three February 1965 recordings ("Ticket to Ride," "Yes It Is," and "I Need You") that would do so electronically: the volume/tone pedal, which could alter the tone's dynamic (or, as in a wah-wah pedal, harmonic) profile after its articulation by the hand. Thus, the ethereal, liquid, shimmering or even-toned and flutelike guitar sounds in these tracks that can retrospectively be understood as predictors of the backwards-guitar sounds of a year hence and even of flutelike backwards-piano tracks such as those heard in "Revolution 9." (The pedal is hardly used at all in the Beatles' last several albums, but can be heard at the end of "Come Together" [at 3:02–3:11]). Also on *Help!*, the Beatles resurrect a performance technique not heard since their early days, where two guitars would double the same line; heard in oldie-covers such as "Dizzy Miss Lizzie" and "Bad Boy" (listen for the mishap-suggesting commentary involving the canary and cat in the latter's Bigsby vibrato), this effect was also achieved in two volume-pedal lines at the end of "Yes It Is" and in octaves in the solo in "The Night Before." Otherwise, we see a strong interest in a great variety of simultaneous guitar sounds, notably in "Help!" (note Harrison's between-verses figuration, electric lines in varying tempi—cautious and then more urgent, undergirded by the strummed acoustic twelve-string guitar), "It's Only Love," "I've Just Seen a Face" (note the acoustic twelve-string solo), and perhaps most of all in "Ticket to Ride," which contrasts Harrison's well-known opening twelve-string Rickenbacker ostinato with three guitar overdubs: a first-scale degree drone Lennon played, Harrison's own volume-pedal enhanced punctuating chords (as at 0:29–0:30), and McCartney's bluesy Casino overdub for the retransition (1:24–1:28).

Help! highlights a few new vocal sonorities: John answered by George in "Help!"; Paul providing descant for Ringo in "Act Naturally"; John's continued focus on his low register ("Tell Me What You See," "I'm Down"); and gravelly multiphonics from both John (in his sensitive Dylan imitation in "You've Got to Hide Your Love Away") and Paul (in his raucous shouting in "The Night Before"). But the album's most significant coloristic innovation is the new incorporation of outside performers, first in the two flutes doubled in octaves for the ending of "Hide" and then in the string quartet added to Paul's solo guitar and voice in "Yesterday." This song's dark and portentous opening owes its effect solely to McCartney's guitar tuning—a very large guitar, the Epiphone Texan, dropped a whole step to accommodate his voice range—and his guitar voicing with the third omitted from the opening chord. And many interesting facets of the string arrangement, particularly the cello line, come directly from the guitar part, which it doubles to a great extent. Other tricks, such as the first violin's inverted pedal in the final verse (an effect used later by electric guitar in "Back in the U.S.S.R."), are original with the string parts, which McCartney and Martin created jointly as they sat at a piano. The listener is also drawn to the parallel retransitions—first violin descending in the first lead-in, McCartney copying this with his vocal melisma in the second lead-in—a musical "remembrance" helping to portray the song's nostalgic theme.

Despite this new approach to personnel and the fact that later Beatles recordings are shaded by all sorts of outside performers including choirs and large orchestras, the Beatles produced all the sounds of *Rubber Soul* and its attendant late-1965 single aided only by two members of their inner circle: producer George Martin and road manager Mal Evans. The most important new aspect to *Rubber Soul*'s rainbow of colors is not the celebrated use in "Norwegian Wood" of the sitar (which often doubles the lead guitar line when not providing a drone), but McCartney's August 1965 adoption of the Rickenbacker bass. Like Harrison's twelve-string guitar, this instrument was serendipitously given to the Beatle by its manufacturer rather than sought out by its player. Its solid maple body provided a much more focused tone than did the hollow-body Höfner, and McCartney also played through a Fender Bassman amplifier for the first time in the *Rubber Soul* sessions. This combination produced a new sound, and it led McCartney to invent highly independent bass lines (see particularly "Drive My Car," "Nowhere Man," "Michelle," "What Goes On," "If I Needed Someone," "The Word," and "You Won't See Me") that would add a new melodic dimension to his continued role as the band's harmonic foundation. McCartney was now and forever after easily disposed to play rhythm guitar or keyboard for basic tracks, adding his bass track as an overdubbed counterpoint.

The registral array of guitar stratification was stretched in much of the year-end album just as much at its upper end as at its lower region, in the group's several uses of the capo. Not only does the capo allow for the easy transposition of parts, it also has just as brightening an effect on resulting timbre as did the dropped tuning darken the opening of "Yesterday." The capo effectively shortens the string length (either a little, in the case of its use at the second fret in "Norwegian Wood," or quite a bit, when at the fifth frets on three different acoustic guitars for "Michelle" or even at the seventh fret—dividing the string in thirds—for an exceedingly brilliant electric twelve-string solo in "If I Needed Someone" and used later on acoustics for the bright "Here Comes the Sun"), artificially creating a sort of soprano guitar. (The final verse of "Girl" uses such a faux-soprano effect along with very rapid decay to emulate a bouzouki added to the accompaniment.) And the capo was not an isolated treble-related accident; we also note that in September 1965 John and George removed the pickups from the neck area of their Gibsons and reattached them near the bridge and that John and George ran their Strats through several sets of faders so the engineers could boost the treble to the utmost, multiple times, to enhance their silvery doubled part in "Nowhere Man," the solo of which culminates in the first natural harmonic featured in a Beatles recording.

"Michelle," which blends Paul's Texan, George's acoustic twelve-string, and John's nylon-string classical guitars (all capoed), also features the group's first significant use of preamp distortion in George's overdubbed electric Casino line. This part gets its beefed-up midrange tone from a choice of the neck pickup and a use of the amplifier's midrange boost control (as if to provide contrast against the trebly Strats of "Nowhere Man"), and gets its beautiful sustain from the very high gain setting on the preamp that overdrives the signal leading to the amplifier. (A later midrange-heavy, clarinet-like guitar solo is heard in "Honey Pie.") Balancing the high-register volume/tone-pedal effects heard in two harmonized lead guitars throughout "Wait" (well separated in the stereo image, now a mix-determined feature of increasing importance in Beatle arrangements) is the new "fuzz" bass effect in "Think for Yourself," where Paul doubles his normal (very independent) bass line an octave higher with extreme distortion for a fuzz effect, perhaps produced with the aid of Vox's Tone Bender, a box that produces an overdriven signal. Elsewhere (as in "Drive My Car" and "The Word"), a more normal guitar timbre is used to double the bass line in octaves, and sometimes (as in "Run for Your Life"— again, note the stereo separation between the constituent guitars—and "Day Tripper"), two guitars double the bass line. And as with "Ticket to Ride," the instrumental break of "Day Tripper" features a wild mixture of different guitar colors/functions, preparing for the vocal climax on the dominant with a new transposition of the ostinato, with a volume/tone-pedal-colored scale rising—one note per measure—through an entire tension-filled twelfth and with a blues-scale solo that fills prior voids in register, rhythm, and inflection of pitch. With this album, guitars are no longer simply an accompaniment for singers, but often become the center of attention, authoring sounds as well as executing them.

As in *Help!*, a new keyboard instrument graces the late-1965 recordings: the wheezing and swelling harmonium that carries the tense suspensions in "We Can Work It Out" and "The Word." Both of these songs also use an effective crash of the suspended cymbal, a sound previously reserved for the announcement of the arrival of a new formal section but now used for its text-painting value, whether it be to portray the crossed-purposes fighting in "We Can Work It Out" or to create a bright mix of partials along with the harmonium to symbolize a spiritual sort of enlightenment at the end of "The Word" (compare the crash-cymbal sunshine here with that in "Good Day Sunshine" recorded a few months later). Similarly, harsh clusters from the organ are heard to blend with the punctuating electric guitar chords following the choruses of "I'm Looking through You." For "In My Life," Martin resurrects his "wind-up" piano, recording a concert grand at half tempo and an octave lower on tape driven at half speed, to approximate the fast decay of a harpsichord for his solo in Baroque counterpoint when replayed at normal speed. This track also features an interesting mix of "Anna"-like syncopated hi-hat, tambourine, and a ringing ride cymbal. Ringo also provides his first of several snare rolls for "Nowhere Man." Clearly, the Beatles were learning to blend as well as contrast their now multitudinous timbres and to do so for novel effects.

Along with a suddenly increased melodic proliferation of accented passing and neighboring tones in the emancipated bass line, the color of the Beatles' arrangements for *Rubber Soul* is also due in part to an increasing emphasis on nonchord tones in "choral" parts, right off the mark in the vocal "car horns" of the album's lead track, "Drive My Car," but also very notably in "The Word." This new command of a suddenly rich counterpoint will allow for a quantum leap in the independence of parts in *Revolver* and with it a vast new explosion of color.

THE BREAKTHROUGH OF *REVOLVER*

We now reach a point in the Beatles' history where emphasizing serially the individual instrumentation of each track or attempting to list all of the new instruments and colors brought to bear in any single collection of songs becomes almost counterproductive because with the exception of 1969's *Let It Be* project (guided by an aesthetic tied to the live stage performance of a simple 1960's rock 'n' roll band), such individuality lies at the core of nearly every track recorded by the band after 1965. Every song has its own mood, theme, structure, and imagery, and timbre is now a central expressive device to these ends. Even tracks from 1966 with traditional instrumentation are treated to color manipulation either at the production stage or in engineering at the mixing board. For instance, Ringo's drums have a punchier sound with little or no decay from 1966 onward because the drumheads themselves are damped (as with a cigarette pack on the snare and with woolen sweaters or piano covers within the bass drum) and because heavy compression is added at the board. Similarly, the horns in "Got to Get You into My Life" are miked in the bells when possible for an unnatural restriction of emphasized partials; John Lennon's voice is run through a revolving Leslie speaker from a Hammond organ (previously noticeable in "Mr. Moonlight") through the second half of "Tomorrow Never Knows" (after 1:26) in an attempt to emulate the sound of the Dalai Lama shouting from a mountaintop. An increased dependence on overdubbing led to combinations that previously would have been ruled out as superfluous but which now create brand-new timbres, such as the doubling of clavichord on top of piano, both played by McCartney before he added his vocal and finally his continuo-supporting bass line, in "For No One" (the continuo notion is also supported by the Baroque horn obbligato, all reminiscent of the texture of a solo Handel cantata). Sometimes, as in "Good Day Sunshine," the extensive overdubbing would require multiple generations of tape, burying the basic track so far in the background that more cymbals or hi-hat would have to be added to keep them sunshine-bright and centered. "Yellow Submarine" is replete with appropriately goofy sound effects, and "Tomorrow Never Knows" becomes all the more mystical for its otherworldly tape effects (including the Beatles' first use of a Mellotron, a keyboard instrument built of sound tapes that—like the guitar treated by the volume/tone pedal—omit the attack-and-decay envelopes from the sounds of traditional instruments) and continuous panning. (Sound effects would be used as late as with the hog grunts of "Piggies" and the tape loops bridging "You Never Give Me Your Money" and "Sun King.") Experimentation in creating new sounds for their own sake almost seemed more important than the crafting of rhythmic, melodic, harmonic, and poetic wonders, although critics have not complained of backsliding in these departments.

In addition to the techniques already mentioned, engineering became more a realm of imaginative play in *Revolver* than in previous work, where the aim had been to present the Beatles as live performers, excepting such universal pop-recording techniques as the addition of reverb and an artificial equalization and limiting of the dynamic range (to aid the record-pressing process and guarantee satisfactory radio transmission). Now, the aim was to create new colors at every possible step: Paul's bass was both miked from his amp's speaker cabinet and injected directly into the board; they even experimented using a large speaker as a "microphone," transducing the amplifier output into a rather unconventional signal that was then run to the board. Tape-speed manipulation allowed Lennon both to speed up his voice in "I'm Only Sleeping" and to slow down the instruments in "Rain," two tracks also notable for the Beatles' first tape-reversed guitar and vocal lines, respectively. Instead of double-tracking their vocals, the Beatles could have a single part "split" onto two separate tracks by an EMI engineer's invention of artificial double tracking (ADT), which would then typically be mixed to separate locations in the stereo image. Note for instance the cinematic effect at 0:32 in "Eleanor Rigby," where ADT washes the left-right spectrum with artificially placed vocal color as Paul's narrator simultaneously shifts authorial voice and spatial location. The coda of "Good Day Sunshine" is drenched with overlapping double-tracked vocals, and the decay of the vocal refrain of "Paperback Writer" (0:47–0:49) is given a heavy artificial tremolo when the tape speed of the echo delay (as opposed to the tape speed of the vocal itself) is slowed down. Such effects are announced as a major player in *Revolver* right at its opening, which satirizes the introductory count-off to the Beatles' first album with tape-manipulated guitar warm-up on the right, a languid count-in from a rehearsal take on the left, and a voice-clearing cough in the center. The central role of the mixing process was also manifested by George Martin's pulling of the mono *Revolver* album on its day of release, necessitating the re-pressing of an already-released Beatles record for the first time to exchange mixes of "Tomorrow Never Knows." Because of all this attention to coloristic detail, many listeners suddenly found wiring themselves to the hi-fi with headphones much more satisfying than dancing with a record playing in the background.

Revolver is scored with numerous instrumental approaches not heard before: the string octet in "Eleanor Rigby" is far more powerful than the unimposing strings of "Yesterday"; a new kind of shimmering is found for "Love You To" in the Indian ensemble of svaramandal, sitar, tamboura, and tabla; the rinkity-tink barrelhouse piano with its metal-tipped hammers and mistuned string courses gives "Good Day Sunshine" a breezy informality; George's new Gibson SG brings many numbers a hot new hard-rock guitar, and this and his Casino are often distorted past the point of blistering feedback (complementing the sympathetic harmonics of the album's sitar, shining variously through the organ or the crash cymbal), as in the acidic trails of "She Said She Said." And the Beatles find new depth in the most basic of their sounds: McCartney and Starr harmonize with each other in strange new ways as the bass doubles each of the drums and cymbals for a bizarre ten-second duet in "Rain" (2:24+), as if to provide registral balance against all the high-partial complexities of the song's blending "shine" emitted by the sustained nasal vocals and nonharmonic tones in strummed guitar chords. Many Beatle albums have been identified in shorthand: *Rubber Soul* is the "guitar" album; *Sgt. Pepper* is the "psychedelic" or the "concept" album; the *White Album* is the "postmodern" collection; *Abbey Road*, the "swan song." Despite a universally growing acceptance of *Revolver* as a masterpiece, this album has not been so glibly characterized. Its wide variety of intentions, directions, and techniques, in color as in all other realms, simply eludes coherent reductive description.

PSYCHEDELIA

Right from the Mellotron and slide-guitar opening of "Strawberry Fields Forever," Beatles colorings had grown to become vaguely impressionistic, like distantly recalled fragrances, as opposed to instantly identifiable guitars and drums. The hyper-vivid shock of highly saturated and contrasting colors that was psychedelia inspired the Beatles' most original and expressive achievements in this domain. Whereas timbral experimentation was certainly going strong in *Revolver*, the recordings released in 1967 display the band's most riotous, brilliant maturity as colorists. The year is marked not so much by the introduction of new sounds in and of themselves, but by the integration of previously discovered timbres through novel combinations and artistic new ways of conceiving of their functions; a plateau had been scaled with *Revolver*, calling for the complete exploration of a wholly new terrain. In 1967 the Beatles can still be heard as a guitar-playing ensemble, but shedding that image is as easy for them as taking on the persona of Sgt. Pepper's band. Some of the group's most imaginative color displays, as in "Strawberry Fields Forever" and

"Lucy in the Sky with Diamonds," are the products of hours-long studio sessions devoted to arrangement and rehearsal, an unprecedented use of competitively booked and expensive studio time that led to *Sgt. Pepper*'s being months in the making. Arranging was now the dominant segment of the compositional process, not to say that the creation of lyrics, melodies, harmonies, rhythm, and form had become simply a matter of routine.

An interesting aspect of the new integration relates to the idea of *Sgt. Pepper* as a "concept" album, although in much more subtle a manner than normally suggested. Each song in this album has its own individual color, giving timbral variety to the motivic references to one song made in another: the dronelike opening g^1/g^2 octaves of "Getting Better," repeated there by a doubling of muted electric guitar and staccato Pianet, are suggested in the same repeated vocal and harpsichord Gs in the "Fixing a Hole" bridge (at "see the people standing there . . . ," 0:51+). Conversely, repeated pitches other than Gs are related to the "Getting Better" opening through their articulation alone, as with the very high repeated staccato violin c^3s in "Within You Without You" (2:42+) or the bass-and-piano's clipped low-register E octaves that introduce the bridge in "A Day in the Life" (2:16+). Related sounds can be achieved in very different ways: the buzz of bass harmonicas in "Being for the Benefit of Mr. Kite" (an idea taken from the Beach Boys' "God Only Knows") is produced with combs and tissue paper in "Lovely Rita," and the album's summary includes a related effect, from the fuzzy acoustic beats the heavily doubled pianos produced in the final chord of "A Day in the Life" (note particularly 4:24–4:36). Even sounds not normally considered to be part of the performance help unite the album, as in the similarly textured whispered or otherwise "off-stage" counting, from George in "Within You Without You" (3:41–3:47), Paul's cue for the Reprise, and Mal Evans's reverb-laden placeholding later (mostly) covered by orchestra in "A Day in the Life." Motivic intersong instrumental interplay takes on more abstract procedural incarnations as well, as in the rapid hockets that recall each other in the two guitars (one heavily distorted) of the "Sgt. Pepper's Lonely Hearts Club Band" chorus (at 0:55–1:01) and in the tubular bell, piano, and bass of the "When I'm Sixty-Four" retransition (at 1:54–2:02; the bass and bass clarinet double in 1:04–1:07 much as the bass and drums did in "Rain").

Then, too, are the timbral puns of 1967: the fireman's bell and barber's bass-viol trim (2:04–2:09) in "Penny Lane" and the bass clarinet adding an ominous tone presaging the threat, "you'll be older too" (0:37+) in "When I'm Sixty-Four," not to mention the colorful choices of words and their clever vocal articulation for text-painting effect, as in the sneezing onomatopoeia of "kitchen," "clutching," and "handkerchief" in "She's Leaving Home" (0:31–0:35) and the familial tongue-rolling burr of all three Rs in "grandchildren on your knee" (1:49–1:52) and elsewhere in "When I'm Sixty-Four." More like the sound effects already known from "Yellow Submarine" are the crowd noise, orchestral tuning, and brass-band concert setting of the *Sgt. Pepper* title track, the laughter appending "Within You Without You," and the circus's swirling steam organs of "Being for the Benefit of Mr. Kite," but much more subtle effects are sought as well, such as the pop of the wine cork over dinner in "Lovely Rita" (1:27). *Sgt. Pepper* introduces a few new sonorities: Ringo emulates in the first of several instances a dance-band drummer with his brushwork in "When I'm Sixty-Four," and Mike Leander provides a rich dictionary of text-painting articulations in his arrangement for harp (initially laden with ADT) plus string nonet of "She's Leaving Home." George Martin provides brilliant new 1967 arrangements in "Penny Lane," "Within You Without You" (note how the dilrubas and then the violins double Harrison's vocal glissandi), and "I Am the Walrus." And the Beatles extend extra care to their performances; note the beautiful blending of backing vocals and clarinets in "When I'm Sixty-Four" (1:48–1:49), most appreciable in the tracks as separated for the 1999 DVD release of *Yellow Submarine*.[10] All this abundance of color gives the bleak opening of the album's final song, "A Day in the Life," a most appropriate reserve in its simple strummed acoustic guitar, grand piano, bass, and its otherworldly reverb-covered vocal. This sparseness, of course, provides the song's and album's perfect foil for the superabundant full-orchestra climax to come.

Perhaps the best way to gain insight into the Beatles' full-grown command of the expressive power of an integrative approach to tone color is to examine its role through a single composition; the many subtle refractions of "Lucy in the Sky with Diamonds" would provide a good example. Color is at the heart of this song's Lewis Carroll–inspired wordplay about a Looking-Glass ride by boat, taxi, and train guided by "a girl with kaleidoscope eyes," imagery initially suggested to Lennon by his four-year-old son's colorful drawing of a classmate, Lucy, pictured floating in the sky.[11] Whereas nearly all Beatles song manuscripts consist entirely of lyrics (either in draft form or fair copy, inscribed either by the composer or by assistant Mal Evans), that of "Lucy" is unique, to my knowledge, in containing any musical information at all. Interwoven through a mere sketch of individual-word cues from various points in the lyrics and the arrival points of a few structural chords is a somewhat detailed scoring outline, indicating at what point certain instruments are to enter, certainly an indication of the unusual importance Lennon places on timbre for this song.[12] Lennon most likely scribbled the preferred indications during the song's eight hours of rehearsal at the EMI Studios on the day before tape started rolling, as group members tried out different instrumental settings.

As he opened Lennon's "Strawberry Fields" with the solo Mellotron, Paul McCartney provides an exotic, brightly gaudy solo keyboard sonority for the "Lucy" introduction. This is played on the Lowrey DSO Heritage Deluxe electronic console organ; Andy Babiuk specifies a registration combining harpsichord, vibraharp, guitar, and music-box stops.[13] McCartney's organ, swimming in reverberation, took the lead through the recording of the song's basic tracks, during which Lennon played piano, Harrison strummed his acoustic Gibson, and Starr played drums; nearly all of these other components were completely muted (only a single D-minor chord remains from Lennon's piano) or otherwise buried in the final mix. Overdubs consisted of Harrison's tamboura (also used for color in selective spots in "Getting Better" as well as its more traditional use as a drone throughout "Within You Without You") and his Stratocaster guitar, McCartney's Rickenbacker bass (its rhythms ornamented in the third verse), two vocals from Lennon and one from McCartney. All elements are blended by the performers and molded by engineers to create an extravagant aural journey. As Lennon begins singing the first verse (0:06+), McCartney begins doubling his own left-hand organ line two octaves below on the bass.[14] If the vocal sounds oddly high, it is because it was recorded at 48.5 cycles per second (CPS), to be replayed at 50 CPS (sped-up vocals are heard elsewhere on the album from Ringo in "With a Little Help from My Friends" and an artificially youthful Paul in "When I'm Sixty-Four"). The A-major verse gives way at 0:32 to a transitional passage tonicizing B-flat. Here, Lennon's voice sounds even stranger, and it is now doubled by Harrison's slide guitar, their articulations and glissandi matched just as carefully as would be done two weeks later for "Within You Without You." The additional strangeness is due to this "transition" vocal having been produced by a different recording than that of the verse vocal; this overdub was taped even further away from the playback speed, at 45 CPS, and treated to massive reverb. Lennon's two vocals overlap throughout 0:26–0:31, making for a smooth transition as the ride is taken from an initial high vocal to one even higher. The conversion is further brushed over by the tamboura (washing the track from 0:16 to 0:34) and an overdubbed open hi-hat struck and partly damped each quarter (and sometimes given a swing shuffle) that enters for vocal phrase endings (first at 0:27 and then earlier in subsequent verses). The monophonic album mix and that for the *Yellow Submarine Songtrack* (1999) compact disc (but unfortunately not the stereo mix used on the now-universal *Sgt. Pepper* CD) also brandish Lennon's sharply struck and deeply reverberating D-minor piano chord at 0:29 (sustaining for two bars and then dropping out until it returns at the same point in the following verse) and Harrison's acoustic strums (from 0:32 through the transitional passage, to 0:50), both of which are treated to hugely weird "phasing" effects through ADT.[15] The entire mix, although economical, weaves a complex blending of high frequencies from tamboura, cymbal, and phased strings (all entering and leaving at different points) that help transport the listener from the strikingly inviting Lowrey introduction to a foreign land of slide guitar and highly sped-up vocal. Lennon had previously guided his listener through a journey ("Let me take you down") in "Strawberry Fields," where the major scene changes are expressed in a subtle manner with the appearances of backward cymbals in the reflective verse flashbacks, but which also startles the listener with the sudden, nightmarish appearance of strings and brass beneath a different vocal speed at 1:00. The shifts in "Lucy in the Sky with Diamonds" are more thoroughly prepared and more eloquently carried out.

The song's G-major chorus (arrived at harmonically through a motion from the tonicized ♭III through IV to V of G—the expansion of a progression played on surface levels even before the days of "Please Please Me") has a more traditional rock instrumentation, as McCartney shifts among Lowrey manuals at this point to play offbeat chords (or on-beat chords, as in the case of the coda) on a more normal reed combination, Starr provides the song's only rock drumming (introduced by three stop-time quarter-note hits, at 0:47+, doubled by both the sticks on floor tom and the kicked beater on bass drum, that modulate from triple to quadruple meter), and Harrison's acoustic guitar continues underneath the Lennon lead vocal and McCartney descant. The one unusual tonal quality in the chorus is supplied by George's guitar, now whirling through the Leslie speaker and doubling not Lennon's vocal but McCartney's bass. A retransition back to each ensuing verse is provided by the sustained vocal "Ah!," both parts doubled by the organ, all of which holds through the blending tamboura to the Lowrey-based verse. These backing vocals seem to fade only gradually, adding to the song's techniques used to blur boundaries. "Lucy" remains today as *the* quintessential psychedelic recording with its timbres just as essential as are its innovative harmonic structure, rhythmic relationships, and formal design in transporting the listener from this world into another.

Despite some high moments, the Beatles' late-1967 projects are anticlimactic in colorations just as in other realms. The title track of *Magical Mystery Tour*, for instance, reworks the audience-grabbing techniques parlayed in "Sgt. Pepper" and the metric modulation of "Lucy"; bass harmonicas come out of the cabinet once again for "Fool on the Hill," several Mellotron settings are heard in "Flying," and the "sampled" backward voices, Leslied lead vocal, and vagrant solo cello (at 3:45+) of "Blue Jay Way" sound like Harrison's attempt to take "Tomorrow Never Knows" to "Strawberry Fields." Lennon discovers a new sound in the Clavioline (a French electronic keyboard) for "Baby You're a Rich Man," but could certainly have gotten a more musical effect with an Indian double-reed instrument, such as the sahnai heard on "The Inner Light." A few very effective new touches appear, including the rhythm guitar's slow amplifier tremolo in "Flying," the comparisons of ladies' swooping chorus with celli glissandi—and men's intoning chorus (perhaps suggested by the "too much!" coda of Harrison's "It's All Too Much," and perhaps in turn anticipating the "hold that line" / "block that kick" chanting at the end of "Revolution 9") with a found broadcast of *King Lear*—in "I Am the Walrus," and the answering of Paul's vocal with violas in thirds in "Hello Goodbye." But *Sgt. Pepper* marks the point at which the Beatles wielded a newly designed palette, brushes, and knife, all applied with masterful judgment.

ROLE CHANGES AND OTHER LATER INTERESTS

Lennon and Harrison had decorated a few of their guitars with psychedelic paint jobs in 1967 but stripped them down to bare wood right after their spring 1968 return from a Himalayan retreat during which they had become much more attached to their acoustics and to a simpler life all around.[16] This shedding is emblematic of a return to a simpler musical style as well, certainly noted in Lennon's finger-picking in "Dear Prudence" (Casino) and "Julia" (Gibson) and McCartney's work on "Blackbird" (D–28), but it does not tell the full story because they also continued with some of the dirtiest overdriven electric guitar distortion of their career, particularly in "Revolution," "I've Got a Feeling," "I Me Mine" (heard on both left and right channels), and the bass line in "Sun King" and "Mean Mr. Mustard." McCartney also showcased his growing skills on an acoustic instrument, the piano, in "Lady Madonna," "Hey Jude," "Martha My Dear," "Let It Be," "The Long and Winding Road," and "You Never Give Me Your Money," although his combined work on electric Pianet and Fender Rhodes in "Come Together" is also striking. (The Rhodes gets its sound from keyboard-controlled rubber mallets striking metal tines, whose vibrations are amplified.) Keyboard from others was also of central importance, as in Chris Thomas's Baroque harpsichord that places irony in the center stage for "Piggies," Nicky Hopkins's central role in complementing the guitars in "Revolution," and Billy Preston's organ and Rhodes work in January 1969 and afterward. Preston's playing was crucial enough to the band that the Beatles strongly considered making him a full member. Lennon and Harrison extended their keyboard skills as well, as with the former's piano played through a guitar amp on "Ob-La-Di, Ob-La-Da" and the latter's flutelike organ on "Long Long Long." The piano glissando threatened to become ubiquitous through the *White Album* as it can be heard in three of the album's first four tracks, as well as later in "Cry Baby Cry" and elsewhere in "The Ballad of John and Yoko." The Mellotron (played masterfully by Chris Thomas in "The Continuing Story of Bungalow Bill") was finally replaced in 1969 by the Moog, which adds colorful countermelodies to "Maxwell's Silver Hammer," "Here Comes the Sun," and "Because."[17] (George Martin also managed to reach back into historical precedents for such instruments in adding the Ondes Martenot to the orchestral score of "Good Night.")

One of the curious things about the Beatles' career involves numerous role changes in the final albums. Part of this can be attributed to the members' growth as musicians, their desire to cover bass while McCartney played keyboard on basic tracks, their looking ahead to solo careers when they would have to do without their bandmates, and perhaps even to boredom with maintaining "assigned" roles. Both Lennon and Harrison have a crack at bass, usually playing the long-neck Fender Bass VI, a six-string guitar tuned an octave below the standard guitar. Thus, both have bass parts in "Back in the

U.S.S.R.," but Lennon shows his lack of appreciation for McCartney's role by strumming chords in "Dig It" and playing undefined tones in his slurpy, insecure work on "The Long and Winding Road." (McCartney's bass itself now blossoms as never before in the Harrison compositions "While My Guitar Gently Weeps" [with fuzz bass], "Old Brown Shoe" [getting a very edgy sound from the Fender Jazz Bass], and "Something" [probably McCartney's most elegant bass line in counterpoint with some fine Telecaster playing by Harrison].) Much better than Lennon's bass playing is heard in Harrison's "bass" lines in the low register through the neck pickup of his custom-made Telecaster for "Two of Us." Perhaps the oddest change in this period is Lennon's apparent desire to sing above McCartney. He had been pushing the upper bounds of his full-voice register since 1966 or so, even though it was generally not the most effective, certainly not the fullest, part of his range. His descant parts above Paul's lead lines in "Hey Jude," "Two of Us," "Maggie Mae," "Get Back," and "Come Together" are successful enough, but that in "The One after 909" is especially unfortunate because this 1969 arrangement lacks the vibrancy and blue-note bends that the duo had in the earlier 1963 voicing. Paul, in turn, works on his bass end, even by singing the bass part to "I Will"; otherwise, he turns in a new color by adding considerable vocal vibrato to his sustained phrase endings in "The Long and Winding Road" (just as his piano playing takes on more dynamic shading there and matches George's vocal colors in the pure harmonizing of his descant line in the bridge and last verse of "Something."

The new role in which Lennon shines, however, is in his growth as lead guitarist. Some of this work appears merely to double his own vocal line while singing, as in "Happiness Is a Warm Gun" and "I Want You (She's So Heavy)" (as George continues to do in "Savoy Truffle"), but his other lead playing is fully independent, as in his bent-note Nashville-style solo for "Get Back," his solo for the album version of "Let It Be," and the fine lap-steel work on "For You Blue." Most amazing is his work on "You Never Give Me Your Money," which most listeners think (and argue) is George's playing. Actually, John plays lead parts on his mellow distorted Casino (starting at 0:09) long before George enters (with chords at 1:20 and bell-like arpeggiations at 1:31) with his magical bright Leslied Telecaster. Both play a magnificent duet, all performed perfectly on the basic tracks, live, and then given a wonderful counterpoint with Paul's overdubbed bass (which enters in understatement only at 0:46), all three achieving perfect unity in the song's transition (2:09–2:28), with Lennon leading and playing on top here and in the coda. The Beatles not only trade guitar roles, but trade guitar solos in "The End," where they alternate colors as well as styles of playing: Paul's hard, sustaining, economical playing on the Esquire is answered by George's sublime, bright, clear, imaginative, and fluid Telecaster work, and then by John's grungy, raucous, belligerent, and dirty Casino before all take further turns.

For the *White Album* and in *Let It Be*, the Beatles return to their rock 'n' roll roots (not exactly abandoned for *Sgt. Pepper*, but certainly return-ing to the forefront in 1968). The texture of "Back in the U.S.S.R.," for exam-ple, is not too far distant from that of *Beatles for Sale* (1964). Part of the hard edge comes from the most powerful doubling of lines since "Day Tripper." "Hey Bulldog" opens with a riff in John's piano octaves, which are then dou-bled in a higher register by George's Gibson SG and John's Casino, and then in a lower one by Paul's bass. Similarly, "Lady Madonna" introduces its bass-line riff on Paul's piano, and then doubles it with bass and John's and George's fuzz guitars played in unison, and goes one step further with saxes joining the line later on. (Even a tuba can double a Beatle bass line, as in "Martha My Dear.") Sometimes the bass line is doubled by two hard-edged guitars, all in three different registers—as in "Birthday" and "Dig a Pony"—pointing to the studio work of Cream and Led Zeppelin, who took as much from the Beatles as from the blues. But sometimes such a doubling could have a mellower effect, such as in the bridge of "Don't Let Me Down" (1:22–1:47), where bass and midrange guitar together provide a beautiful countermelody (composed by Harrison) against Lennon's double-tracked vocal, a color that also contrasts with the heavier amp tremolo with which George blends his Telecaster's tone alongside Billy Preston's Fender Rhodes in other passages (while Lennon's Casino provides a brighter background, noticeable only in textural "holes," such as at 0:39–0:41). An unusual double-tracked vocal in two octaves from Lennon in "Happiness Is a Warm Gun" (1:03–1:34) makes for a transition from a fully open, warm opening vocal sound to one that is highly pinched through compression (reminding one of a different but related vocal transfor-mation in "Tomorrow Never Knows"), and also highlights the ambivalence Lennon seems to feel about his preferred register.

Of course, a few new sounds work their way into the late Beatle record-ings. Female voices, present in choruses for "Yellow Submarine," "All You Need Is Love," and "I Am the Walrus," return with solo roles in "Revolution 9" and "Bungalow Bill" as well as unison doubling in "Birthday" and "Across the Universe." The whistling heard at the endings of "Bungalow Bill" and "Two of Us" convey an offhand informality. New guitar sounds include Paul's bottleneck slide in "Wild Honey Pie," George's tamboura-enhanced and Om-inspiring wah-wah pedal "ringing through my open ears" in "Across the Uni-verse," Eric Clapton's fluid, distorted, and highly phased guitar solo in "While My Guitar Gently Weeps" (phased by an oscillator used to "flange" the tape in and out of sync with itself), and—most imaginatively—George's Leslied Telecaster harmonics that close "Oh! Darling," the bridge of which features some extremely hot but frustrated damping of arpeggios. The Beatles can also be said to have anticipated twenty-first century artists Beck, Björk, and Por-tishead by including the scratchy sound of surface noise from a vinyl record (or in this case, from a shellac 78) for a period touch in the opening of "Honey

Pie." In addition to the Kandinsky-like nonrepresentational approach to color celebrated in the *musique concrète* of "Revolution 9," new electronic effects include the glissando-like gradual stopping of a tape machine to force the ending of "Glass Onion," the rattling of a wine bottle atop an amp at the end of "Long Long Long," and Phil Spector's full tape echo on an isolated hi-hat in the album release of "Let It Be." Finally, first-time instruments include Chinese blocks ("I Will"), anvil ("Maxwell's Silver Hammer"), sleigh bells and fiddle ("Don't Pass Me By"), and an entire Indian ensemble recorded in Bombay ("The Inner Light") that includes instruments not heard on any previous Beatles tracks.

At a time in their career when the Beatles are usually thought to have worked independently from each other, they actually achieved some very tight ensemble. Some of this is illusory, as with Harrison's own two overdubbed guitar parts that stab in alternation in the second chorus of "Savoy Truffle" (1:04–1:09) and with Lennon's own two overdubbed Casino parts in "The Ballad of John and Yoko" (as at 0:06–0:10). Some of it has more to do with their producer, who decided such things as the manner in which brass doodles are composed around loud, distorted, and syncopated chords from Lennon's fuzz Casino in the chorus of "Revolution 1." In all of these songs (at 3:09+ in "Revolution 1"), the alternating instruments rapidly switch sides in the stereo image, one of numerous panning devices commonly used for intensifying such contrasts in the *White Album* and *Abbey Road*. But such hockets, more subtle than those noted from 1967, are basic to the conception of the phrase in the dynamic piano/bass chord that interrupts the orchestral stabs in "Carry That Weight" (1:05) and as the heavy tape echo of Lennon's vocal "shoot me" carries over the hi-hat triplets and pair of rack toms (the second mounted tom being new in Ringo's 1969 Ludwig kit), all subdividing the deep murkiness of the bass and electric piano in the introduction to "Come Together." This effect marks an auspicious beginning to an album full of exquisite arrangements, flawless ensemble, ears full of color, and imaginative and crisp engineering.

Throughout their career, the Beatles discovered countless sonorities and put all resulting colors, alone and in every conceivable combination, to imaginative and expressive service. Their interest in color involved much more than choices of instrumentation, manipulation of register, subtle details of timbre, sound envelopes, and recording techniques, extending to combinations of lines and other matters of contrapuntal and textural interest, articulation and phrasing, to the definition of harmonic function and rhythmic identity, even to the phonemes of word choices and pronunciations. Their chronological development of sophisticated and flexible melodic, harmonic, rhythmic, formal, contrapuntal, and poetic aims and techniques by the end of 1965 provided more than a necessary foundation for the great experimentation in tone color that was to coincide perfectly with a great flowering of psychedelic imagery. In their masterpieces of 1966 and 1967, the Beatles opened gallery upon gallery of unmistakably original watercolors, oils, pastels, and collages that stand among the most alluring and yet the most challenging works of rock history. Thirty-plus years hence, generations of listeners continue to revel in the aural analogues of the satins that came in chartreuse, fuchsia, sky blue, and tomato.

NOTES

1. The seven brief quotations of lyrics in this paragraph are taken from, respectively, "Lucy in the Sky with Diamonds," "Savoy Truffle," "Fool on the Hill," "Happiness Is a Warm Gun," "Mother Nature's Son," "It's All Too Much," and "The Inner Light."

2. I have outlined the roles of many of these musical elements in my essay, "The Beatles as Composers: The Genesis of *Abbey Road*, Side Two," as well as in my books, *The Beatles as Musicians: The Quarry Men through Rubber Soul* and *The Beatles as Musicians: Revolver through the Anthology*.

3. Norman Smith, the Beatles' recording engineer through 1965, recalls that for their June 1962 audition for EMI, "there was as much noise coming from the amps as there was from the instruments; Paul's bass amp was particularly bad" (Babiuk 65; see also Everett, *Quarry Men* 122). Brian Epstein, the Beatles' manager, replaced John's and George's amps with much better Vox equipment in July 1962. Andy Babiuk (50) says that McCartney usually played his Höfner with the neck pickup switched on and the bridge pickup switched off. Owing to the physics of string vibration, this setting would have emphasized the two or three lowest, most basic, partials of most open and stopped notes and de-emphasized the more colorful upper partials that would have been amplified by the instrument's hollow body and projected near the bridge, yielding a simple bass tone. Babiuk (67) also describes the new Vox amps as "well made, with a loud, clear, punchy sound." In addition to the instruments mentioned herein, John and (to a lesser extent) George strummed matching Gibson amplified acoustics in many recordings; the Duo-Jet became a back-up instrument in May 1963 when replaced by the Gretsch Country Gentleman, and George acquired a Gretsch Tennessean at the end of that same year.

4. Here and elsewhere in this chapter, timings are those programmed into the canon of Beatles albums as regularized on compact disc.

5. McCartney discusses the group's attempt to find its sound in Latin qualities in Everett, *Quarry Men* 127. The original recording of "Devil in His Heart" by the Donays includes the guitar part with parallel thirds but no maracas; this model carries no hint of any Latin style.

6. Andy Babiuk (105) points out that the Tennessean has single-coil pickups, as opposed to the hum-bucking dual-coil pickups (wired with opposite poles) on the

Country Gent, "providing a more cutting sound." Unlike the single-coil Fenders, however, the Tennessean also boosted midrange colors with its hollow body.

7. The "Words of Love" instrumentation is asserted by Babiuk (147).

8. See Babiuk 159.

9. George Martin finally resorted to trumpets for the mariachi effect in "Magical Mystery Tour." The parallel thirds are inverted for parallel sixths in both Harrison's Telecaster in "Dig a Pony" and Lennon's Casino in "The Ballad of John and Yoko."

10. The new digital remastering for the soundtrack of this surround-sound video, created directly from the Beatles' original four-track working tape, is also presented with each track heard in isolation on the CD release, *5.1 Degrees of Separation* (2000).

11. Julian's colored drawing is reproduced in Turner 123.

12. The "score" is given in Davies 282. On the same scrap on which this working "score" appears is information that Lennon has copied from the title page of the pamphlet, "The Doctrine of Kabalism," a manual pertaining to the Egyptian Tarot by the mystic C. C. Zain. The Tarot cards illustrating the second edition of the booklet (1936), that of interest to Lennon, are unusual in that they include constellations of stars much like the "diamonds" in Julian's drawing. See "A History of Egyptian Tarot Decks."

13. Babiuk 202. Later, for "Because," Lennon achieves a timbre related to that which opens "Lucy" by doubling George Martin's part on a Baldwin Combo electric harpsichord with his reverb-enhanced Casino.

14. The timings in this discussion refer to the mix heard on the *Sgt. Pepper* CD, even though other mixes are occasionally referred to.

15. The monophonic mix of "Lucy" is also presented a half-step slower than is the stereo, reducing the effect of the sped-up vocal but greatly heightening the phasing and reverb effects.

16. The Casinos of each were stripped to bare wood, as was Lennon's Gibson J–160E. Harrison's Strat remained painted, and indeed he added to its decor in 1969. McCartney's Rickenbacker bass retained its 1967 paint until the 1970s. The Beatles had brought new Martin D–28s to India.

17. The qualities heard in the Moog IIIp in these songs, and their relationships to the coexisting texture, are treated in some detail in my essay, "The Beatles as Composers: The Genesis of *Abbey Road*, Side Two" and in my book, *The Beatles as Musicians: Revolver through the Anthology.*

PART II

"A splendid time is guaranteed for all"

Theorizing the Beatles

CHAPTER 5

Mythology,
Remythology,
and Demythology

The Beatles on Film

KENNETH WOMACK
AND TODD F. DAVIS

I N THEIR VARIOUS FILM EXCURSIONS, the Beatles appropriated the power of "Beatlemania" and self-consciously established a cultural mythology to ensure their commercial and popular dominion. This chapter traces the infancy, maturity, and ultimate disillusionment the Beatles experienced during the production of their four feature films—*A Hard Day's Night* (1964), *Help!* (1965), *Yellow Submarine* (1968), and *Let It Be* (1970)—as well as the television movie, *Magical Mystery Tour* (1967). In addition to devoting particular attention to the cult of personality that the Beatles developed via such myth-making ephemera as lunchboxes, Beatles wigs, jigsaw puzzles, cartoons, and coloring books, an analysis of the Beatles' films demonstrates the ways in which the band members employed *A Hard Day's Night* and *Help!* to fashion the overarching cultural identity that they would resurrect during the middle of their career in *Magical Mystery Tour* and *Yellow Submarine*. Finally, a reading of the band's filmic epitaph *Let It Be* argues that the Beatles' documentary failed to demythologize their cultural persona completely because their breakup created a larger sense of cultural absence that has served only to cement their mystique in the ensuing decades.

Next to the Apple Boutique, Apple Electronics, and the Apple corporation's many other disastrous subsidiaries, the Beatles' films—with the notable exception of *A Hard Day's Night*—will surely go down in history as some of the band's least successful ventures, if only for their lack of artistry. "Although the group had achieved a remarkable amount of international success prior to its forays into film," Bob Neaverson perceptively observes, "the phenomenon of Beatlemania could not and would not have been either as substantial or as durable without the identificatory process afforded by cinema" ("Tell Me" 152). Although three of their films generated sizable box-office receipts, the Beatles' celluloid excursions usefully demonstrate their self-consciousness about themselves as a material and infinitely marketable good. Inspired by a scene in *Blackboard Jungle* (1955), the Beatles fashioned a chant in their earliest days in Hamburg that functioned as a rallying cry of sorts. In his 1980 *Playboy* interview, Lennon recalls that "I would yell out, 'Where are we going, fellows?' They would say, 'To the top, Johnny,' in pseudo-American voices. And I would say, 'Where is that, fellows?' And they would say, 'To the toppermost of the poppermost!'" (*All We Are Saying* 159). A combination of self-confidence and panache, their somewhat calculated vision of success would begin to change the landscape of popular culture after Brian Epstein famously strolled into one of their lunchtime performances at Liverpool's Cavern Club in November 1961. Whereas Epstein's acumen as a businessperson would prove to be illusory—his statesmanlike control of the Beatles' empire, it seems, was a mere juggling act—their new manager possessed an innate sense about how to repackage the Beatles for the wide world beyond Liverpool and the North Country. Ridding them of their notoriously unkempt hair and their leather jackets and pants, he restyled the band's image with more exacting grooming and brand new suits.

Interestingly, Epstein began negotiating the Beatles' film debut well before the band's landmark appearance on the *Ed Sullivan Show* in February 1964. In October 1963, as Beatlemania conquered England, Epstein and the Fab Four availed themselves of the pop musical, the marketing tool that existed during the 1960s as the principal artistic venue for their most notable precursor and, by early 1964, their singular rival, Elvis Presley. In films such as *G.I. Blues* (1960), *Girls! Girls! Girls!* (1962), and *Fun in Acapulco* (1963), Elvis fashioned the economic model that the Beatles appropriated for three of their filmic narratives.[1] The Beatles would take the paradigm a step further and share in the creation of the phenomenon that we now understand, via Hollywood blockbuster productions and their ilk, as the multimedia, multi-market sales campaign. Such media blitzes function as synergistic revenue-generating engines that propel not only the film—the Ur-text of the marketing campaign—but also the soundtrack album, the sheet music, the action figures, the T-shirts, the posters, and every other imaginable bit of Beatles-related paraphernalia. The pace of the Beatles' genesis as self-conscious promoters of their various products dwarfs the explosion of Beatlemania itself. When Epstein negotiated their contract with United Artists for *A Hard Day's Night* in October 1963, they wanted to make the film "for the express purpose of having a soundtrack album," according to the film's producer Walter Shenson *(You Can't Do That)*. In one instance, Lennon even told Epstein "we don't fancy being Bill Haley and the Bellhops, Brian" (qtd. in Barrow, "*A Hard Day's Night*" 5). By the end of February 1964, they came to envision the film as an opportunity for blazing trails into new marketing vistas well beyond the teenage demographic.

The alacrity with which the Beatles came to perceive themselves as a marketing juggernaut also dovetails precisely with their triumphant visit to the United States in 1964. Yet by the summer of that year, the Beatles lost millions of dollars in copyright infringements across the globe, and they could do little more than stand by as idle observers while the revenues drifted into the pockets of vast numbers of unscrupulous manufacturers.[2] "The vaguest representation of insects, of guitars, or little mop-headed men had the power to sell anything, however cheap, however nasty," Philip Norman writes in *Shout!: The Beatles in Their Generation* (1981). "And so, after one or two minor prosecutions, the pirates settled down, unhampered, to their bonanza" (207–8). For the Beatles, the world of film afforded them with a means for securing control of themselves as a commodity and for establishing the self-image that would fuel their marketing engine. As Jacques Attali remarks in *Noise* (1985), the popular music industry's economic emergence in the 1950s and beyond spawned a new, media-driven era of production in which acts of representation and repetition serve as the mechanisms for engendering and sustaining success. The evolution of this multiplicative marketing phenomenon "fundamentally changes the code of social reproduction," Attali writes, and consumers—the recipients of iteration after iteration of deftly constructed signs and messages—begin responding to the "mysterious and powerful links [that] exist between technology and knowledge on the one hand, and music on the other" (146, 147). As this awe-inspiring marketing machine developed throughout the latter half of the twentieth century, its promoters, for whom Epstein functioned as a pioneer, came to understand that the art of any effective media campaign originates in its capacity for communicating its message to a target audience. With *A Hard Day's Night*, the Beatles accomplished this end by deftly crafting images for each of the band members that their later films, in one fashion or another, would attempt to echo.

MYTHOLOGY

The idea of mythology finds its roots in our desires to tell stories about ourselves. We do this, of course, in an effort to make sense of our experiences, to imbue our lives with meaning. The act of myth-making possesses a peculiarly social dimension as well. By mythologizing our experiences, we establish a narrative frame through which people may contextualize their own lives in relationship with other human beings. In this way, we introduce points of convergence in our various mythologies that allow us to create spaces of interaction. These moments of intersection can be genuine instances of our longing, as humans, for interpersonal connection. Yet they can also be calculated maneuvers to control—indeed, to manipulate—the ways in which audiences come to perceive the mythologized subject. The stories that we tell about ourselves assume much greater power when placed in a public context driven by media, marketing, and economic imperatives. At the same time, our identities become obscured, subservient to myth's machinery, a legend-making mechanism that, by virtue of its very existence, must tell and retell story after story to keep our dreams of a comprehensible, unified narrative alive.

Quite obviously, the Beatles themselves—as human beings and as artists—sought to establish their own micronarratives within their real, workaday lives. As we know from the juggernaut of Beatles-related paraphernalia, these personal myths were ultimately subsumed by the awesome myth-making power of Beatlemania. Yet can we really perceive the genuine nature of their personae in such a hypersurrealized context? Clearly, the screaming fan at a random U.S. concert in 1964—tears running down her cheeks as she pushes her way to the front of the pack in an effort to touch the hem of Paul McCartney's suit coat—was looking into the mythologizing frame of Beatlemania in an effort to catch a glimpse of the "real" Paul. Surely, this fan would have wanted no truck with the less fantastic stories that McCartney might tell about himself, stories that bear little resemblance to the plasticine image of him as a lovable, nonthreatening Mop Top. Rather, she hoped—as so many of us do—to encounter the mythologizing accoutrements that she had already projected onto him via Capitol Records' media-generated desire to "meet" the Beatles. In short, Beatlemania's grand illusion accrued its power through the financially advantageous collision between a growing international fan base's need for a facile mythology and the willingness of the Beatles' relentlessly regenerating marketing engine to sustain the Fab Four's media-friendly story.

Yet these are not artfully created narratives. As a highly constructed sociocultural text, the Beatles—in concert with legions of marketeers and a compliant global audience—appropriated their preexisting pop-cultural personae to cobble together a film that merges their mythological identities with the cinematic tropes in which their audience was already well versed. Hence, *A Hard Day's Night* capitalizes on each band member's image as it had been established by the adeptly choreographed news conferences and appearances on such popular fare as *Thank Your Lucky Stars* (in Great Britain) and the *Ed Sullivan Show*. Perhaps even more significantly, the audience for the Beatles' films would already have been well schooled in the generic myth-making conventions of the pop musical by movies such as *The Girl Can't Help It* (1956) and *Rock Around the Clock* (1956), not to mention Elvis's various cinematic forays. The audience's desire to see their heroes fulfill their preconceived roles as the Fab Four allows them to anticipate—and thus share in the construction of—the existing characters and plot mechanisms inherent in *A Hard Day's Night*.

Obviously, the Beatles' films are hardly the best venue for exploring the vast sweep of their artistic legacy. Any fan would be better served by revisiting *Rubber Soul* (1965), *Revolver* (1966), or *The White Album* (1968) to register the impact of the band's cultural significance. Of their five films, *A Hard Day's Night* continues to enjoy the most sustained critical acclaim. Produced on a budget of some $350,000, principal photography for *A Hard Day's Night* began in early March 1964. Amazingly, the film wrapped in April and premiered on July 6 at the London Pavilion in Piccadilly Circus. Directed by Richard Lester, the film grossed $11 million worldwide and $1.3 million in the first week of its U.S. release—both of which were astounding figures for that era. As with the Beatles cartoons that would premiere on ABC television in September 1965, *A Hard Day's Night* assisted the band in fomenting the mythology about their different personalities that lingers to the present day. As a pop musical that splices together micronarratives about each band members' experiences during a "hard day's night," the film features various montages and performance pieces devoted to the six new Beatles' songs recorded explicitly for the movie. Neaverson notes that films such as *A Hard Day's Night* attempt to draw their audiences into a voyeuristic relationship with their subjects, to afford their spectators with a glimpse into the band's constructed "lives": "The audience is allowed to see a pop group in intimate, 'behind-the-scenes' scenarios which are essentially 'real,' or at least, realistic," Neaverson writes. "Ultimately, [the film] enabled them to leave the cinema feeling that they had come to 'know' (and love) the group as 'real' people, rather than that they had merely been 'entertained' by a pop group acting out a totally fictitious plot" (*Beatles Movies* 21). But, of course, a fictive and self-consciously constructed text is exactly what audience members experienced.

In addition to marketing the band as a happy-go-lucky group of unthreatening young men, *A Hard Day's Night* concretized the Beatles' individual images for the current generation, and—thanks to videocassettes, DVDs, and cable television—generations to come.[3] Henceforth, Lennon became known for his sarcastic intelligence; McCartney for his boyish charm and good looks; George Harrison for being the "quiet one"; and Ringo Starr for his affable personality and good-natured humor. The Parlophone album cover for *A Hard Day's Night* is itself a study in this form of identity creation. The album's cover art features five playful photographs of each Beatle mugging for the camera. Lennon can be seen striking slyly introspective poses. Harrison's various guises underscore his reputation as the quiet Beatle; one of his photographs even depicts him with his back to the camera in monochromatic silhouette.[4] McCartney is portrayed in the act of pursuing innocent and unself-conscious antics, and Starr seems intentionally muted. His photos make him appear bland and unobtrusive, as if more palpable characteristics might shatter his good-natured image.

Paramount to the construction of the Beatles' media personalities was the notion that none of them be perceived as being romantically involved. As Lester remembers, "It was an instinctive thing that fans would be quite happy with them as four available people as opposed to, I suppose, the Elvis Presley pictures, where there was always a love interest" (qtd. in Neaverson, *Beatles Movies* 25). Epstein and the Beatles' handlers were so paranoid regarding any public knowledge of Lennon's marriage to Cynthia Powell in August 1962, for example, that their relationship was kept secret until well after the emergence of Beatlemania.[5] After the release of *A Hard Day's Night* in the summer of 1964, John, Paul, George, and Ringo became household words. As Roger Ebert observes, "After that movie was released everybody knew the names of all four Beatles—*everybody*" *(You Can't Do That)*. As Epstein and the Beatles had intended, *A Hard Day's Night* allowed them to establish inroads into demographic bases beyond the teenagers who worshipped them after their *Ed Sullivan Show* appearance. In short, the Beatles had won over, in Neaverson's words, the "non-believers" (*Beatles Movies* 27).

With *Help!* the Beatles cemented the collective, carefree image that they began fashioning in *A Hard Day's Night*, while creating additional opportunities for deepening the highly orchestrated nature of their public "personalities." Originally titled *Eight Arms to Hold You*, *Help!* enjoyed an ample budget of $600,000. Directed by Lester and filmed between February 23 and May 11, 1965, *Help!*'s narrative relies on the same zany humor of *A Hard Day's Night*. In contrast with the band's earlier film, *Help!* employs a James Bond-inspired spy text as its central crisis: Ringo has come into the possession of an exotic diamond ring coveted by various desperate people, including hit men, Eastern mystics, and mad scientists among a host of others. Numerous car chases and skiing shenanigans ensue as the drummer's mates attempt to rescue him from his predicament. In *Help!*, one can glimpse the future of such equally screwball oddities as the Monkees and the Banana Splits in the film's campy ridiculousness. As with *A Hard Day's Night*, *Help!* labors to maintain the mythology of the group's collective identity. In one unforgettable scene, the Beatles return home to four adjacent row houses. After unlocking each of their separate doors in unison, each member enters what turns out to be a single, gigantic flat that they all share. For the Beatles themselves, the irony of that scene must have been simply staggering at the time. As Ann Pacey, a critic for the London *Sun*, astutely observes, the Beatles seem "as trapped as four flies" in *Help!* (qtd. in Neaverson, *Beatles Movies* 42). Despite their obvious efforts in the first two films, the Beatles' attempts at fashioning a wholesome public image would be undone, rather precipitously, in March 1966 by Lennon's infamous remark that the Beatles were bigger than Jesus Christ and in 1967 by rumors and ultimately admissions about their experimentation with various drugs, particularly LSD.

REMYTHOLOGY

At some juncture or another in our lives, we are forced to confront the past, to reflect on the mythological narratives that we construct (and allow to be constructed by others) about ourselves. How can we not be dissatisfied about—or at least uneasy with—the discrepancies between our lived experiences and the necessarily artificial reconstruction of those experiences? For the Beatles, such dis-ease becomes apparent as early as June 1966 with the U.S. release of *Yesterday . . . and Today* and its notorious cover art. Known by Beatles fans and music critics alike as the "butcher" cover, Robert Whitaker's gory photograph featured the Beatles dressed in white laboratory coats, clutching decapitated baby dolls, and surrounded by raw meat. Although Capitol Records withdrew the cover artwork and released the album five days later with a benign photograph of the group playfully posing around a steamer trunk, the butcher cover clearly demonstrates the band's dissatisfaction with the cultural mythos that had subsumed their identities as artists.[6] In one of the last interviews before his senseless murder, John attributes the cover's origins to the band's "boredom and resentment at having to do *another* photo session and *another* Beatles thing. We were sick to death of it," he recalls, and "the photographer was into Dali and making surreal pictures" (*All We Are Saying* 219). Although the Beatles were willing, quite obviously, to attend to the myth-making machinery of fame and fortune, John's remarks underscore the band's competing desires to take themselves more seriously as creative artists and, potentially, to explore different artistic—and, later, spiritual—forms. Yet as the *Yesterday . . . and Today* episode reveals, Beatlemania had become a constraining and self-perpetuating mechanism, and, even more pointedly, the Beatles themselves had become visibly jaded by the marketing activities (photo sessions, concert tours, press conferences, and the like) that were necessary to achieve its continuation.

For the Beatles, the act of remythology allowed them to account for their evolving artistic interests and continue to stoke the fires of global celebrity at the same time. Their concomitant desires for wealth and artistic freedom were at loggerheads with one another, yet remythology—the process of reconfiguring one's own mythos in an effort to approximate more closely the nuances of our projected identities—afforded them with a narrative bridge connecting the story of who they were (the four Mop Tops of 1964 and 1965) with who they were becoming (the recording artists and cultural figures who would emerge as equally unknowable legends for the tailor-made consumption of future generations). And they could only accomplish this end, as history shows us, by grafting signs of their earnest explorations of new musical and hallucinogenic vistas, the spiritual possibilities of transcendental meditation, and the ethics of pacifism onto the more innocent and wholesome images of *A Hard Day's Night* and *Help!*

Perhaps the most poignant example of this transformation is evidenced by Peter Blake's cover art for *Sgt. Pepper's Lonely Hearts Club Band*, which depicts the competing narratives of the paradigmatic Fab Four with the incarnation of the Summer of Love-era Beatles, decked out, as they are, in psychedelic military regalia as Sgt. Pepper's fabled troupe. Literally, the album's cover depicts the group's former mythological selves standing stage right of their remythologized contemporary counterparts, themselves surrounded by similarly mythologized figures from the annals of history, religion, Hollywood, music, sports, and literature. Whereas the album's cover art prefigures the newly remythologized identities that the group would bring to life in *Magical Mystery Tour* and *Yellow Submarine*, it also finds the Beatles implicitly recognizing the constraints inherent in the mythologizing process itself. From the iconic depiction of Marlon Brando in *On the Waterfront* (1954) to the stereotypically one-dimensional portrait of boxer Sonny Liston, *Sgt. Pepper's* cover reminds us that nuance and complexity have little value in the act of mythmaking. Although remythology ostensibly provides the Beatles with avenues for exploring new artistic spaces, their culturally inscribed identities insist that they adhere to many of their narrowly defined character traits as prescribed by the mythos of Beatlemania. Despite obvious evidence of the band's forays into counterculture—*Sgt. Pepper* finds them replete with moustaches and sideburns while standing amidst a garden of cannabis and flower power—the lads continue to perform certain character traits in *Magical Mystery Tour* and *Yellow Submarine* that reaffirm the mythologized aspects of their former selves. In this reified world, Lennon still winks for the camera, Starr bumbles for comic relief, McCartney effects a benign Adonis, and Harrison remains ever so quiet.

After scuttling any plans for concert tours in August 1966 and achieving new artistic heights with *Sgt. Pepper* in the summer of 1967, the Beatles would seem to have drifted well beyond the carefully crafted identities that they established via *A Hard Day's Night* and *Help!* With Epstein's sudden death in August 1967 and a renewed desire to consolidate their popularity and become the masters of their own economic and artistic destiny, the band shrewdly attempted to remythologize their media personalities in *Magical Mystery Tour* and *Yellow Submarine*. It was a gamble that failed somewhat miserably in the first instance, while succeeding far beyond their aspirations in the second. As perhaps their single greatest artistic failure, the film version of *Magical Mystery Tour* showcases the band members in beguiling comic villanelles that are memorable solely for their utter disarray. The film's chaotic narrative features musical iterations from Beatles films past (including a marching band's intentionally cloying version of "She Loves You" and a string arrangement of "All My Loving"[7]) and, in the movie's finest moments, quasi-music videos for "The Fool on the Hill," "I Am the Walrus," and "Blue Jay Way." The film reaches its ridiculous nadir in a series of car chases and a variety of nonsensical skits that attempt to recall the zany vignettes inherent in *A Hard Day's Night* and *Help!* Their efforts at remythologizing their public personalities especially fail when they attempt to graft their early Beatles' identities onto their post-1965 profiles as spiritually and psychotropically inclined artists. By the advent of *Magical Mystery Tour*, there is simply no avenue for going back to the heady (or, in retrospect, perhaps not so heady) days of *A Hard Day's Night* and *Help!* The poor reviews that *Magical Mystery Tour* received after its debut on BBC television confirmed the awful reality of its failure. ABC television, which owned the rights to broadcast *Magical Mystery Tour* in the United States, opted not to air the film at all.

In contrast with *Magical Mystery Tour*, *Yellow Submarine* put the Beatles back on the cinematic map with an original and, for the time period at least, significant artistic accomplishment. Directed by Canadian animator George Dunning, *Yellow Submarine* was produced by Al Brodax, one of the creative forces behind the Beatles cartoons. Cowritten by Brodax, Lee Minoff, and Erich Seagal, who would later author the screenplay for *Love Story* (1970), *Yellow Submarine* featured little actual input from the band. Initially skeptical about the value of making another film, the Beatles only contributed four new songs, a few script alterations, and a brief appearance at the end of the movie. Yet the finished product clearly exceeded their expectations. As former Apple press officer Tony Barrow notes, the Beatles were "so pleased with the way the whole production had been put together that they were only too happy to associate themselves with it more closely from then on" (qtd. in Barrow, *"Yellow Submarine"* 13). And indeed they should be: in addition to contributing yet again to the promulgation of their constructed celluloid personalities, *Yellow Submarine* added another layer to their remythology by portraying their genuine interests in pacifism. In the film's climactic scene, for example, Lennon's character battles an insidious flying Glove by hurling the word *Love* at the accessory while singing "All You Need Is Love." Although Lennon would betray his own pacifist ideology in "Revolution 1,"[8] a song that the Beatles recorded for the *White Album* during the month in which the film premiered, *Yellow Submarine*'s cartoonish vision of the Beatles living a near-Utopian existence in Pepperland coheres rather easily with their earlier, equally carefree narratives about life as members of the Fab Four. Perhaps even more intriguingly, *Yellow Submarine* demonstrates that acts of mythology and remythology are never controlled by a single author.[9] The Beatles' tacit (and, ultimately, enthusiastic) approval of *Yellow Submarine* reminds us that myth-making is an inherently collaborative process in which intentionality plays a comparatively minor role in relation to the star turn of celebrity culture.[10] And the release of *Magical Mystery Tour*, although a commercial and critical failure, highlights the ways in which the iconic image nevertheless becomes dispersed and figures in the public consciousness, as well as in our larger, mythologically informed understanding of who and what we believe the Beatles to be.

DEMYTHOLOGY

Why, then, do we seek to demythologize the past? What is the motivation for dismantling the myths that we have so carefully constructed and nurtured? Demythology finds its origins and impetus in the act of reading our own mythologies, where we discover that the narratives of our lives have begun to assume meanings well beyond our ken. As we remarked earlier, mythology must reiterate story after story to sustain itself, codifying human experience in such a manner that it begins to seem even more "real" to the listener (and at times to the speaker as well). On listening to such tales, two responses often arise: either we are satisfied with the mythology and allow it to be perpetuated, or, conversely, we find the mythos so at odds with our perceptions of the lived experience that we seek to deconstruct or dismantle it.

For the Beatles, the mythology that they (along with Epstein and the band's handlers) had constructed now afforded them with far more than financial security and fame. In fact, it had begun to seep into every facet of their creative and biographical lives. An edifice of truly frightening proportions and imposing impenetrability, the Fab Four's mythology had transmogrified into a prisonlike structure that would not allow the Beatles, who had grown progressively more devoted to their roles as artists and musicians, the space for exploring other creative venues and opportunities. Although celebrity clearly provided Lennon, for instance, with a massive international forum for expressing his views, how, indeed, could he focus his attentions on the antiwar movement and his hunger for peace when the mask of Beatlehood required him to wink mischievously at the camera and conjure up Beatle John? How, moreover, could McCartney lose himself in a particular melody, experimenting with new musical forms and avant-garde ideas, when his admirers, caught up in the fan culture and rapture of Beatlemania, were willing to believe the most ridiculous of myths: that Paul was dead?

As an attempt to remove their overwhelming veil of celebrity, the Beatles' final film, *Let It Be*, finds them working, consciously or unconsciously, to document their lives as artists, fashioning a film that they believed would move beyond the tired mythologies that had evolved over the previous six years. With cameras rolling on a brightly lit movie set, the Beatles' best efforts to undo the shackles of their mythology were bound to fail. Once again, they discovered themselves mired in artifice. The seeds of their dissolution are evident in nearly every frame, save for the rooftop concert that closes the film. For much of *Let It Be*, their petty disagreements and intractability merely shift the narrative from a film about a working rock band into the story of their eventual breakup. Disbandment is, in itself, a significant aspect of rock 'n' roll's archetypal structure. It is also a signal form of demythology. Originally titled *Get Back* to communicate the notion of the Beatles "getting back" to their roots, *Let It Be* instead illustrates the Beatles in a desperate attempt, scene after scene, to stave off and yet gesture toward their inevitable demise. At one juncture, Harrison even quits the group, if only briefly, after a dispute with Lennon.[11]

Directed by Michael Lindsay-Hogg and filmed throughout January 1969, *Let It Be* demythologizes the media-created personalities of the four Mop Tops through a series of brutally honest and frequently unsettling moments. Suffering within the dank, creatively stagnant atmosphere of London's Twickenham Film Studios (the same soundstage where they filmed *A Hard Day's Night* five years earlier) the Beatles clearly struggled to find a new sound in the wake of the *White Album*. Far afield from the comfort zone they established after years of working at Abbey Road Studios, *Let It Be* depicts the band in various states of unrest and disagreement. In one instance, Harrison reacts to McCartney's patronizing attitude about his guitar arrangement for the song "Two of Us": "I'll play whatever you want me to play or I won't play at all if you don't want me to play. Whatever it is that will please you, I'll do it." For the first time on film, such unvarnished moments unveiled the Beatles' genuinely *human* personalities, albeit after years of interpersonal strain. As Lennon later recalled, the release of *Let It Be* "would break the Beatles, you know, it would break the myth. That's us, with no trousers on and no glossy paint over the cover and no sort of hope. This is what we are like with our trousers off, so would you please end the game now?" (*Anthology* 322). In the film's famous conclusion, the Beatles assemble on the roof of their Savile Row office building for their final concert. Amazingly—or perhaps not so amazingly, given the band's previous film efforts—the concert sequence seems to energize the Beatles, nearly erasing the dismal images of the group in the act of recording a lackluster album. In this way, the Beatles' myth seems to emerge even during their most self-conscious acts of demythology.

Considered in its entirety, the *Let It Be* project "serves its duty as a chronicle of January 1969 *too* well," according to Doug Sulpy and Ray Schweighardt, "revealing a group of four unhappy musicians generally giving the worst performances of their otherwise illustrious career" (316). Several months later, the Beatles would reassemble to record *Abbey Road*, their musical swan song and, for many listeners, their finest album. Soon thereafter, they disbanded before devolving into the bevy of lawsuits that would occupy them throughout the 1970s. The cultural mystique that has emerged regarding the band in the ensuing decades clearly dwarfs their own deconstructive efforts in *Let It Be*.[12] As the success of *The Beatles Anthology* miniseries in 1995 and their recent bestselling compilation album demonstrates, the Beatles' myth that they effected via *A Hard Day's Night* and *Help!*—and to a lesser extent through the *Ed Sullivan Show* and the Beatles cartoons—looms much larger than the infinitely more complicated nuances of their real lives. Like it or not, they will always be the "four lads from Liverpool." After all, they scripted it that way.

NOTES

1. With Beatlemania's global onslaught in 1964, Brian Epstein self-consciously crafted an economic model for the Beatles that included the completion and release of two albums and one film per year. The band succeeded in fulfilling this expectation in 1964 and 1965, when they released four albums—*A Hard Day's Night* (1964), *Beatles for Sale* (1964), *Help!* (1965), and *Rubber Soul* (1965)—and two films—*A Hard Day's Night* (1964) and *Help!* (1965).

2. In *The Love You Make: An Insider's Story of the Beatles* (1983), Peter Brown suggests that ineffectual business deals Epstein negotiated led to many of the Beatles' merchandising failures during this era. The Reliant Shirt Corporation, for example, had negotiated for the rights to manufacture Beatles T-shirts for a licensing fee of a mere $100,000. In one three-day period, Reliant sold more than one million T-shirts and earned back their licensing fee three times over (117). Brown estimates that by 1967, "$100 million had slipped through their [the Beatles'] hands" (149).

3. In one of the most interesting examples of the band's efforts to cement their media-created personalities in the public mindset, the Beatles authorized the publication of a novelization of *A Hard Day's Night* in July 1964. Written by John Burke, the volume purports to be an insider's look at "the Beatles as nobody ever before has known them." The book's dust jacket promises that "in this fabulous new novel you'll get the chance of a lifetime to spend a whole, fantastic day with them. Loving and romancing, twisting and singing, cutting up and cutting out—here are Ringo, Paul, John, and George at their irresistible best. Yeah, yeah, yeah!"

4. One of the great misnomers of the Beatles myth concerns George's allegedly "quiet" demeanor. As his friend David Hedley fondly recalled after Harrison's death in November 2001, "He was such a private man, but not a quiet one. He didn't like fame and the irrational behavior that fame brings, but he was a very outgoing person and a very lovely man. He was hugely sociable and would talk on equal terms with everybody" (qtd. in Barlow).

5. After the media discovered the existence of John and Cynthia's secret marriage in late 1963, Epstein persuaded the Beatles to "make the best of it," according to Peter Brown: "A married Beatle with an adorable baby son [Julian] was wholesome

enough for their image—as long as none of the newspapers pointed out that Cynthia was obviously pregnant before John married her" (102).

6. The cover fiasco ensured that *Yesterday . . . and Today* became the only Beatles album to lose money for Capitol Records. Ironically, the company ultimately failed in its effort to eradicate the offending cover. During the long weekend in which Capitol employees were busy removing *Yesterday . . . and Today*'s cover artwork—at a reported cost of more than $200,000—many fatigued workers resorted to pasting the new photograph over the "butcher" cover. As a result, numerous fans discovered that they could carefully extricate the original photograph. The butcher cover has since become a much-desired item of Beatles memorabilia among serious collectors (Schaffner 56–58).

7. The Beatles offer a similarly self-referential moment in *Help!* via a scene in which sitar players perform "A Hard Day's Night" in an Indian restaurant. In *Let It Be*, the Beatles continue this process of looking backward when they recite a series of rock standards, including "Shake, Rattle, and Roll," "Rip It Up," "Kansas City," and "You Really Got a Hold on Me," from their pre-Beatlemania past in Hamburg and the Cavern.

8. See Jeffrey Roessner's chapter herein for additional discussion regarding Lennon's intentional indecision in "Revolution 1" about whether to embrace radical acts of destruction.

9. Interestingly, Lennon pointedly counters the notion that the Beatles were fully committed to propagating their media-friendly personae. Referring to his experiences during the production of *A Hard Day's Night*, Lennon remarks:

> You see, there's another illusion that we were just puppets and that the great people like Brian Epstein and Dick Lester created the situation and made this whole fuckin' thing. But it was really precisely because we were what we were—and realistic. We didn't want to make a fuckin' shitty pop movie. . . . We were always trying to make it more realistic, even with Dick and all that, but they wouldn't have it. (qtd. in Yule 19)

10. Although much of the biographical and autobiographical material related to the Beatles suggests their genuine endorsement of *Yellow Submarine*, Lennon characteristically remembers things differently. The filmmakers behind the project, he contends, "were gross animals apart from the guy who drew the paintings for the movie. They lifted all the ideas for the movie out of our heads and didn't give us any credit. We had nothing to do with that movie, and we sort of resented them. It was the third movie that we owed United Artists. Brian had set it up and we had nothing to do with it. But I liked the movie, the artwork," he nevertheless concedes (*All We Are Saying* 204). Robert R. Hieronimus's *Inside the Yellow Submarine: The Making of the Beatles' Animated Classic* (2002) offers a useful rejoinder to Lennon's claims, particularly his feelings of resentment about the Beatles' ostensible role (or lack thereof) in the film's production (50–51).

11. See Doug Sulpy and Ray Schweighardt's *Get Back: The Unauthorized Chronicle of the Beatles' Let It Be Disaster* (1997) for a day-by-day, song-by-song analysis of the band's activities in January 1969.

12. The release of *Let It Be . . . Naked* (2003), the band's unvarnished recordings from the *Get Back* sessions, demonstrates, once again, that the surviving Beatles have yet to make sense of the complex of interpersonal events and the strictures of all-consuming fame they experienced during *Let It Be*'s convoluted production.

CHAPTER 6

Vacio Luminoso

"Tomorrow Never Knows" and the Coherence of the Impossible

RUSSELL REISING

I N 1966 ABIMAEL GUZMAN visited the People's Republic of China, met with Chairman Mao, and returned, galvanized as a revolutionary who urged his Peruvian comrades to follow El Sendero Luminoso, or the "Shining Path." Equally revolutionary, "Tomorrow Never Knows," the first and ultimate fruit of the Beatles *Revolver* (1966) recording sessions that same year, urges us to surrender to a "Shining Void." This was still a full two years before the Beatles would actually title a song "Revolution." Rather than signing up with any particular sectarian group, John and company sang, "We all want to change your head" and gave the following advice:

> You tell me it's the institution,
> Well you know,
> You better free your mind instead.

The Beatles had already planted the seeds of this line of "political" thinking on *Revolver*, an album that illuminates a path dedicated to personal freedom and mind expansion, and that album represents what many fans, scholars, and critics of popular music elevate as a far more "revolutionary" recording than anything else the Beatles ever did.

Even for today's listeners educated in, or at least habituated to, innovative and challenging electronic effects in popular music ("experienced," in at least one of the ways endorsed by Jimi Hendrix), "Tomorrow Never Knows," the final track on *Revolver*, signals a revolutionary launch from the album's first thirteen songs into the circumambient strains of its grand finale. Although the Beatles' *Revolver* revolution makes some claims to our political consciousnesses by critiquing some "institutions," they really aim, throughout the album but especially on "Tomorrow Never Knows," at our psychospiritual and aesthetic sensibilities instead. Their "shining path" does not lead to London, Beijing, or to Washington, D.C., let alone to Lima, Peru. What is revolutionary and "shining" for the Beatles on *Revolver* is nothing less (or nothing more) than what John Lennon, following Timothy Leary and Richard Alpert, called the void: a pathless path that one reaches by relaxing and floating downstream, not by beating against the current, and certainly not by firing machine guns, rifles, or revolvers.

Revolver is, as I have called it elsewhere, "an album of firsts," and many of its fourteen cuts represent striking lyrical innovations and musical departures.[1] "Eleanor Rigby" is the first song on which none of the Beatles plays an instrument; "Love You To" pulses as the Beatles' first thorough immersion in Asiatic soundscapes; "Yellow Submarine," a song often (and unjustly) mocked, represents the Beatles' first extensive use of ambient sound effects. Even by these extreme measures of newness heaped on newness, "Tomorrow Never Knows" still virtually explodes on the listener's awareness, especially after the traditionally brassy, Motown-soaked soul of "Got to Get You into My Life." Paradoxically, the revolutionary accomplishment of "Tomorrow Never Knows" precisely provides *Revolver* with a traditional sense of musical and lyrical coherence, even as it propels us into hitherto unexplored musical and psychospiritual space. This revolutionary rupture is also the evolutionary apogee, or, to put it another way, the break is the bridge.

Sonically, none of *Revolver*'s cuts seems very clearly related to any other, and the album is virtually defined by abrupt transitions from one musical universe to another.[2] Listen, for example, to the transitions from the hard rock of "Taxman" into the chamber strains of "Eleanor Rigby," from Paul's mellow "For No One" to John's exuberant "Doctor Robert," or from either the mellifluous "Here, There, and Everywhere" into "Yellow Submarine" or from the affirmative choral ending to that song into the strained desperation of "She Said She Said." Philosophically and thematically, however, the album twists, turns, and surges toward the transcendent vision of "Tomorrow Never Knows," a lyrical tour de force that unites all of the album's tracks. We might be used to such "concept albums" by now, having learned how to listen to totalizing musical and lyrical visions via such accomplishments as the Who's *Tommy* and *Quadrophenia*; Jethro Tull's *Aqualung* and *Thick as a Brick*; Yes's *Tales from Topographic Oceans* (a symphonic piece in four movements); Pink

Floyd's *Dark Side of the Moon*, *Wish You Were Here*, and *The Wall*; Genesis's *The Lamb Lies Down on Broadway*; and even works such as Willie Nelson's *Red Headed Stranger*; Bruce Springsteen's *The Ghost of Tom Joad*; the Red Hot Chili Peppers' *Californication*; or Tom Petty and the Heartbreakers' *The Last DJ*. Earlier in the history of popular music, the folk era produced unified albums by the likes of Woody Guthrie who collected a variety of "protest" songs, but those albums never aspired to the level of coherent, conceptual works of art. In early 1966, the idea of a concept album or of lyrical and philosophical coherence uniting a wildly different and wildly experimental ensemble of songs challenged and propelled rock 'n' roll fans around the world into a newly ambitious idea of popular music and its potential.

Jon Savage recently described "Tomorrow Never Knows" as the greatest British psychedelic song ever: it "takes you right into the maelstrom . . . it immediately impacted on pop culture" (61). Reviewers quickly responded to *Revolver*'s newness and embraced its musical, lyrical, and psychospiritual aims. Richard Goldstein's *Village Voice* review predicted, "we will view this album in retrospect as a key work in the development of rock 'n' roll into an artistic pursuit" (26). Jules Siegel similarly situated *Revolver* within the bracing altitude of "high culture" when he enthusiastically praised the Beatles' lyrical accomplishment:

> Now the fate of the Beatles lies in the hands of those who someday will prepare the poetry textbooks of the future, in which songs of unrequited love and psychedelic philosophy will appear stripped of their music, raw material for doctoral dissertations, just as the songs of John Donne, William Shakespeare, and John Milton, once a special kind of seventeenth-century Top 40, are now locked inside the groves of the academy, armored in footnotes and frozen out flat on the dry, cold paper of expensive variorum editions. (14)

Moreover, Richard Poirier astutely cautions those critics who import high-toned criteria to popular music that, "by giving the new a distinguished social label of the old, [they] merely accommodate it [and] sap it of its disruptive powers" (116–17). As many fans hyperbolically spouted in those bracing years between 1966 and 1969, the esteemed trio of B's—Bach, Beethoven, and Brahms—became a quartet with the addition of the Beatles. Although we all want to protect *Revolver* from the dubious distinction of being "locked inside the groves of the academy" and from being sapped of its power, Siegel's appreciation of the album's poetry and Poirier's of the group's power and impact surely recognize that the Beatles were introducing us to "another kind of mind," another kind of cultural world, embodied in the grooves of *Revolver*'s vinyl.

I believe that the Beatles were fully aware of, if not fully intent on, the theoretical dimension of *Revolver*. By originally giving "Tomorrow Never

Knows" the title "Mark I," the Beatles signaled a new musical departure. Although we cannot argue definitively that the Beatles wrote and arranged the rest of the tunes to establish the prehistory of human evolution taken to such a quantum leap in the final cut, the coherence resulting from the complex interweaving of the album's lyrics suggests such a trajectory. In a remarkable accomplishment of summation, virtually every word of "Tomorrow Never Knows" revisits, recapitulates, and supercharges an earlier phrase from *Revolver*. After the brief but hypnotically rhythmic instrumental introduction, "Tomorrow Never Knows" begins with the now famous lines,

> Turn off your mind, relax, and float downstream
> It is not dying, it is not dying.

Similar to Robert Frost's brilliant "Directive" with its initial injunction to "Back out of all this now too much for us," and anticipating the psychedelically charged "I'd love to turn you on," from *Sgt. Pepper's Lonely Hearts Club Band*'s concluding "A Day in the Life," the Beatles urge us to turn something off, not on, although the drift of their meaning is virtually identical. Drawn from Leary and Alpert's *Psychedelic Manual*, their LSD user's guide to *The Tibetan Book of the Dead*, these lines advocate an engaged withdrawal, a turning off that is actually a tuning in to what George Harrison would call "The Inner Light." Paradoxically, only when the Beatles have engaged us with the most ambitious soundscape of their recording careers, one that fully engages and challenges our minds to make sense of the sonic onslaught of their instrumental, electronic, and ambient effects, do they request we "turn off" to the very stimuli that, along with Sly and the Family Stone, "want to take us higher." So, whether by virtue of the paradox of the lyrical content or of the emotional frustration precipitated by the lines, *Revolver*'s final cut begins by distancing itself from everything that has preceded it.

Alternately, however, the initial line roots us deeply in the album's lyrical project. In their injunction to turn off our minds and "relax," the Beatles return us to the hectic, contemporary social scenarios dramatized in several of *Revolver*'s songs. In "I'm Only Sleeping," for example, Lennon characterizes his times as, "Running everywhere at such a speed / Till they find there's no need (there's no need)." Adding to this critique in "Love You To," Harrison mourns the many ways in which we fritter away our lives in useless craving and by "living" at an exhausting pace: "Each day just goes so fast / I turn around—it's past." "Turn off your mind [and] relax," then, emerges as the Beatles' diagnosis of a world gone crazy with what Henry David Thoreau called "quiet desperation," with people living "what was not life." Other songs suggest an antidote. In "I'm Only Sleeping," for example, Lennon strikes the album's first explicit verbal anticipation of "Tomorrow Never Knows," even as he offers an alternative to the frantic pace of existence with his line, "Stay in bed, float upstream (float upstream)." Floating upstream, floating down-stream, whichever way you "picture yourself in a boat on a river" ("Lucy in Sky with Diamonds"), the ease of a life floating, or relaxing in bed, offers a palpably antiestablishment challenge to the "Five O'Clock World" and its devotees "running everywhere at such a speed." So, rather than advocating laziness, "I'm Only Sleeping," again like Thoreau's *Walden*, comes across more as a doctor's (perhaps even Doctor Robert's) advice for recuperation. Elsewhere on *Revolver*, the Beatles suggest similarly relaxed modes of existence: "As we live a life of ease" ("Yellow Submarine") and "I could wait forever, I've got time" ("I Want to Tell You"). To be sure, the silly seriousness of "Yellow Submarine" lies in its participation in this dimension of *Revolver*'s lyrical counterculture, its affirmation of living life to its fullest rather than enduring some kind of death in life.

In its willful transcendence of death, "It is not dying, it is not dying" also links up fully with *Revolver*'s earlier songs. Throughout the album, the Beatles maintain a running dialogue with thoughts of death and life, of morbidity and exuberance, rejecting or transcending them at every step of the way. In the album's inaugural track, "Taxman," Harrison's rant against the British taxation system includes the following lines: "My advice to those who die / Declare the pennies on your eyes." Of course, images of death and waste permeate the lives documented in the elegant "Eleanor Rigby." Recall, for example, "Eleanor Rigby died in the church and was buried along with her name" and "Father MacKenzie wiping the dirt from his hands as he walks from the grave / No one was saved." All these lonely people, "Eleanor Rigby" suggests, have wasted their lives, squandering their breath on detached and antiquated occupations such as picking up rice from other people's weddings, keeping their faces in jars by the door, and darning their socks in the night "when there's nobody there." As if to preempt such a bleak ending, Harrison, in "Love You To," urges someone to "Love me while you can / Before I'm a dead old man." Recorded during the *Revolver* sessions but not included on the album, "Rain" suggests how pervasive this commitment to life was for the Beatles at this time. In that song, they strike a similar chord when they castigate those who "run and hide their heads" when the rains come, by noting, "They might as well be dead." The polarity could hardly be starker, a life dedicated to love and engagement set against one of alienation, detachment, and death. This unnatural commitment to death repels the persona in Lennon's "She Said She Said." Throughout that song, the lyrics stage the tense sparring between Lennon and some unnamed other. The actual trigger for Lennon's composition of "She Said She Said" occurred during Lennon's second LSD trip when Peter Fonda began talking about a time when, as a child, he claims to have died on the operating table but was brought back to life. Lennon's feminizing of the interlocutor in "She Said She Said" belies the experiential origin of the song's lyrics; it might be one of those numbers in which his misogyny lurks in the margins.[3] Throughout the song, Lennon recalls a dialogue that strands its subjects in a bleak world reminiscent of all those lonely, alienated souls from "Eleanor Rigby." But this speaker finally transcends the downward drift of what "she said" by affirming, "I know that I'm ready to leave / 'Cause you're making me feel like I've never been born." Although it documents an exchange reminiscent of the interpersonal confusion recorded by R. D. Laing in *Knots* (1970), "She Said She Said" reconnects with life-affirming energies as redemptive alternatives to the despairing situation. As "Tomorrow Never Knows" puts it: "It is not dying." "She Said She Said" concludes the first side of *Revolver*, and the album's commitment to life is reinforced by the very next cut—the giddily optimistic "Good Day Sunshine."

But *Revolver*'s dialectic leaves room for one more downturn prior to the transcendence of "Tomorrow Never Knows." Surely one of the more traditionally beautiful songs on *Revolver*, "For No One" was originally titled, "Why Did It Die?" (Everett 1999, 53–54). Mourning the loss of a lover, Paul's line, "And yet you don't believe her when she said her love is dead" revisits the sadness of love gone wrong. But the title change and the placement of "Got to Get You into My Life" (Paul's other brassily optimistic composition celebrating new love found) shortly after "For No One" suggests the transience of emotional setbacks. While losing a lover might seem like the end of the world, it surely "is not dying" from the perspective of *Revolver*.

The song's next couplet—"Lay down all thoughts, surrender to the void / It is shining, it is shining"—enjoins the listener to deeper passivity and quietude by relinquishing all hold to ego and consciousness, and, by its affirmative articulation, suggests that "it *is* shining," an affirmation stripped of the song's initial negation of "it is *not* dying" (emphasis added). The passivity encoded within these lines also recalls moments of purposive, if luxurious, relaxation from earlier on *Revolver*. The speaker in "I'm Only Sleeping," for example, finds himself "Lying there and staring at the ceiling." "Yellow Submarine" celebrates living "a life of ease," and the speaker of "She Said She Said" repudiates a companion whose bleakness makes life miserable. Finally, Paul's vocals indicate that the entire drift of "Here, There, and Everywhere" is a poised realization that "to lead a better life I need my love to be here" and of the value of spending time "running my hands through her hair." "It is shining," of course, most clearly recapitulates the veritable orgy of shining from the lyrics of "Good Day Sunshine" with its line, "We take a walk, the sun is shining down," and its multiple repetitions of the title phrase performed with various vocal inflections and electronic effects. Once again, "Rain" furthers its critique of those who would escape life's mysteries in similar terms: "When the sun shines / They slip into the shade." Neither rain nor shine satisfies those intent on avoiding life. Again, according to "Rain," "they might as well be dead."

Of course, given the Beatles' initial experiences with LSD just prior to and during the recording of *Revolver*, the "shining" to which John refers here probably references psychedelic transformations. Leary recreates psychedelic "shining" in breathtaking terms in *High Priest*:

> I opened my eyes. I was in heaven. Illumination. Every object in the room was a radiant structure of atomic-god-particles. Radiating. Matter did not exist. There was just this million-matrix lattice web of energies. Shimmering. Alive. Interconnected in space-time. Everything hooked up in a cosmic dance. Fragile. Indestructible. (328)

Such a shatteringly beautiful experience as this most likely powered John Lennon's creation.

"Tomorrow Never Knows" elaborates on the notion of visionary luminosity implicit in "shining," expanding on both its conceptual and its ocular ranges of meaning. In this song, and throughout *Revolver*, seeing is meaning just as much as it is believing:

> You may see the meaning of within
> It is being, it is being.

Appropriately, "Taxman" opens the album by suggesting the equivalence of blindness with death: "And my advice for those who die / Declare the pennies on your eyes." Literally opaque, the pennies merely accentuate the eyes shut after the moment of life's cessation, but the Beatles use their opening volley to suggest the blindness of the world, again echoing writers such as Thoreau, who, in *Walden*, similarly equated blindness with death, or at least with those "living what was not life." *Revolver* examines various scenarios, positive and negative, in which they contrast blindness and nothingness with seeing and insight.

"Love You To," for example, bemoans the fact that:

> There's people standing round
> Who screw you in the ground
> They'll fill your head with all the things you see.

"For No One" personalizes and inverts this moment of visual fullness equaling nothing of value:

> And in her eyes you see nothing
> No sign of love behind the tears
> Cried for no one
> A love that should have lasted years.

Just as the dead's eyes are blank and covered with the dead dullness of pennies, the eyes of a lost love "might as well be dead" in that they neither reflect the passion that once lit up two lives nor form a visionary, or as Hendrix would call it, rainbow, bridge between two people.

The perpetually enigmatic "And Your Bird Can Sing" traffics extensively in various negations, nearly all of them focused on some sensory fullness compromised by sensory loss. For example, the hypothetical addressee of the song's lyrics may have heard "every sound there is," but he or she "can't hear me"; that is, the song's speaker. The same pattern holds true for vision:

> You say you've seen seven wonders and your bird is green
> But you can't see me, you can't see me

Here, rather than explicit criticism of some oppressive "Other" or explicit grieving over a lost lover, John Lennon's song suggests something similar to Ralph Waldo Emerson's dictum, "Traveling is a fool's paradise." Harrison's "The Inner Light" makes much the same point with lyrics such as, "without going out of my door / I can know all things on earth" and, "the farther one travels / The less one knows."[4] This person may have traveled the world and seen all the human and natural wonders that one can hope for, but he or she really cannot *see* the song's persona. "Doctor Robert" revisits this notion, albeit in its celebrity form. The infamous Doctor Robert, a composite of various dispensers of LSD and other mind-expanding chemicals during the years of the Beatles' early psychedelic experimentation, has achieved a certain "star status." Certain of his devotees, however, seem to have missed the deeper dimension of the psychedelic trip, and they see Doctor Robert as someone whose celebrity cachet itself proves alluring. Rather than gaining insight into their own inner worlds, they want others to see them with the Doctor. In other words, certain forms of seeing, here touristic belt-notching and paparazzi visual clips, fall far short of the genuine seeing-within that "Tomorrow Never Knows" elevates to the only sight worth seeing.

Not until McCartney's brilliant "Got to Get You into My Life" does *Revolver* suggest the fullness of seeing that "Tomorrow Never Knows" celebrates. In that brassy communiqué of joy and exuberance, Paul opens by singing:

> I was alone, I took a ride,
> I didn't know what I would find there
> Another road where maybe I could see another kind of mind there
> Ooh, then I suddenly see you,
> Ooh, did I tell you I need you
> Every single day of my life.

As I have developed elsewhere in more detail, "Got to Get You into My Life" celebrates mind expansion in all its possible forms: psychological, passionate, and psychedelic (Reising, "Not Dying" 248–49). Prefiguring numerous other rock songs that develop some mode of transportation to suggest the psyche-delic "tripping" experience (Pink Floyd's "Bike" and "Interstellar Overdrive," the Moody Blues' "See Saw," the Who's "Magic Bus," and Steppenwolf's "Magic Carpet Ride," for example), "Got to Get You into My Life" is partic-ularly lucid and definitive in this respect. Taking a ride to encounter a differ-ent kind of mind codifies what many theorists and practitioners regard as the very essence of the psychedelic experience. Anticipating "Tomorrow Never Knows," Paul's song focuses on what one "sees" on this ride, whether it be "another kind of mind" or the song's celebrated "you," the very "you" that the Beatles call "Lucy in the Sky with Diamonds" and that Eric Burdon and the Animals christened "A Girl Named Sandoz" (after Sandoz, the Swiss phar-maceutical company that manufactured LSD).

Even before they proclaimed with necessary redundancy that "all you need is love" and "love is all you need," the Beatles had issued their manifesto for the so-called love generation, and they did so on *Revolver*:

> Love is all and love is everyone
> It is knowing, it is knowing.

Loving and knowing twine together in the pantheon of virtues and energies celebrated in "Tomorrow Never Knows." As with every other one of the song's motifs, images of both "love" and "knowing" permeate *Revolver*'s earlier tracks. One could argue that "Taxman" is loaded with rage, and, therefore, introduces the theme of love by virtue of its vitriolic negation of love and com-passion. Similarly, the loneliness and alienation characteristic of Eleanor Rigby's world strand all of its characters in loveless and quietly desperate iso-lation. "I'm Only Sleeping" pleads for its speaker simply to be left alone in his solitary bed. Not until we reach side two's "For No One" does *Revolver* actu-ally addresses the sadness and pain of failed love directly with the lines:

> No sign of love behind the tears
> Cried for no one
> A love that should have lasted years.

Apparently not all romances last forever such as those celebrated in songs such as "Here, There, and Everywhere."

However, "Love You To" introduces what will become one of *Revolver*'s primary energies, almost as though they need to be imported from the exotic other worlds evoked by his Asian styling, so dead to magic and mystery is their own. "Love You To" urges its auditor to "Love me while you can," to "Make love all day long," and in a wonderfully self-reflexive rock 'n' roll moment (which anticipates Jefferson Airplane's manifesto to "Make Love

Flying") to "Make love singing songs." "Here, There, and Everywhere,"
Revolver's next song, domesticates the love that "Love You To" insinuated in
its sitar-drenched strums, "To lead a better life I need my love to be here."
Here, not somewhere else. Here, wherever one is, not ensconced in some
ashram or perched atop some Himalayan peak on the other side of the world.
But Paul's song quickly complicates the very deictic locator he just provided
by noting, "But to love her is to need her everywhere / Knowing that love is
to share." "Here" becomes "there" becomes "everywhere." Moreover, the line
"Each one believing that love never dies" immortalizes, or, as Herman
Melville's Ishmael might put it, ubiquitizes the concept of love in time, and,
by so doing, offers a counterpoint to the love that dies in "For No One." So
"now" becomes "then" becomes "eternity." In one final lyrical gesture, "Here,
There, and Everywhere" stresses the transpersonal nature of love itself in the
phrase "knowing that love is to share." "I" becomes "you" becomes "everyone."[5]
Of course, "Good Day Sunshine," the most conventionally optimistic song on
Revolver, offers two giddily affirmative paeans to the power of love. McCartney sings in consecutive verses, "I'm in love and it's a sunny day" and "I love
her and she's loving me." For McCartney, in a distinct negation of the mourn-
ful complaint represented by Bill Withers in "Ain't No Sunshine," it is sunny,
and, in dramatic contrast with Withers's tune, the female protagonist is decidedly present. Hence, even in these mellifluous love ballads about rootedness,
immediacy, and love, the Beatles prepare the way for the universalizing
designs of "Tomorrow Never Knows."

    "It is knowing," the other primary motif from this couplet, is introduced
on "Taxman" with its monological diatribe against the British tax system, pro-
ceeding as though it "knows it all" and that nothing more could possibly be
said on the subject. The speaker of "I'm Only Sleeping" betrays a similarly
definitive tone, suggesting that his luxuriance is irrefragable, beyond reproach,
without alternative. Knowing in its affirmative, mind-expanded sense emerges
quietly in "Here, There, and Everywhere" with its gently emphatic opening
line, "To lead a better life I need my love to be here," and culminating in the
repeated verse:

> I want her everywhere and if she's beside me
> I know I need never care
> But to love her is to need her everywhere
> Knowing that love is to share.

Intimate interpersonal relations provide another context for "knowing" in
"She Said She Said," albeit more in a manner of self-protection and defense.
There, assaulted by his partner's despairing discourse on death (she *knows*
what being both dead and sad is like), Lennon's speaker counters by declaring, "I said even though you know what you know / I know that I'm ready

to leave." The escapism these lines suggest differs significantly from that "I'm Only Sleeping" implied in that this speaker opts to leave a hostile environment in which he is made "to feel like [he's] never been born." "I Want to Tell You," the final Harrison track on *Revolver*, expresses the desire for knowing, a knowing that provides a bond of intimacy between Harrison and his addressee:

> Sometimes I wish I knew you well
> Then I could speak my mind and tell you
> Maybe you'd understand.

Escaping from the knotted oppressiveness of "She Said She Said," Harrison's song imagines a perfect interpersonal bond in which communication flows freely, unwarped by dark agendas or hidden motives. And, in "Got to Get You into My Life," McCartney celebrates both an affirmative plunge into the unknown, "I didn't know what I would find there," and the certainty that such a leap of faith can generate: "You knew I wanted just to hold you." Thus, throughout *Revolver* the Beatles plumb the depths of knowing, unknowing, not knowing, wisdom, and ignorance. When we reach the final declaration of "It is knowing," then, the Beatles have freed up knowing from all local particulars and have cast it in the broadest possible terms as a state of untrammeled being.

The couplet that begins with the line, "That ignorance and hate may mourn the dead" occupies an anomalous position on *Revolver*. Unlike any of the other verses from "Tomorrow Never Knows," this one functions primarily to recapitulate earlier notions, not to advance new ones. Seemingly negating all earlier references to "knowing," "love," and "life," the opposites of "ignorance," "hate," and "dead" erupt as a temporary collapse of the song's thematics. In so doing, however, they serve as an intralyrical moment of paradox and negation, similar to those occasionally present in the trajectory of every other theme *Revolver* advanced and "Tomorrow Never Knows" resolved. And it is not only by its own recapitulation of the album's motific play on the concept of belief and doubt, but also by transcending the negativity the previous line staged that the couplet concludes with the line, "It is believing, it is believing."

Throughout *Revolver*, however, belief and the risk of believing (leaps of faith, as it were) emerge as viable rejoinders to doubt, fear, and alienation. "Here, There, and Everywhere" puts it quite clearly when Paul sings, "Each one believing that love never dies." Here, the optimism and commitment of lovers communicates a variety of eternity. Paul's "For No One" suggests the desperate power of believing, even in the face of tragedy and loss. In that song of love gone sour, Paul sings of his subject, "You don't believe her when she said her love is dead." Denial, maybe; repression, perhaps. Inspired by his "belief" in his lover's place in his life, this optimist, like John's persona in "She

Said She Said," refuses to be daunted merely by what someone says. Anticipating the song's next verse, Paul's response moves beyond the speaker's leaving in "She Said She Said." In "Doctor Robert," the Beatles pay particular
tribute both to the physicians who supplied LSD to their friends as well as to
the psychedelic concoctions themselves when they insist, "he's a man you must
believe." What *Revolver* traffics in, then, is belief, not necessarily mere knowing. In fact, even the magisterial proclamations of "Tomorrow Never Knows"
need to be tempered in that they can only stand as choices, options, and leaps
of faith the Beatles experimented in and provisionally endorsed.

The cognitive status of any one of the claims "Tomorrow Never Knows"
makes borders on the Technicolor transience of our dreams: "But listen to the
color of your dreams / It is not leaving, it is not leaving." The quasi-oxy-
moronic act of dreaming does not necessarily equate with leaving or slipping
into some other state of consciousness detached from the immediacy of lived
experience. But on *Revolver*, not all visions are visionary, not all dreams
dreamy. We must recall that two of the earliest cuts on the album explored
contradictory dream states. The dream state of "Eleanor Rigby [who] lives in
a dream," is one of bleakness, of black-and-white starkness, similar to the
cover art of *Revolver*, which made its appearance amidst the color-drenched
excesses of mid-1960s art. Immediately following "Eleanor Rigby," "I'm Only
Sleeping" poses a radical alternative to the alienated unreality of dream state
in which "all the lonely people" find themselves. Here, dreaming emerges
almost as a prescription for the blues examined in "Taxman" and "Eleanor
Rigby." Indeed, "I'm Only Sleeping" problematizes the apparent opposition of
"waking" and "dreaming" in its first lines:

> When I wake up early in the morning,
> Lift my head, I'm still yawning.
> When I'm in the middle of a dream,
> Stay in bed, float up stream (float up stream).

Identical adverbials of time ("when") begin each sentence, and another set of
chronological markers ("still" and "in the middle of") also link them internally,
suggesting a vague state somewhere between sleeping and waking. Together
with internal rhymes interlinking lines two and four ("head" and "bed"), and
with concluding near rhymes linking both couplets, "I'm Only Sleeping"
refuses to declare whether "waking up" or remaining "in the middle of a
dream" are alternative, or at least different, states of existence or whether they
are roughly equivalent alternatives to those "running everywhere at such a
speed." In either case, when the speaker requests, "Please don't spoil my day;
I'm miles away" and "Please don't wake me, no, don't shake me," and when he
urges others to "Leave me where I am—I'm only sleeping," he makes a case,
not for mere lethargy, but for an alternative to the anger and loneliness that

have plagued the characters in *Revolver*'s first two songs. Almost Thoreauvian (again) in its marching to a different drummer mentality, Lennon's speaker wakes to a different alarm clock. As the verse concludes, this kind of dreaming "is not leaving."

But *Revolver* addresses this crucial concept in numerous other ways, all focused on rootedness and immediacy. The theme pervades *Revolver*, emerging as something similar to its ethical center. "Here, There, and Everywhere" presents the matter very clearly when it begins: "To lead a better life I need my love to be here." Another love song, Paul's "Got to Get You into My Life," similarly expresses deep satisfaction with a domestic/emotional status quo in its line, "When I'm with you I want to stay there." Two other songs reinforce this notion, albeit from a negative angle. In "For No One," a tune mourning the loss of love, McCartney suggests these telling differences with the line, "You stay home, she goes out." In other words, the woman strays, or at least wanders, whereas the man remains squarely at "home." The speaker of "She Said She Said" declares, "I know that I'm ready to leave / 'Cause you're making me feel like I've never been born," thus "leaving," but to maintain his own sense of self when confronted by someone who threatens to "bring him down." So, whether lying in bed, gathered with companions in a "Yellow Submarine," or lounging with a lover on a beautiful summer's day, *Revolver*'s primary subjects articulate a shared commitment to a sense of place. It—whether transcendence, happiness, or intellectual and spiritual poise—is not about leaving.

In the ultimate couplet of "Tomorrow Never Knows," the Beatles finalize their concluding song by projecting it, themselves, and their audience into a realm where play is serious and where endings are beginnings, and vice versa: "So play the game 'Existence' to the end, / Of the beginning, of the beginning." Most directly, the "game" Existence contrasts with "The games [that] begin to drag me down" in Harrison's "I Want to Tell You." Indirectly, those same "games" of emptiness and negativity make the speaker of "She Said She Said" feel as if he has "never been born." These "games" must surely be different from the playful attitude characteristic of those who "live in a yellow submarine," where they live a life of ease and relaxation, the same sense of equipoise that defines the speakers in "I'm Only Sleeping" and "Good Day Sunshine." In those songs, as in most others throughout *Revolver*, "Existence" is imagined as simultaneously playful, serious, tender, and relaxed. And yet the mere fact of *Revolver* representing fourteen fictional tableaux suggests that it offers "games," or plays, minidramas of comic exuberance as well as of tragic sadness, of existence. Moreover, the very cohabitation of those extremes packaged within the vision of one "album" suggests the dynamism and the Möbius-strip complexity of the final line.

I have argued elsewhere that, through its intricately related cuts, *Revolver* enacts something of a dialectical drama of consciousness surging through an evolutionary spiral from rage and grief ("Taxman" and "Eleanor Rigby") to confidence, joy, and transcendence ("I Want to Tell You," "Got to Get You into My Life," and "Tomorrow Never Knows"). Only once, in "And Your Bird Can Sing," does *Revolver* visit anything resembling circularity, and even there, only with the line, "Look in my direction, I'll be round, I'll be round." And yet the final doubling of "Of the beginning, of the beginning" seems to stage a return within the album's final line through the doubling of the phrase "of the beginning." Moreover, "Tomorrow Never Knows" literally revisits the beginning by virtue of McCartney's guitar solo from "Taxman," the album's first cut, being sampled, slowed down, cut up, reversed, and electronically altered to create one of the most bracing instrumental moments in "Tomorrow Never Knows." In other words, "Tomorrow Never Knows" returns us sonically to "the beginning" of the entire album. In another moment of sonic recapitulation, the tinny, dance-hall piano at the song's conclusion refers to the ragtime piano from "Good Day Sunshine," while also anticipating the end of "Within You Without You" *(Sgt. Pepper)* with its enigmatic laughter.

But rather than suggesting some pointless circularity, the Beatles return us to another kind of beginning, one reached by the historical and psychological journey through *Revolver* and its newly psychedelicized take on the human condition. Sonically, *Revolver* ranges widely through time, sampling the sounds of ancient India ("Love You To"), eighteenth-century Europe ("Eleanor Rigby" and "For No One"), and the swinging and experimental 1960s ("She Said She Said" and "Got to Get You into My Life" to name only two). In its final recapitulative moment, "Tomorrow Never Knows" also symbolically expands the geo-logic of *Revolver*. On "Yellow Submarine," the album had explored the ocean depths, but in "Tomorrow Never Knows," Lennon originally wanted to re-create the sound of 1,000 Tibetan monks chanting in the background (MacDonald 152). But Lennon's perspective from mountaintops functions more than atmospherically and culturally. Theorists of the psychedelic experience repeatedly stress its ability to complicate one's sense of place, to situate one "here, there, and everywhere" or to be simultaneously within one and without one, as it were. Indeed, the integrative nature of psychedelic experience is often felt to be an initiation into the realm of the historical, cultural, racial, and geographical ubiquity. For example, after ingesting the Amazonian ayahuasca brew, William Burroughs wrote to Allen Ginsberg:

> The blood and substance of many races, Negro, Polynesian, Mountain Mongol, Desert Nomad, Polyglot Near East, Indian—new races as yet unconceived and unborn, combinations not yet realized passes through your body. Migrations, incredible journeys through deserts and jungles and mountains (stasis and death in closed mountain valleys where plants sprout out of the

Rock and vast crustaceans hatch inside and break the shell of the body), across the Pacific in an outrigger canoe to Easter Island. The Composite City where all human potentials are spread out in a vast silent market. (44)

During his first LSD trip John Coltrane recalled having "perceived the inter-relationships of all life forms" (qtd. in Lee and Shlain 79). So, just as psychedelic experience seems to enable the powerful integration of self with all others and all of history, "Tomorrow Never Knows" operates as the integrating rhetoric of *Revolver*, providing, perhaps even discovering, the coherence and unity that evolves symbiotically out of the album's songs.

Moreover, the emotional negativity, alienation, and despair present in varying degrees on several of *Revolver*'s cuts are all resolved, "left," transcended within the psychedelic dialectic of its unfolding. In this respect, "Tomorrow Never Knows" offers the band's most complexly psychedelic experience. "It is not dying" dramatizes the symbolic "death and rebirth" that many psychedelic journeys enable one to experience. "Merely" dying or being symbolically reborn does not form the crux of these transformative experiences, but rather the sense of having been reborn into a life which, as one of Masters and Houston's psychedelic case studies put it, is "a new life exactly like someone who has died and been reborn, leaving behind all the torments of the old life" (188). The newness of the song's soundscape, then, mirrors the renewed appreciation of existence following the symbolic death of the psychedelic trip, which in turn emerges because of having transcended the troubles of loneliness, alienation, failed communication, and withdrawal as represented throughout *Revolver*'s individual cuts.

Moreover, the concept of the album provided a vehicle and a philosophy capable of transcending the discrete units of songs usually packaged together to constitute an album. Whereas albums prior to *Revolver* merely packaged 13 or 14 largely unrelated songs into the popular album format, *Revolver* gathered 14 dialectically related statements on the human condition into a unified and coherent vision. In one sense, it is popular music's first celebration of the human as technological and the technological as human. No two transitions are the same, no two songs sound the same, and yet *Revolver* articulates a vision of human existence both evolutionary in its dynamic and unified in its themes. Unity within diversity and diversity punctuating unity: take your pick. Through its synthesizing ambitions, *Revolver* achieves something similar to the grand unification of experience that many regard as the hallmark of psychedelic experience itself.

"Tomorrow Never Knows" was the first song recorded for the album, and, perhaps unlike any song before it or since, it serves as both the linchpin of *Revolver* as well as its apotheosis. Without "Tomorrow Never Knows," the album *Revolver* makes no sense and, because of the absence of any overarching perspective or point of view, might simply fizzle out into oblivion. Without the rest of *Revolver*, "Tomorrow Never Knows" may still shock its listeners and take them higher, in the manner Sly Stone wanted to, but it probably would not stand as the towering accomplishment it is. The violence of the transition into "Tomorrow Never Knows" clashes with the fact that the lyrical essence of the song revisits and recapitulates every one of the album's primary motifs. It is the quintessence of the album's coherence, similar to the fourth movement of Dvořák's Ninth Symphony *(From the New World)* or of any other orchestral work whose final movement echoes and closes its themes. In this way, the "sound" of the song belies its seamless integration with the rest of the album. The Beatles' two versions of "Revolution" pose an important comparison. The faster version, released as a single, "sounds" more revolutionary, at least in its hard-edged rocking core. In the slower version of the song—"Revolution 1" featured on the *White Album*—the band pointedly follows the lines, "But if you talk about destruction / Don't you know that you can count me out," by adding "in" to replace "out." In other words, the slower, mellower version carries a harder revolutionary punch. Function, or meaning, does not, in other words, always follow form in some simple, linear way.

"Tomorrow Never Knows" and, for that matter, *Revolver* as a whole, then, occupy critical and problematic places in the history of the Beatles' careers as well as in the evolution of rock 'n' roll (and here I use that phrase in its widest possible sense) as a musical genre, both in its relationship to itself and its own history as well as to the lyrical and musical conventions of so-called high culture. I suggest in my introduction that *Revolver*'s break from earlier rock practices simultaneously constitutes its *bridge* with more traditionally agreed-on works of "high" culture. I would like to conclude by suggesting the highly complex set of values embedded within that claim and within this chapter. As is the case in the preceding example of the Beatles' two versions of "Revolution," form and function can coexist, but they can also strain against each other. Revolutionary/conservative, innovative/traditional, pop/high culture: such pairings might be either/or situations, or they might be both/and; but they are more likely to be both both/and and either/or scenarios. And the general carnivalization enacted by popular culture in the 1960s certainly produced many such complex cultural negotiations.

"Tomorrow Never Knows" might fully realize a bridge between rock 'n' roll and serious music, but how is that particular revolution to be understood? Yes, *Revolver* ushers rock 'n' roll into a newly sophisticated, newly ambitious, newly intellectual era, and subsequent releases by the Beatles, as well as grandly unified, or at least thematically coherent albums such as *Beggar's Banquet* by the Rolling Stones and the numerous works to which I have referred, all testify to the fruits of the Beatles' achievement. Rock 'n' roll would never again be "merely" about beaches, cars, and kisses. But the excesses and the oft-lampooned pomposity of the psychedelic era (witness beautiful monstrosities such as Vanilla Fudge's cover of "You Keep Me Hanging On") and of "progressive" rock (Emerson, Lake, and Palmer's *Tarkus* or their rock interpretation of Mussorgsky's *Pictures at an Exhibition*, for example) might suggest something has been lost from rock even as it aspires to mature themes and visions. To be sure, we find anger and social criticism throughout *Revolver* and much of the rock tradition up to about 1980, but not until punks such as the Ramones, the Sex Pistols, Elvis Costello, the Clash, and Gang of Four would popular music return in any consistent and unified way to the intensity and outrage of the Who's "My Generation," the Rolling Stones' "Street Fighting Man," or the Animals' "We Gotta Get Out of This Place" or "It's My Life."

The Beatles' own trajectory is an important case in point. *Revolver* is a very serious and a very heady album, both in terms of its sonic experiments as well as in its lyrical drift. Even the love songs (and there are no "silly love songs" on *Revolver*) relate deeply and seriously to its darker, more tragic elements. By *Sgt. Pepper's Lonely Hearts Club Band*, with the exception of Harrison's compositions, the Beatles have already retreated lyrically into predominantly banal, occasionally schmaltzy, and often trivial vignettes about the kinds of subjects Lennon later admitted to having hated ("When I'm Sixty-Four," "Lovely Rita," "She's Leaving Home"). Sonically, of course, *Sgt. Pepper* is magnificent, but its magnificence lies more in the realm of the most exquisite ear candy rather than of philosophical or poetic sublimity. Lyrically, irony and detachment dominate *Sgt. Pepper*. Such may be the case of some inevitable development within the Beatles' project; perhaps other developments in rock and in Anglo-American society affected the Beatles, or perhaps the beginnings of the serious rift between Lennon and McCartney would eventually fragment the group's existence. As with the differences between the 45 rpm version of "Revolution" and the version of "Revolution 1" from *The Beatles* (the *White Album*) the revolution enacted by *Revolver* and "Tomorrow Never Knows" may, like many revolutions—political, social, and aesthetic—ultimately be defined more by its complexities, ambiguities, and ironies than by any definitive transformation.

NOTES

1. See my introduction to *"Every Sound There Is."*

2. See the essays by Ger Tillekens, Stephen Valdez, and Naphtali Wagner in *"Every Sound There Is"* for excellent discussions of the musical coherence within *Revolver*.

3. Other instances include Lennon's misogynistic lyrics to *Rubber Soul*'s "Run for Your Life" and his lyrical confessions about spousal abuse in *Sgt. Pepper*'s "Getting Better."

4. Thanks to Jim LeBlanc for reminding me of George's lines, for his excellent reading of an earlier draft of this chapter, and for more than thirty years of friendship. Many thanks also to Alma Reising for her editorial expertise. Both Jim and Alma made this a better chapter.

5. For a humorous take on this matter, please listen to the Bonzo Dog Band's "Kama Sutra" with its lyric: "In position seventy-two, you were me, and I was you!"

Chapter 7

The Spectacle of Alienation

Death, Loss, and the Crowd in *Sgt. Pepper's Lonely Hearts Club Band*

WILLIAM M. NORTHCUTT

> All the lonely people
> Where do they all belong?
> — Lennon and McCartney, "Eleanor Rigby"

> See the people standing there who disagree and never win
> And wonder why they don't get in my door.
> — Lennon and McCartney, "Fixing a Hole"

SGT. PEPPER'S LONELY HEARTS CLUB BAND comes to us accompanied by a thirty-five-year legacy of critical and fanzine commentary, of inanities such as the "Paul is Dead" conspiracy, of overdetermined interpretations, of our own memories, of references, allusions, and appropriations in mass media. It comes to us today as the original culture product, whose cover has been lampooned and honored by Frank Zappa and *The Simpsons*, and whose melodic strains show up in the music of acts as diverse as the Butthole Surfers and William Shatner.[1] Whether we have just bought our first copy or are listening to it for the thousandth time, *Sgt. Pepper* comes to us, like literary and cultural texts, as a work "already read." Criticism of the album generally eschews fanzine espousals of concepts and conspiracies for the de-historicized assumption of unity in *Sgt. Pepper*'s audience.

Steve Turner concludes, "for anyone who was young at the time, the music automatically evokes the sight of beads and kaftans, the sound of tinkling bells and the aroma of marijuana masked by joss sticks" (144). Likewise in *Beatlesongs*, William Dowlding asserts that "*Sgt. Pepper* not only changed pop music, but transformed how we perceived that music, and, in a very literal sense, how we perceived ourselves" (152). In *Flowers in the Dustbin*, James Miller reports his 1967 experience of hearing the album everywhere across the Occident as he traveled from California to Greece, an experience he says echoes Langdon Winner's trek across America at the time of *Sgt. Pepper*'s release (344) and Kenneth Tynan's remark that the album was a "decisive moment in the history of Western civilization" (344). Miller counters, "That was an illusion, of course. But that is how it really felt" (260). The Beatles themselves have helped to perpetuate the idea that the summer of 1967 was a unique moment of social unity. Ringo Starr says in *The Beatles Anthology*, "*Sgt. Pepper* was a special album. . . . It was Flower Power coming into its fullest. It was love and peace; it was a fabulous period, for me and the world" (248). In what would prove to be one of George Harrison's last extensive discussions of the Beatles' legacy, he says:

> The summer of 1967 was the Summer of Love for us. . . . A lot of it was bullshit; it was just what the press was saying. But there was definitely a vibe: we could feel what was going on with our friends—and people who had similar goals in America—even though we were miles away. You could just pick up the vibes, man. (254)

The audiences who received and continue to receive *Sgt. Pepper* were and are more heterogeneous than such zeitgeist commentary allows. In the American South, *Sgt. Pepper* came with the apparatus of Lennon's 1966 oft-quoted comments on Jesus Christ to rock-journalist and friend Maureen Cleave:

> Christianity will go. It will vanish and shrink. . . . We're more popular than Jesus now; I don't know which will go first—rock 'n' roll or Christianity. Jesus was all right, but his disciples were thick and ordinary. It's them twisting it that ruins it for me. (*Anthology* 223)

Christ's "disciples" in the southern United States answered en masse. Record burnings and protests, death threats and bomb scares dogged the Beatles on their last tour through the South. Harrison would later comment, "the repercussions were big, particularly in the Bible Belt" (*Anthology* 225). Lennon related their experience as particularly harrowing:

One night on a show in the South somewhere [Memphis] somebody let off a firecracker while we were on stage. There had been threats to shoot us, the Klan were burning Beatle records outside and a lot of the crew-cut kids were joining in with them. Somebody let off a firecracker and every one of us . . . looked at each other, because each thought it was the other that had been shot. It was that bad. (*Anthology* 227)

By the end of 1966, the Beatles began to see their relationship to the crowd as an antagonistic one.

Sgt. Pepper finds Lennon, McCartney, Harrison, and Starr retreating from the public that had so harassed them with Beatlemania and Beatle bashing. Ironically, part of that desire to abandon live performance was prompted by the repressive South, from which their chief influences—rock, blues, country, and jazz—had come and against whose repression these forms had sprung. Such tensions presented the group with a crisis of identity, which the Beatles tried to resolve on *Sgt. Pepper*—through new "readings" of their musical influences, newly developed philosophical ideals, the developing drug culture, and the world they wanted to change. In significant ways, these solutions were contradictory, and they echo a host of other contradictions that inform the album and its receptions. As my analysis will show, *Sgt. Pepper* is as much about separation and alienation as it is about unity.

Specifically, I want to look at the "political unconscious" of *Sgt. Pepper*, rather than prove thematic unities. Fredric Jameson explains, "the assertion of a political unconscious proposes" that we "explore the multiple paths that lead to the unmasking of cultural artifacts as socially symbolic acts" (*Political Unconscious* 20). Central to my reading is the understanding that *Sgt. Pepper* arrived during a great time of social unrest, technological development, and the growth of media culture. The Beatles responded by, to emend Ian Macdonald's term, "revolutions in the head." These revolutions were based not only on the Beatles' sociopolitical stances to the establishment, but also by the Beatles' relationship to the masses. The young men were still strongly connected to their Liverpool working-class origins, but were drawn to the freedom they enjoyed as members of the growing celebrity class, which they were helping to define. As for the masses, *Sgt. Pepper* classifies the crowds:

• as masses of record buyers "invited" to the spectacle;
• as unenlightened, moral and political hypocrites, supporters, and reproducers of restrictive mores and laws—the establishment and its public and private agents;
• as an enlightened, but elite set of *art* appreciators and rock 'n' rollers who were feeling "the vibes";
• as screaming Beatlemaniacs—who buy records, but make real contact and real music impossible.

As their fame grew, so did their discomfort with celebrity. The wildness of Beatlemania and the rigors of Memphis and Manila[2] forced them to confront their positions as individuals outside the Beatle spectacle. At the same time, they realized that their celebrity afforded them the chance to air political beliefs. The Beatles found themselves in a position more elevated and enlightened than that of the masses, and although they roundly condemned the moralistic ideology of postwar England, they steadfastly tried to connect with the ordinary person on the street. In addition, the Beatles sensed the contradictions inherent in their part of the spectacle: they were at once protesting aspects of capitalism while promoting a product of image and music to be sold and accepted; they felt alienated from the crowd, yet they felt the need to express admiration and criticism of the extraspectacle crowd and to sell them records. As they developed worldviews differing greatly from those of Liverpool's working class, they made attempts at both reconciliation and provocation. Caught between loyalty to the working class and their position among the elite, the band members began to see their relationship to establishment culture as an antagonistic one as well. In Barry Miles's official biography, McCartney says "a rubbing-up . . . occurred" between the Beatles and what McCartney calls the "cusp" of the British establishment. At the time of *Sgt. Pepper*, McCartney says that they had the feeling that the "cusp . . . were on their way out, we were on the way in" (126). *Sgt. Pepper's Lonely Hearts Club Band* in all its multiplicity represents a disparate set of responses to these contradictory, social forces. On the album, the Beatles explore and exploit the elements of performance and presentation in an attempt to control irresolvable social and personal issues.

From 1964 on, the lyrics of Lennon, McCartney, and Harrison return repeatedly to themes of death, loss, and alienation in connection with various crowds. "Eleanor Rigby" narrates the story of a lonely old woman whose funeral is unattended by the crowds of "lonely people" for whom she had fretted all her lonely life. Her alienation from the crowd and from herself reflects McCartney's pity for the masses, but it also evinces a growing concern with his place in relation to the crowd. Lennon's "In My Life" reflects bittersweetly on the "friends and lovers" of whom "some are dead and some are living." In Harrison's "Taxman," a response to British taxation, the dead have to "declare the pennies" holding down their lifeless eyelids. And Lennon's "Tomorrow Never Knows" is about Lennon's Leary-inspired and metaphorical attempt to "kill" the ego,[3] as he paraphrases Leary's invitation to LSD experimenters: "Turn off your mind, relax, and float downstream." Each of these songs is involved in a dialogue with the crowd, but none comes to a final resolution. The *Sgt. Pepper* sessions would become the space where the Beatles explored the limitations and possibilities of the spectacle.

ROCK 'N' ROLL IDENTITY AND AVANT-GARDE AGITATION

Sources such as Mark Lewisohn's *The Beatles: Recording Sessions* tell us that the first real recording sessions for *Sgt. Pepper* began with no concept and only a few songs that Lennon and McCartney had written separately or were still writing. In November 1966, the Beatles met with George Martin at EMI's Abbey Road Studios.[4] There they began the first of several versions of Lennon's "Strawberry Fields Forever." After finishing off McCartney's "When I'm Sixty-Four," they began work on "Penny Lane." In *All You Need Is Ears*, Martin says, "*Sgt. Pepper* originated with a song which was never on it" (199), and he expresses regret that "Strawberry Fields Forever" and "Penny Lane" were released as a double-A-sided single and that they were excluded from the final album.

But their place at the beginning of the *Sgt. Pepper* sessions indicates that early on, Lennon and McCartney were concerned with questions of identity and the spectacle. "Strawberry Fields," where "nothing is real," sees Lennon contemplating his place among the people, and "Penny Lane" finds McCartney searching out his fellow-creatures via a "barber showing photographs," a "nurse . . . selling poppies from a tray," a "fireman" holding "an hourglass," and a banker who "never wears a mac." Each song is a nostalgic, utopian version of its author's boyhood Liverpool: an area known as Penny Lane and the garden of an orphanage named Strawberry Field.

As much as these tunes are about warm memories, those memories are of a time now lost, when Lennon and McCartney could have walked through the area without the hassle of fans. Both songs reflect an era before they found themselves directly involved in the spectacle of celebrity. By late 1966, exclusion and conditional inclusion seem to be their answer to the crowd. In "Strawberry Fields Forever" Lennon begins, "Let me take you down, cause I'm going to Strawberry Fields. / Nothing is real, and nothing to get hung about." A lover of puns, Lennon invites the listener to enter into a world where "nothing is real" and where nothing will cause "hang-ups"—or possibly a place where no one would get hanged to death for their differences. As quickly as he invites his listener to come along, however, he sings that "no one" is in his "tree" and that "you can't, you know, tune in, but it's all right."

Lennon's feelings of superiority, clashed violently with his urge to champion the working class and to acknowledge his own working-class roots. Until the end, Lennon bemoaned the furor of Beatlemania, and in his last *Rolling Stone* interview, he showed that he still felt ambivalent about the crowd, even about the elite crowd involved in the Cultural Revolution:

> For the few of us who did question what was going on . . . I have found out personally—not for the whole world!—that I am responsible for it, as well as them. I am part of them. There's no separation; we're all one, so in that

respect, I look at it all and think, "Ah, well, I have to deal with me again in that way. What is real? What is the illusion I'm living or not living?" And I have to deal with it every day. (qtd. in Cott and Doudna 191)

Meanwhile, back in late 1966, he sang of the place of the unreal as a space separate from the world of spectacle. And though MacDonald classifies it as "another of Lennon's hallucinogenic ventures into the mental interior" and a continuation of Lennon's fascination with Leary (173–74), its language is simple. Its complexities grow out of the gaps in Lennon's view of the spectacle and the crowd. In the end, Lennon invites the crowd to investigate something they cannot understand, to appreciate his brilliance, but to enjoy the journey vicariously through him—even though cognition will fail them. In the end, the spectacle is Lennon's own genius.

Although the song excludes the crowd, we know from the *Anthology* recordings that it started as a folksy ballad in what Lennon would have considered the more direct style of Dylan. The final recording comprised two versions of the song in different keys and recorded a week apart. The final version of the song is a hybrid, melded together via the studio ingenuity of George Martin and engineer Geoff Emerick. Ironically, the song's text was meant to be a "direct" address to the audience and clashed with Lennon's ideals. As Walter Everett (1999) says, "it must be remembered that Lennon was genuine in his lifelong adulation for the most simplistic and visceral rock and roll" (10); at this point, Lennon was just learning the potential of avant-garde techniques for political protest. Even though he admitted shortly after the Beatles' demise that *Sgt. Pepper* was "a peak," he also revealed his dissatisfaction with "Strawberry Fields," saying, "I don't like production so much" (*Lennon Remembers* 138). "Locked" into what Jameson calls "the category of the individual subject" (*Political Unconscious* 68), Lennon attempted to reproduce the "sincerity" of his American influences, but this folksy approach conflicted with the song's experimentation—and with the crowd to whom he "directly" sang. Both "Strawberry Fields Forever" and "Penny Lane" see the Beatles furthering their engagement with orchestral music—a trend that would become cliché by the end of 1967 and one that would create tension during the recording of *Sgt. Pepper*.[5]

PERFORMING THE DISTANCE, DISTANCING THE PERFORMANCE

"Sgt. Pepper," the souped-up reprise, "Getting Better," "When I'm Sixty-Four," "Lucy in the Sky with Diamonds," and "With a Little Help from My Friends" set a sunny, seemingly unified tone for the rest of the album. Yet the concept for the song "Sgt. Pepper," the eventual album title, and the packaging of the album made it all seem more cohesive than is obviously true. The packaging of *Sgt. Pepper*, its gatefold sleeve, cardboard cutouts, and printed lyrics were firsts in the industry, and they were a concerted effort to sell the product to the masses. The cover's printed lyrics indicated the Beatles' self-confidence as artists, and it indicated a desire to preach to the masses—to praise and condemn them for their parts in the spectacle.

Guy Debord's 1967 theorization of "the spectacle" might help us to understand the Beatles' relation to celebrity and the crowd. Debord explains, "all the life of societies in which modern conditions of production reign announces itself as an immense accumulation of spectacles. All that is directly experienced is distanced in a representation" (3).[6] And whereas the spectacle projects an appearance of unity, it is the "alpha and omega" of "separation" (13), "the heart of ir-realism in the real society" (5), the "contrary of dialogue" (9), and the "omnipresent choice—already made—in the production, and its corollary consumption" (5). Debord says that the spectacle is "not an ensemble of images, but a social rapport, mediated by images" (4). He portrays a self-interested media age, which is, as Jameson tells us, organized by the "faceless" masters in a new age of burgeoning multinational corporations in which the "restraints" of hegemonic power structures "are reproduced by the culture industry" (*Postmodernism* 17). Debord, however, points out that in the struggle against such totality, one has to "speak in the language of the spectacle" to criticize it, implying that struggle from within was possible. The Beatles found themselves fighting the spectacle from within, and McCartney had an idea that would give them a way to separate themselves from spectacle and its spectacle crowds.

After coming up with the concept for the album, McCartney wrote the title song as a quasi-direct statement to the crowd and as an indirect reproach of England's and the United States' involvement in Asia. Whereas he had previously sung from the third-person point of view, his use of identity becomes more complex by 1966. *Sgt. Pepper* was an attempt to appease his and Lennon's rock sensibilities, but it was also an effort to reconcile social conflicts and unite Beatles and fans in the spectacle while practically distancing them. In a 1984 interview with *Playboy*, McCartney says that *Sgt. Pepper* "was an idea I had, I think, when I was flying from L.A. to somewhere. I thought it would be nice to lose our identities, to submerge ourselves in the persona of a fake group. We would make up all the culture around it and collect all our heroes in one place" (qtd. in Dowlding 159).

Lennon helped to explain McCartney's rationale for creating the band's alter egos.[7] He says that McCartney was looking for a name such as those en vogue on the California scene:

> Fred and His Incredible Shrinking Grateful Airplanes. . . . He was trying to put some distance between the Beatles and the public—and so there was this identity of Sgt. Pepper. Intellectually, that's the same thing he did by writing "she loves you" instead of "I love you." (*Anthology* 241)

As Allan Moore reminds us in his book-length analysis of *Sgt. Pepper*, "the spectacle of celebrity was growing in London, and popular culture had become central, symbolized by the arrival of 'celebrities' [who] were primarily famous simply for being famous" (*Beatles* 11). The Beatles were always suspicious of mass adulation, although they also realized such adulation had to be sustained. Lennon commented shortly after the group stopped touring in 1966, "I reckon we could send out four waxwork dummies of ourselves and that would satisfy the crowds. Beatles concerts are nothing to do with music any more. They're just bloody tribal rites" (*Anthology* 329).

They felt that their performances were suffering and that the Beatles roles Brian Epstein had assigned them had become too restrictive, publicly and privately. John and George had begun to speak out about their opposition to the Vietnam War, but their reluctance to hurt sales in the United States must certainly have created tensions in their public and private thoughts. In any case, it helped to create the conditions by which McCartney envisioned Sgt. Pepper and his band as a means of bridging the gaps—but also of creating others. The cover featured those wax effigies of them—to the side, in mourning clothes—a representation of the distance the band was putting between themselves and the spectacular image of Mop-Top Beatles. As McCartney explains:

> We were fed up with being the Beatles. We really hated that fucking four little Mop-Top boys approach. We were not boys, we were men. It was all gone, all that boy shit, all that screaming, we didn't want any more, plus, we'd now got turned on to pot and thought of ourselves as artists rather than just performers. . . . Then suddenly on the plane I got this idea. I thought, Let's not be ourselves. Let's develop alter egos so we're not having to project an image which we know. (qtd. in Miles 303)

The Beatles usually toyed with identity, playing under various incarnations as the Quarry Men, Johnny and the Moondogs, the Silver Beetles, the Silver Beatles, and the Nurk Twins. McCartney, under the name "Bernard Webb," had penned the number-one record "Woman" for Peter and Gordon. And Richard Starkey always worked under his professional alias "Ringo Starr."

"Sgt. Pepper's Lonely Hearts Club Band" opens with a string ensemble that never disappears. Its classical replacement, a brass band, plays its music to an audience laughing inexplicably over the band's foregrounded solo. It implies the loss and rebirth of a time past—"20 years ago," before the band began "going in and out of style"—and makes an ingenuous invitation: "We'd like to take you home with us. We'd love to take you home." The song's ambivalence toward the crowd is also seen in its mock apology, "I don't really want to stop the show." An overture sets the stage for a brass band—which seems (but is not necessarily) comprised of Sgt. Pepper's players, whose members perform an antiquated march over distorted and tightly compressed power chords. Although the song represents an ingenious pairing of high and low culture, the establishment and burgeoning youth culture, it is also a provocation to the unhip. Rather than reinstating the status quo, it insists on pulling it into its world of youth culture rock. The song remains rock but the horns do not remain classical. The song's backing vocals are appropriations of Motown and Beach Boys harmonies, and they are punctuated by the bluesy sevenths that Lennon and McCartney associated with rock 'n' roll. In "Sgt. Pepper" the Beatles distance themselves from the spectacle, conditionally inhabiting Sgt. Pepper and his band, withdrawing to the distance as creators and artists, omniscient and firmly rooted in rock.

Obviously, inherent contradictions are found in such a method. Some saw *Sgt. Pepper* and its cover as a nod to the establishment. Iconoclast Frank Zappa made that point abundantly clear via the parodic *Sgt. Pepper* cover on his 1968 release, with the album's title, *We're Only in It for the Money*, emblazoned across Sgt. Pepper's bass drum, surrounded by Zappa, his Mothers of Invention, and the images of Jimi Hendrix, Castro, and Lee Harvey Oswald at the moment in which Jack Ruby shot him.[8] This sort of criticism and a belief in rock's directness prompted Lennon to dismiss some of his own songs on *Sgt. Pepper* as "poetic" (*Lennon Remembers* 40). As for the *Sgt. Pepper* concept, Lennon says, "You see, Paul said come and see the show, I didn't. I said, 'I read the news today oh boy'" (40).

Nevertheless, McCartney viewed the title song and its eventual (if loose) concept as a mockery of contemporary England's antiquated Edwardian values and Western involvement in the Vietnam War. George Martin insists that the military aspect of *Sgt. Pepper* "was partly a send-up of the U.S. in Vietnam." (qtd. in Moore, *Beatles* 21). Sheila Whiteley *(The Space between the Notes)* points out that "by wearing the uniform of the past within the context of a psychedelically charged album, *Sgt. Pepper* undercuts traditional values and the military man becomes yet another showman, a figure of fun" (41). Zappa's reading shows that some listeners took the military wear as an endorsement of England's imperial past and present. As album designer Peter Blake says in the CD's liner notes, Jesus, Gandhi, and Hitler almost made it into the images of heroes and celebrities dotting the album's cover, but were nixed as being too controversial. The final group of people featured on the cover (everyone from Muhammad Ali to Lenny Bruce) speaks not of inclusivity, but of select heroes. The average citizenry of "Penny Lane" is nowhere in evidence here. The Beatles had come to see themselves as having something to say; they and their music take center stage, surrounded by great thinkers and great celebrities.

"With a Little Help from My Friends" furthers the appearance of unity, and it may be the song most responsible for the feeling that *Sgt. Pepper* is about unity. Cowritten by Lennon and McCartney, this composition is the first song on the album to avowedly endorse marijuana, although it was recorded a considerable time after "A Day in the Life" and its mantra, "I'd love to turn you on." And although critics may belittle such behavior, cannabis's contemplative properties seem to have encouraged the Beatles in their questioning of the spectacle and its position to the repressive strictures of the establishment. Vis á vis the crowd, "With a Little Help" expresses the singer's (perhaps for real in Ringo's case) fear of losing the audience by singing off-key. But again, the Beatles put distance between the singer and the spectacle. Within the performance on the record, it is understood that conditions of studio recording will prevent the record from coming out with Ringo singing terribly off-key. The question, "Would you stand up and walk out on me?" is, then, a rhetorical statement based on the broader question of identity. As with the title song, the crowd remains on the outside, let in only as a spectacle attendee. The introductory segue is reminiscent of the introduction to the earlier hit "Eight Days a Week" and seems to appeal to Beatlemaniacs. Added later, it is a brave contrast to their new sound, but it represents a firm good-bye to the Beatles' past, and, presumably, to its audience.

In "Getting Better," Lennon's lines of regret over his past misogyny contrast with McCartney's sunny optimism, which truly seems to be in order as the speaker compares past and present ways of thinking and behaving. He contrasts his brilliance and psychedelic openness against the brutal stupidity of the teachers "who weren't cool" and who tried to fill them up with "rules." Still, the song rings a plaintive note of alienation in personal relationships, implying that directness and free love are the answers. But not everyone is welcome in this world. McCartney brings the song to a peak, singing in his best rock 'n' roll voice about the "people standing there who disagree and never win and wonder why they don't get in my door."

"She's Leaving Home" and "When I'm Sixty-Four" are often cited as songs that bridge different generations of Beatle listeners. MacDonald says, "The Beatles offered an inclusive vision, which, among other things, worked to defuse the tensions of the generation gap" (185). The truth of this may be that audiences have mainly perceived it as a gap-shoring album, but the songs show obvious splits with establishment culture and the crowd. "She's Leaving Home" is a story told partly by an "objective" third-person narrator and partly by first-person narrators (the girl's parents). The third-person narrator speaks directly of what has happened, whereas the parents' selfish responses expose their morality. The narrator judges their punishment to be a significant one: their daughter is running away with someone from the lower class and will obviously gain sexual experience. McCartney clearly saw the antiquated ballad as a means to promote the youth rebellion, but this kind of ditty created tensions among the band members, who suspected such work as "soft."

"When I'm Sixty-Four" was written as a sincere tribute to McCartney's aging father James, and its rooty-toot style makes it seem a tribute to the older generation. But many critics have pointed out that the song pokes fun at the music and ideals of the time. The song's first-person narrator is a young man, presumably in the 1920s, proposing to an unnamed woman, asking her for a lifetime guarantee. His attempts to get her to "fill in" a "form" and "indicate precisely" what she "mean[s] to say" point to his dumb, uncarnal innocence. This innocence here is not looked at with nostalgic warmth; instead, it stands as one with staid Britannica and its unnatural ideology. McCartney establishes a dichotomy resonant with Romanticism. The staid mores of the establishment generation are as unnatural as the spectacle. Indirect speech is spectacle speech, whereas rock speech and youth culture operate under the laws of nature. As with "She's Leaving Home," "When I'm Sixty-Four" allows the narrative to emerge from an establishment point of view. And like its counterpart, it ultimately speaks of a generational standoff. As MacDonald reminds us, "the 'generation gap' which opened in the Fifties turns out not to be a quarrel between a particular set of parents and children but an historical chasm between one way of life and another" (25). However inclusive the album seemed in effect, songs such as "She's Leaving Home" and "When I'm Sixty Four" are not meant as dialogue with the album's other fare. The speaker in "When I'm Sixty-Four" evinces a deep attachment, a nostalgia even, for an increasingly distant and romanticized past, whereas the narrator in "Lovely Rita" enjoys himself with "a sister or two" while Rita busies herself elsewhere.[9] The contrast could not be more striking.

STUCK INSIDE THE CROWD

Near the end of the sessions for the album, Harrison composed and recorded "Within You Without You" without the other Beatles and with the accompaniment of an Indian quartet playing traditional Indian instruments. His quickly dispatched "Only a Northern Song," a dark and comic in-joke about the band's publishing contract, was rejected for the album. Leaving the theme of economics, Harrison chose to sing of his new philosophy in the form of a sermon. Everett (1999) says that around the time of *Sgt. Pepper*, "Harrison immersed himself in all things Indian, turning from Leary to Yogananda to the *Bhagavadgita*" (98)—referring to the swami whose teachings Harrison read alongside the Vedas. In an even fuller integration of Indian music than in *Revolver*'s "Love You To," "Within You Without You" presents its audience with a religion meant to supplant Christianity. It shows Harrison taking control of the Beatles' transcendental discourse. In later years, Harrison expressed doubt over whether Lennon, composer of "Tomorrow Never Knows," had understood his own lyrics (*Anthology* 210). He continues, setting the record straight about what Lennon's song meant:

> The whole point is that *we* are the song. The self is coming from a state of
> pure awareness, from the state of being. All the rest that comes about in the

outward manifestation of the physical world . . . is just clutter. The true
nature of each soul is pure consciousness. So the song is really about transcending and about the quality of the transcendent. (210)

In an interview with *Melody Maker* around the time of *Sgt. Pepper*, Harrison
defended the Beatles against charges that they were skirting reality. "Reality is
a concept," he says, and:

Everybody has their own reality (if they are lucky). Most people's reality is
an illusion, a great big illusion. . . . I am not George. . . . The physical body
will pass but this bit in the middle, that's the only reality. All the rest is the
illusion, so to say that somebody thinks that we, the ex-Beatles, are removed
from reality is their personal concept. (44)

For all its mysticism and manufactured mystery, "Within You Without You"
is a clear and direct song that bemoans "the space between us all / And the
people—who hide themselves behind a wall of illusion." The song contains
one of the most humane lines on the album with Harrison singing, "with our
love—we could save the world—if they only knew." He places himself among
the crowd, "within" whom and "without" whom "life flows on," but again,
"they" refers to the unenlightened crowds of Beatlemania and of the establishment. Harrison's space, like McCartney's in "Fixing a Hole," is reserved for
the initiated and enlightened.

Part of Harrison's message is the idea that life is transitory and that death
is just another condition, nothing to get hung up about. Its message, that
death is simply another concept such as reality, is itself a retreat from reality,
but it is also an indirect response to those in power orchestrating the Vietnam
War. The inexplicable laughter at song's end echoes the laughter in the title
track. Here, however, classical (Eastern) culture is not being mocked. If anything, the laughter is directed at the establishment culture that the song con-
demns. Still, this instance and the laughter in "Sgt. Pepper" remain inexplicable, opening questions for the listener, who is only conditionally admitted to
this summer spectacle of love.

OPENING THE MIND, CLOSING THE DOOR

Because "Strawberry Fields Forever" was not released on *Sgt. Pepper*, Lennon's
contribution to the album proper may seem less significant than McCartney's.
Timewise this may be true, but Lennon's songs, even "A Day in the Life,"
helped to add a more textured, bluesier edge to the album's overall impression.
Whereas "Lucy in the Sky with Diamonds" may begin as a near waltz, its title
refrain reestablishes the distorted guitars heard in "Sgt. Pepper." Lennon's

songs show an engagement with the spectacle equally as powerful as McCartney's, and they reveal a greater concern with issues of class and the crowd.

Lennon and McCartney had similar childhoods: both lost their mothers during their teen years, and each came from working-class homes with middle-class aspirations. As McCartney recounts, his mother and father "aspired to a better life. That idea that we had to get out of here, we had to do better than this. This was okay for everyone else in the street but we could do better than this" (Miles 6). Lennon was always more openly class-conscious than McCartney and always betrayed his personal conflicts when discussing class issues. Explaining his politics in the last *Playboy* interview, Lennon says:

> In England, there are only two things to be, basically: You are either for the labor movement or for the capitalist movement. Either you become a right-wing Archie Bunker if you are in the class I am in, or you become an instinctive socialist, which I was. That meant I think people should get their false teeth and their health looked after, all the rest of it. But apart from that, I worked for money and I wanted to be rich. So what the hell—if that's a paradox, then I'm a socialist. But I am not anything. What I used to be is guilty about money. That's why I lost it, either by giving it away or by allowing myself to be screwed by so-called managers. (*All We Are Saying* 94)

Lennon's views were obviously not so clearly defined in 1966 and 1967, but even in 1980, he still felt the need to justify his separation from the masses.

Whereas McCartney's response to the Beatles' class conflicts found their nonresolve in identity play, Lennon mistrusted such trickery. Such mistrust emanated from his wariness of avant-garde art and techniques (even though they had been used extensively on his *Revolver* work), from his rock 'n' roll consciousness, and from the conflicts between working-class rock culture and high-culture, educated-class aspects of avant-garde work. According to all accounts, until McCartney's consistent urging and later Yoko Ono's influence, Lennon had little interest in the avant-garde and its forms of expression. In the *Playboy* interview he says that "A Day in the Life," "Lucy in the Sky with Diamonds," and "Strawberry Fields Forever" were written under pressure after McCartney surprised him with the November recording date. He also maintains that part of his resentment toward McCartney stems from the experiments of *Sgt. Pepper*. With such experiments, he claims, McCartney "subconsciously" attempted to "destroy" his rock 'n' roll (*All We Are Saying* 192).

"Lucy in the Sky with Diamonds" is perhaps the album's most (in)famous song, mostly because of its accidental acronym "LSD." Its title taken from Julian Lennon's drawing of a kindergarten playmate, "Lucy" again finds Lennon returning to the theme of the crowd. Whiteley *(The Space between the Notes)* claims that in the song, "The singer takes on the role of experienced user and in the verse leads the novice . . . into a changed reality" (43). Although I do not doubt Whiteley's claim about LSD's influence on the progression of images in the song, the political subtext is more complex. MacDonald has documented Timothy Leary's theories and their influence on Lennon and the hallucinogenic philosophy in Lennon's work. Even Lennon dismissed his narcotic thinking at the time. In his retrospective post-Beatles interviews with Jann Wenner, Lennon says:

> I got a message on acid that you should destroy your ego, and I did. I was read-ing that stupid book of Leary's and all that shit. We were going through a whole game that everyone went through. And I destroyed meself. . . . I didn't believe I could do *anything*. (*Lennon Remembers* 53–54)

All four Beatles were experienced pot smokers by *Sgt. Pepper* and felt a certain freedom to refer to it explicitly on the album and in public: "I get high with a little help from my friends," "Went upstairs and took a smoke," and "I'd love to turn you on." But "Lucy in the Sky with Diamonds" is also a continuation of the spectacle contained in *Sgt. Pepper*. Its images of "newspaper taxis" (McCartney's line, according to Lennon) and a "girl with kaleidoscope eyes" tell a story of alienation and loss. Lennon says the images of the song:

> were from *Alice in Wonderland*. It was Alice in the boat. She is buying an egg and it turns into Humpty Dumpty. The woman serving in the shop turns into a sheep and the next minute they are rowing in a rowing boat some-where and I was visualizing that. There was also the image of the female who would someday come save me—a "girl with kaleidoscope eyes" who would come out of the sky. (*All We Are Saying* 181)

However the public read the song, Lennon was trying to create a space apart from reality, outside the very spectacle he was creating. In the first verse, the song asks the listener to "picture yourself in a boat on a river, / with tangerine trees and marmalade skies." The language is childlike, but unlike "Strawberry Fields," it lets the audience see what the singer is seeing. Instead of offering a vision of the past, it plants the listener in a fantasia. Here, "rocking horse peo-ple eat marshmallow pies"; "Newspaper taxis" actually "wait"; and "Everyone smiles as you drift by the river." The song ends with a surprise for the jour-neying imaginer: "Suddenly someone is there at the turnstile, / the girl with kaleidoscope eyes." This song, mostly of Lennon's doing, allows the crowd to intrude, but only for a visionary moment. Here, the ability to imagine sets him apart from the crowd. The sudden arrival of a savior with kaleidoscope eyes is a personal cry for help, lost in the images of the spectacle.[10] But the song is ultimately fantasy. And like "Strawberry Fields," it allows the listener no closer behind the mask of the *Sgt. Pepper* spectacle.

Similarly, "Being for the Benefit of Mr. Kite," a song that Lennon took almost verbatim from an old circus poster, presents another spectacle within the spectacle. Placed on the album after "She's Leaving Home," the song brilliantly melds the sounds of calliopes and organs with the beat-heavy rock combo. "Being for the Benefit of Mr. Kite" is an antiquated advertisement promising danger in the "hogshead of real fire" that awaits the "men and horses." Here, Lennon highlights the spectacle, but the listener is not the audience of the circus; the listener remains on the outside of the crowd that is beckoned to see "Mr. K" as he prepares to "challenge the world." The circus barker's pitch is made to an audience that never was, invited to a show that never will be, and he sells sensationalism (as any good barker would). While he sells the show, he addresses the crowd aggressively, telling them "Don't be late!" and warning them, "Mr. K performs his tricks without a sound." Even when he claims, "Messrs. K and H. assure the public / their production will be second to none," he keeps the crowd at a distance by addressing them ("the public") through the indirect voices of "Messrs. K and H." Lennon's circus is a maelstrom of distance between the crowd and the performer. The crowd that thrives on spectacle, but pays its money (the "benefit of Mr. Kite"), must be kept in its place. The barker, like Lennon, was intent on keeping the crowd at bay.

In "Good Morning Good Morning," Lennon borrows again, here from a Kellogg's cereal ad slogan, a sound bite of the growing media culture. The ad's sunny message, however, is undercut by the doctor's diagnosis, "Nothing to do to save his life, call his wife in." But this situation sits beside other "everyday" morning activities. In this particular world, though, the second-person "you" (whom we assume is not the doctor) heads out to "roam," but:

> Everybody knows there's nothing doing
> Everything is closed it's like a ruin
> Everyone you see is half asleep.
> And you're on your own you're in the street

The world of "Good Morning Good Morning" is a place where you are eventually "on your own" because of the dimwitted crowd who is "half asleep." The lyrics end with "you" being saved by the possibility of a romantic liaison, but this resolution seems half-hearted after the diagnosis of death in the opening lines. At the song's conclusion, taking the Beach Boys' *Pet Sounds'* and its use of animal noises one step further, Lennon sent a subtle message to the "half-asleep." Lewisohn reports that "John had decided that he would like to end his song with animal sound effects, and asked that they be compiled in such a way that each successive animal was capable of frightening or devouring its predecessor" (*Complete* 250). Subtle though that message might be, this song's concluding food-chain romp is directed at the "half-asleep" and is analogous to the implied "late-comers" of Mr. Kite's circus.

Interestingly, in his two books of witticisms, Lennon had pitted such a crowd against the individual, most notably in the story entitled "The Wumberlog" in the book *A Spaniard in the Works*, which tells the story of a young boy in search of the "Wumberlog"—people "Wot lived when they were dead" (126). A "carrot" (shades of *Alice*) leads him to the Wumberlogs, who are digging industriously at the boy's grave. As they throw the dirt over him, they mock him by "shouting out / 'Here's mud into your eye'" (133). The cliché of the crowd's "toast" is seen as a cruel gesture. As comic as it is, it shows Lennon's conflicting feelings about the crowd.

Although he dismissed much of his work on *Sgt. Pepper*, he was proud of "A Day in the Life," even up to the end. I mean to imply neither that Lennon was wholly reluctant to experiment with his songs, no that McCartney was the reigning genius of *Sgt. Pepper*. Lennon must have been somewhat open to the avant-garde techniques McCartney espoused or "A Day in the Life" would not have happened. Lennon and McCartney wrote the two main sections as separate songs, and only after they started to integrate them did they come up with the idea for the track's orchestral transitions. Recorded immediately after the orchestral experiments of "Strawberry Fields" and "Penny Lane," "A Day in the Life" revisits the Beatles' engagement with classical instrumentation, and thus, establishment culture. Turning the recording session into a party, they and friends Mick Jagger and Marianne Faithfull handed out joints, flowers, and silly costumes to the orchestra.[11] On the orchestral score, the band had written, "From here, you're on your own," referring to their loose instructions for the orchestra (*Anthology* 247). Alternating conducting chores with George Martin, Paul wore a kitchen apron while leading the orchestra. Although the Beatles were most certainly not mocking the musicians in attendance, they were satirizing the orchestra's position as establishment culture. The Beatles always saw themselves in competition, and they strove with songs such as "A Day in the Life" to earn the recognition from the very establishment that they themselves rejected. For all the awards and recognition the Beatles earned, Lennon and Harrison felt justifying their own legitimacy as musicians in opposition to trained players necessary; McCartney and Starr continue to admit their lack of technical ability, but boast of their home-grown talents, staple claims of *legitimate* rock musicians. A final, somber, and enduring piano chord (recorded on multiple pianos by Martin, Lennon, McCartney, and Starr) concludes "A Day in the Life." Almost two weeks after the song was finished, "A Day in the Life" received its final piano chords. But just as the tuning (thus, *out-of-tune*) orchestra is excluded from "Sgt. Pepper," the orchestra is excluded here from those final piano chords. The Beatles have taken control of a classical instrument, and the orchestra is forgotten. The song is followed by the repetitive "run out" sample, from which a voice sings of those who "never do see any other way" or who are "never to see any other way." On the original album, the "run out" has a repeating groove, and the message repeats eternally to the "half-asleep." From beginning to end, the Beatles have classified and ordered the crowd.

Part of what was expected of the crowd was their understanding of the Beatles' experimentation with drugs. When working on the transitions in "A Day in the Life," Lennon and McCartney chose to openly state, "I'd love to turn you on." Lennon and Harrison were eventually arrested for small amounts of narcotics—albeit small amounts that, in the late 1960s, carried the threat of jail time. McCartney's ten days in a jail in Japan testify to the fact that much of the world did not (and continue not to) want to be turned on. In the 1960s, marijuana use was clearly taboo in most minds of establishment England. McCartney says that coming up with and singing "I'd love to turn you on" was liberating, similar to writing about "sexual" matters (Miles 325). But as its title implies, "A Day in the Life" is about the diurnal and mundane, at least on the surface. Even death is seen as mundane because the focus is on the crowd, not on the death. Lennon's sections of the song come from the point of view of Lennon himself reading the newspaper. In the *Playboy* interview, Lennon explains:

> Just as it sounds: I was reading the paper one day and I noticed two stories. One was the Guinness heir [Tara Browne, a Beatle acquaintance] who killed himself in a car. That was the main headline story. He died in London in a car crash. On the next page was a story about 4,000 holes in Blackburn, Lancashire. In the streets, that is. They were going to fill them all. . . . I thought it was a damn good piece of work. (*All We Are Saying* 183–84)

The crowd in the song is a spectacle crowd, who "stood and stared" at the young upper-class man. They gaze at his death not out of pity, but out of a fascination with sensationalism. The crowd views death as a spectacle, and Lennon presents the crowd as the spectacle itself. Whereas they were absent in "Mr. Kite" and nestled out of view in "Good Morning Good Morning," here they are present, yet mesmerized, by the spectacle. Browne is no longer a person, but is instead a prop in the spectacle, his death tacitly equated with such other events as the discovery of how many potholes "it takes to fill the Albert Hall." The song's anthemic "I'd love to turn you on" may refer to drugs, but it is also Lennon's message to the half-asleep masses, inviting them to enlightenment. As MacDonald astutely remarks, "A Day in the Life" is a "song not of disillusionment with life itself but of disenchantment with the limits of mundane perception. [It] depicts the 'real world' as an unenlightened construct that reduces, depresses, and ultimately destroys" (181). In many ways, this is precisely why *Sgt. Pepper's Lonely Hearts Club Band* remains a cultural product continually "reread" over and over again in our popular culture, and in our private homes, with a story to tell of class-consciousness and class conflict, as well as of love, peace, unity, and rebellion.

NOTES

1. Shatner's inadvertently comic version of "Lucy in the Sky with Diamonds" has become a cult favorite.

2. See the *Beatles Anthology* (219–21) for additional discussion regarding the traumas that beset the band during their 1966 world tour.

3. See Ian MacDonald on "Tomorrow Never Knows" (148–53), where he discusses Leary's *The Psychedelic Experience* and its influence on Lennon's thinking.

4. For additional discussion of the producer's experiences during the *Sgt. Pepper* sessions, see Martin's *With a Little Help from My Friends*.

5. The Moody Blues' "Nights in White Satin," from *Days of Future Passed*, released in November 1967, depicts a wandering soul who "loves" the crowd outside the knight's quest. Justin Hayward's line, "Letters I've written, never meaning to send," embarrassingly emulates the conundrumic language of Lennon's *Pepper*-y lyrics.

6. All of the Debord quotations are my translations of his original French text.

7. McCartney would create a similar set of characters (the "Jailer Man" and "Sailor Sam") for Wings' 1973 album, *Band on the Run*.

8. The cover was only officially released in 1995, when Ryko reissued Zappa's album.

9. In *Many Years from Now*, McCartney tells Barry Miles that his father, Jim McCartney, was happy for his son because technology had perfected contraception and hence allowed the younger generation to enjoy sex in a more liberated fashion. McCartney describes the sexual freedom of the 1960s as equivalent to Moses's "parting" of the sea with the waters coming back down with the rise of fatal STDs in the 1980s (142–43).

10. In his final *Playboy* interview, Lennon claims that the "girl" in his song was his premonition of meeting Yoko Ono.

11. This ensemble's appearance could have explained the audience's laughter in *Sgt. Pepper* had they been, indeed, the brass band of the title song.

CHAPTER 8

We All Want to Change the World

Postmodern Politics and the Beatles' *White Album*

JEFFREY ROESSNER

S INCE ITS RELEASE IN 1968, the Beatles' self-titled album, which quickly became known as the *White Album*, has generated a variety of responses from musicologists, rock journalists, historians, and critics from the New Left. Based on the music, lyrics, or even the album's place in John Lennon's development as an avant-garde artist, these reviews range from favorable to severely critical. In the reviews that focus on the music, such as Wilfred Mellers's *The Twilight of the Gods*, little attention is paid to the album's historical context, for example, how it relates to the counterculture of the late 1960s. Likewise, critics who concentrate on the political relevance of the lyrics, especially in the two versions of "Revolution," ignore or dismiss the significance of the catalogue of musical styles on the record. The assumption here is that only songs with heavy lyrical "messages" address or constitute a legitimate response to specific historical and political circumstances. In other words, it is either pop—even if it is highbrow pop—or politics. My contention is that the *White Album*, through its disparate musical styles and self-reflexivity, contests this arbitrary distinction. The *White Album* outlines a way of being political, a postmodern politics, which was and still is largely judged as being pure escapism.

The criticism of the album from the New Left generally centered on the charge that the eclectic style and self-consciousness of the record were means of eluding the pressing political concerns of the time. This argument resembles the Marxist position of Fredric Jameson in "Postmodernism and Consumer Society," who criticizes the use of what he calls "pastiche" in postmodern culture as a means of evading "real" history. Such an argument, however, assumes that there is one way of being political and fails to consider the context, or the specific historical circumstances, that gives any use of parody its particular significance. Seen in this context, the *White Album* shows how parody and eclecticism can serve as specific political commentary. By 1968, the corporate/capitalist attempts to manipulate rock artists and fans were reaching a peak, and early rock 'n' roll had lost much of its initially subversive power. Concurrently, the Beatles found themselves lauded in highbrow art circles because of their "masterpiece," *Sgt. Pepper's Lonely Hearts Club Band*. At this point in their career, then, the Beatles' turn to parody serves not as an escape from but as a specific response to key cultural tensions: the self-reflexivity and ironic appropriation of various styles on the *White Album* allowed the Beatles to contest the commodification of rock music even as they helped redefine the relationship between artistic style and political relevance.

WHEN YOU TALK ABOUT DESTRUCTION

Released in November 1968, the *White Album* marked a significant departure from the psychedelic sounds the Beatles had cultivated on *Sgt. Pepper*, which had come out well over a year earlier. Although the Beatles' self-titled double album includes a variety of instruments and maintains a heady sense of experimentation, the record does not exude the aura of disciplined perfection so apparent on *Sgt. Pepper*. Perhaps the most original aspect of the *White Album*, however, concerns the diverse musical styles of its thirty songs. The album includes straightforward rock songs ("Birthday"); campy blues ("Yer Blues"); country-and-western numbers ("Rocky Raccoon" and "Don't Pass Me By"); a 1920s music hall song ("Honey Pie"); a lush, orchestral ballad ("Good Night"); and an experimental sound collage ("Revolution 9"). Given this extreme diversity in style, critics generally complain that the album lacks unity, and that the Beatles at this point were not functioning as a group any longer, but as sidemen playing on each other's songs. In 1968, however, the harshest criticism of the eclectic style of the songs came from the New Left.

Largely abandoning the labor struggles and the communist sympathies of earlier radicals, the college students who comprised the bulk of the New Left took their inspiration from the civil rights movement and dedicated themselves to protesting the United States' racial, social, and economic inequities (Breines 25). The groundwork for this movement was laid in the early 1960s, largely through the work of the Students for a Democratic Society (SDS) founded in 1960. Increasingly skeptical that change could occur through traditional political parties, the New Left sounded its call for radical change throughout the often violent political and social circumstances of 1968. The most promising sign of initial success occurred during the student uprising in Paris on May 6, a revolt symbolizing the hope that bureaucracy could be successfully resisted by mass protest. Meanwhile, the violent suppression of demonstrations at the Democratic National Convention in Chicago foreshadowed what would become a fierce battle between police and protestors of the Vietnam War. The assassination of Martin Luther King Jr. and Senator Robert F. Kennedy underscored the high stakes of this conflict. In light of the rash of violence in 1968, critics from the New Left vigorously attacked the *White Album* for its allegedly frivolous style and its disregard of serious political issues.

The Beatles' response to these protests and murders seemed evasive and outworn—a continuation of the "All You Need Is Love," nonviolent ethic of flower power. The most pointed attack centered on Lennon's "Revolution," the single version of which was released a little over three months after the Paris uprising. Lennon has remarked that he conceived of the song as his attempt to break the Beatles' silence on political issues; he was angry that in their touring years they had been forced to remain silent on controversial topics such as the Vietnam War (Sheff 196). But when Lennon finally spoke out in "Revolution," he did not give an answer that many wanted to hear. In "Revolution 1," the slower version of the song that appears on the *White Album*, Lennon did not take a stance on violent confrontation, but he offered a statement of his own confusion. He sings, "When you talk about destruction, / Don't you know that you can count me out . . . in." In his indecision, he gives equal weight to both the "out" and "in." By the time the Beatles recorded the faster, raunchier version of "Revolution," however, Lennon had made a commitment: seeing the violence to which he was adamantly opposed, he made clear that if destruction were involved, he wanted to be counted "out." Hoping for a more radical statement, the political left felt betrayed by Lennon's refusal either to condone the violence or to offer a solution.

Along with their refusal to offer explicit political directives on the *White Album*, the Beatles were criticized for presenting an eclectic mix of songs as a means of evading important political issues. The major fault most critics found with the album was that "its playfulness and gentle satire had become at best irrelevant and at worst reactionary" (Wiener 65). Writing for the *London Daily Times*, Jon Landau argued, "the Beatles have used parody on this album precisely because they were afraid of confronting reality. It becomes a mask behind which they can hide from the urgencies of the moment" (qtd. in Wiener 65). Equating parody on the *White Album* with escapism, Landau chastises the Beatles for failing to address the political issues he thinks are important and for doing so in a way—using parody—that Landau sees as politically invalid or even evasive. In his dismissal of parody, Landau ultimately aligns himself with the Marxist criticism of postmodern culture Jameson offered.

Perhaps the most important—and by now infamous—statement on parody in postmodern culture occurs in Jameson's "Postmodernism and the Consumer Society." In his essay, Jameson makes a distinction between parody and what he terms *pastiche*. Although both parody and pastiche involve "the imitation of a peculiar or unique style, the wearing of a stylistic mask," Jameson argues that pastiche is "a neutral practice of such mimicry, without parody's ulterior motive . . . without that still latent feeling that there exists something *normal* compared to which that which is being imitated is rather comic" (114). Pastiche is the failed postmodern attempt at parody. Jameson believes this failure results from the loss of a norm or standard of judgment, which he links to the "death of the subject" in postmodern society (114). Dazzled by pyrotechnic but ultimately shallow displays of style, the postmodern subject remains trapped by history as if in a bewildering maze. The subject thus never attains a vantage point on history from which to make crucial political judgments or to resist the forces of consumer capitalism. Just as Landau charges the Beatles with donning a mask to evade cultural and political urgencies, so Jameson sees pastiche in contemporary art as a shimmering stylistic surface without depth or a norm against which any significant judgments can be made.

In their longing for an authentic politics, both Jameson and Landau exhibit a disturbing nostalgia for a unified subject position from which to make judgments and take a political stance; they refuse to acknowledge that a particular historical context can give specific meaning to pastiche. Dismissing eclecticism in all contemporary art as escapism, neither Jameson nor Landau considers how the context of its creation or reception might give any particular use of eclecticism a political valence. As Landau calls for an explicit statement by the Beatles on urgent issues, he ignores the circumstances that make the Beatles' use of parody more than a mask. Reading the *White Album* as the Beatles' response to their position as rock artists circa 1968, then, not only clarifies the politics of the band, but also helps define the stakes of parody as a postmodern practice.

JUST LET ME HEAR SOME OF THAT ROCK 'N' ROLL MUSIC

In large measure, the Beatles' turn to parody on the *White Album* came in response to the culture of rock 'n' roll in the mid-1960s. By that point, the early wave of rock 'n' roll had lost much of its rebellious edge. Music by Elvis Presley, Chuck Berry, and Buddy Holly no longer represented radical defiance of authority, parental or otherwise. In its sexual beat and its association with juvenile delinquency, 1950's rock was aimed at a particular generation of young listeners who used it as a radical symbol of their defiance. By the time the Beatles made their first record in the early 1960s, however, the London music industry had already created Cliff Richard, a sanitized, whitewashed version of Presley, and so capitalized on the image of rock's first sex symbol, the man who a few years earlier could only be shown from the waist up on the *Ed Sullivan Show*. Chuck Berry too had been recycled for middle-class consumption by Brian Wilson through the fun-in-the-sun style of the early Beach Boys' records. As the decade wore on, rock music continued to gain acceptance through increased radio play and performers who homogenized the raucous style of earlier artists such as Berry, Little Richard, and Elvis. As rock music came of age and its commercial appeal became evident, its early association with sexual and social deviance waned; it no longer stood prima facie as a sign of defiance.

Although rock existed as a commodity from its earliest days, corporate attempts to control the music were also reaching a peak in the late 1960s. In 1967, MGM attempted to create an East Coast alternative to the San Francisco sound with their failed "Boss-Town" sound from Boston (Wiener 5). Along with such blatant attempts to manipulate musical trends came an even more disturbing attempt to manipulate fans. In 1969 Columbia Records ran a series of ads in underground newspapers that read, "The Man Can't Bust Our Music" (Wiener 3). Claiming solidarity with record buyers, Columbia aimed to capitalize on the political struggles of the counterculture. Record companies had never so explicitly tried to control the meaning of the music for its fans, and ultimately, such tactics would force both fans and artists to acknowledge rock's existence as a commodity. If the music felt as though it belonged to the listener, it was also literally for sale, produced and manufactured by companies: rock artists, especially those with political aims, would have to come to terms with their complicity in this process.

Recognizing the increasing corporate control of rock music, the Beatles responded in one way by forming their own company, Apple Records, in 1968. As Lennon remarked in a news conference at the time, Apple was a business that would deal in records, films, and electronics; he baited the industry and the media by claiming that the Beatles "wanted to set up a system whereby people who just want to make a film about anything don't have to go on their knees in somebody's office—probably yours" *(Compleat)*. Here, Lennon grasps the extent of corporate power over the artistic productions of the counterculture. Given the effort involved to establish and run their own company as an alternative, the Beatles clearly had such manipulation on their minds during the recording of the *White Album*, the first record released on their new label.

Along with wresting a measure of artistic freedom from the hands of record company executives, the Beatles at this point in their career also confronted their growing reputation as rock "artists." Consistently evolving as musicians through the 1960s, the Beatles seemed to offer an unprecedented leap in lyrical and musical sophistication with each new record. In particular, *Rubber Soul, Revolver*, and *Sgt. Pepper's Lonely Hearts Club Band* all represent significant shifts in the direction of the Beatles' music and sent seismic shock waves through the rest of the music and art world. Not until *Sgt. Pepper*, however, did they begin to be regarded more widely as serious musicians. Although the Beatles had been favorably compared with classical composers from their earliest records, this was no preparation for the critical response to *Sgt. Pepper*. Mellers identifies *Sgt. Pepper* as the record that marked the turning point "when the Beatles stopped being ritual dance music and became music to be listened to" *(Compleat)*. The idea that the Beatles had created a work of art rather than merely a pop album dominated the reception of the record in intellectual and artistic circles. And critics such as Mellers made clear that they were not descending to the level of the Beatles, but that the Beatles, with their "masterpiece," had finally become worthy of serious attention.

Such reception was mildly ironic given that *Sgt. Pepper* is self-consciously a stage show: taking their cue from McCartney's suggestion that they reinvent themselves for this record, the Beatles adopted a new identity as Sgt. Pepper's fictional band. They underscored this in the cover shot on the record, which shows the Beatles, dressed in fluorescent band uniforms, backed by a multitude of cardboard cutouts of friends and celebrities. Beside four dour, wax Mop Tops from Madame Tussaud's museum, the live, mustached Beatles are standing at their own grave. If the album thus firmly buries the "She Loves You" era, it also marked the height of their career as musicians. But we should not forget that we are being put on or we risk missing the show: the fake crowd and orchestra tuning at the beginning, the laughter following the otherwise serious "Within You Without You," and the forty-five-second chord, the dog whistle, and the chatter that conclude the record. It is highly experimental, but it is also funny. Apparently, most critics took the music too seriously for Lennon and McCartney.

During the last years of the Beatles and on into their solo careers, both Lennon and McCartney satirized those who insisted on finding hidden meaning in their work or intellectually analyzing their music. Lennon especially showed his disdain for this type of analysis of his music or words. He ultimately claimed that musicians have a choice: they can either play rock 'n' roll or "go bullshitting off into intellectualism" (Wenner 75). Given his bluntness, we should not be surprised that Lennon had held that point of view for some time. He offered a more elaborate statement of such feelings to Beatles' biographer Hunter Davies shortly after completing *Sgt. Pepper*:

> It's nice when people like it [our music], but when they start "appreciating" it, getting great deep things out of it, making a thing of it, then it's a lot of shit. It proves what we've always thought about most sorts of so-called art. It's a lot of shit. We hated all that shit they wrote and talked about Beethoven and ballet, all kidding themselves it was important. Now it's hap-

pening to us. . . . Let's stick that in there, we say, that'll start them puzzling. I'm sure all artists do, when they realize it's a con. I bet Picasso sticks things in. I bet he's been laughing his balls off for the last 80 years. (321)

Lennon here shows his distaste for the very response that *Sgt. Pepper* generated. He wanted nothing to do with the Mellers of the world who tried to aestheticize the Beatles' music or find deeper messages in the lyrics. In discussing his urge to "stick something in there" to start them "puzzling," Lennon also notes the band's penchant for giving the critics false leads—a tactic that the Beatles would exploit most fully on the *White Album*. Perhaps the most significant idea Lennon expresses, however, concerns the Beatles' contempt for high art. Increasingly determined to be a politically visible artist, he knew that could not happen with critics treating the Beatles' music as rarefied; ultimately, then, the *White Album* would have to distance Lennon's band from the pretensions associated with *Sgt. Pepper*.

Given its place in the history of rock 'n' roll in general, and in the Beatles' development in particular, the *White Album* offers a complex response to the discourse of rock in the late 1960s. The shifting meaning of musical style—especially rock's loss of subversive power through commercialization, corporate manipulation, and the Beatles' growing stature as artists—surely informed the band's approach to songwriting. Hence, rather than seeing the record as escapist (and the criticism of it as part of what sparked Lennon's attempt at more traditional political actions later on), reading the album as the statement of a singer and band already politically engaged is possible. The album does not explicitly say "yes" to revolution or "no" to the Vietnam War. But the Beatles do employ style, especially parody and reflexivity, to address significant political issues within the rock culture of their era.

THIRTEEN WAYS OF LOOKING AT "BLACKBIRD"

Starting with its very cover, the *White Album* parodies the high art aesthetic that had become associated with *Sgt. Pepper*. After the psychedelic extravagance of that album, the band chose to title their ninth album simply *The Beatles*. Assuming their identity again after having played as a fictional band, they opted for a stark white cover that stood in marked contrast to the florid excess of the *Sgt. Pepper* jacket. The *White Album* cover does not depict an art work per se, and it contains no pictures of the band: it simply has "The Beatles" embossed crookedly on the lower right side of the all-white jacket. Ian Inglis has argued that the cover thus "does not invite interpretation but restricts it, since the only visible words are, explicitly, 'The Beatles'" ("Nothing" 95). But the jacket here does indeed make room for listeners by offering a virtual blank canvas onto which they can project their fantasies. Such openness to interpretation, in fact, points up the avant-garde impulse behind the cover, designed by pop artist Richard Hamilton. Explaining his minimalist approach as a self-conscious nod to contemporary art, Hamilton says, "To avoid the issue of competing with the lavish design treatments of most jackets, I suggested a plain white cover so pure and reticent that it would seem to place it in the context of the most esoteric art publications" ("100 Classic" 93). The rejection of the supposedly rarefied aesthetic of *Sgt. Pepper* could hardly be more complete. Rather than attempt to build on the reputation of their masterpiece, the Beatles here opted for an avant-garde design as a response to the highbrow reception of pop they had initiated with *Sgt. Pepper*.

But can the *White Album* be taken seriously as an avant-garde work? The context of its production undercuts any such pretension. Hamilton says of the cover, "I took it more into the little-press field by individually numbering each cover. The title *The Beatles* was embossed in as seemingly casual a manner as possible, and the numbering had almost the appearance of a hand-numbering machine" ("100 Classic" 93). The language is significant: the title was embossed in a "seemingly" casual manner and the numbering had the "appearance" of being done by hand. Hamilton implies that the avant-garde appeal is skin-deep. Moreover, he suggested that the Beatles produce a limited edition of several hundred thousand numbered copies, mimicking the tradition of hand-numbered art prints. Ultimately, by using a machine to increase the album's avant-garde appeal, Hamilton apes the fetishized, individually crafted art work, the very aesthetic that Lennon earlier characterized as a "lot of shit."

The irony in the *White Album*'s cover depends on the fact that its avant-garde appearance was mechanically reproduced. Walter Benjamin has argued that such reproduction "emancipates the work of art from its parasitical dependence on ritual" by destroying its "aura" (221). The artwork's aura depends on the existence of a single and irreplaceable original, and duplication in itself deflates this mystical value. In parodying the fetish of the original art work with the cover of their album, the Beatles at once align themselves with the avant-garde and critique it. The stark jacket not only eschews the psychedelic trappings of the era (trappings the Beatles themselves helped put in place), but it also ironically distances them from the avant-garde fetish of the new: they undercut the aura of their product by highlighting its very existence as a manufactured commodity.

Along with sporting a cover that foregrounds the Beatles' complex relationship to consumer culture and high art, the *White Album* offers radically eclectic musical styles in marked contrast to the self-conscious artistry of *Sgt. Pepper*. The Beatles parody everything from 1920s music hall songs, country-and-western ballads, English blues, and 1950s doo-wop to Chuck Berry, the Beach Boys, and themselves. Given its seemingly eccentric catalog of styles, the record has often been dismissed as the chaotic product of four individual musicians rather than a cohesive band. Philip Norman refers to the "disorganization" of the *White Album* as opposed to the "discipline" of *Sgt. Pepper* (348). He also notes that George Martin, the producer, thought the songs on the record "reeked of the argument and self-indulgence that had gone into their making" (342). In fact, Martin has claimed several times that he wanted to edit the album down to a single record composed of the fourteen best songs.

Martin's impulse to clean up the record stems from what he and others feel is the record's disunity or disorganization. But in curbing the album's excesses, what could be cut beyond the obvious material that is short or radically experimental ("Wild Honey Pie"; "Why Don't We Do It in the Road?"; "Revolution 9")? In his song-by-song analysis of the Beatles' catalog, Tim Riley argues that editing the record would eliminate "not a few but many great tracks" (260). Aside from losing strong material, however, a greater difficulty would arise in editing the album: although conveying a feeling of excess and disorganization, it also—in a way that's difficult to express—coheres. Discussing the Beatles' use of parody on the record, Riley notes that "by placing 'Birthday' next to 'Yer Blues' and 'Revolution' next to 'Honey Pie,' it is as though the Beatles mean to pair each musical extremity with its opposite" (260). Offering an alternative to the demand for stylistic unity, Riley identifies this balance of polarities as the quality that gives the album that elusive sense of cohesion, which is why removing any track seems disruptive. Ultimately, then, the eclectic range of music at once thwarts any attempt to define the style of the record and replaces the totalizing concept of style with an emphasis on the relationship between songs.

Further undercutting attempts to interpret the record's deeper meaning, the Beatles also create a disorienting maze of intratextual references on the *White Album*, most notably in Lennon's "Glass Onion," which contains lyrical and musical references to at least five other Beatles tunes. The song provides a perfect example of what Lennon meant when he said the Beatles put things into their lyrics to start the critics "puzzling." Lennon sings about "Strawberry Fields" ("the place where nothing is real"), the "walrus and me," "Lady Madonna trying to makes ends meet," the "fool on the hill," and "fixing a hole in the ocean." The music, too, underscores this self-reflexive romp through Beatles history as flutes mock the tune of "Fool on the Hill" when he refers to it. Using references to other songs to construct his tune, Lennon openly admits he is distributing clues so listeners can solve this Beatle puzzle: "Well here's another clue for you all / The walrus was Paul." Through this misleading clue, Lennon pokes fun at those who want to find out what the songs "mean." This is not a detective novel: it has no answer or solution to it. In satirizing the urge to find a stable meaning, John emphasizes what the critics of the album fail to see in its alleged disorganization: the album does not offer much closure, and any coherence it has depends on the interplay of eclectic material. Lennon's final jab at the too-serious critics comes at the end of the song when he admits, for those puzzling over the clues, that he is simply "trying to make a dove-tail joint"—another allusion to the carpenter in *Alice in Wonderland*, as well as a sly in-joke for pot smokers.

Following Lennon's example, George Harrison also mocks anyone assembling clues to solve this Beatles' riddle. In "Savoy Truffle" (perhaps the only pop song about losing your teeth from eating sweets), Harrison sings, "We all know Obla-Di-Bla-Da / But can you show me, where you are?" With a self-assured tone, he offers "Ob-La-Di, Ob-La Da" as a common point of reference, but of course, that song comes three sides earlier on the same album. Smugly referring to "Ob-La-Di, Ob-La-Da," and mispronouncing the song's title in the same instance, George sends up those who want to find the meaning, who want to know the song. And being asked "where you are" must seem an ironically rhetorical question after having already listened to three sides' worth of the album's radically eclectic contents.

Far from being an escape from history, the intertextual references and the play of styles on the *White Album* in fact can be read as an acknowledge-ment of the past. As Umberto Eco writes in his essay "Postmodernism, Irony, the Enjoyable," the postmodern "reply to the modern consists of recognizing that the past, since it cannot really be destroyed, . . . must be revisited: but with irony, not innocently" (67). As an example, Eco argues that a man can-not say "I love you madly" to a cultivated woman because both of them know the expression has already been made a cliché by Barbara Cartland;[1] to avoid false innocence, then, the man must say, "As Barbara Cartland would put it, I love you madly" (67). Enclosing the saying in quotation marks, the speaker both avoids false innocence and conveys his feeling. Viewed from this per-spective, the Beatles' appropriation of various styles on the *White Album* does not suggest exhaustion or escape; instead, it signals their knowledge of and implication in the musical past. In 1968 they could no longer naïvely play 1950's rock 'n' roll for its association with rebellion. The widespread accep-tance of rock 'n' roll, along with corporate attempts to harness its meaning for fans, were historical trends that impinged on the possible significance of the style. Rather than play music for its initial subversive value, the Beatles made ironic reference to earlier musical styles, thus both distancing themselves from the past and reinscribing those styles into a new historical moment with new meaning. They gave the music specific political and cultural relevance for their times.

The *White Album* contains several such appropriations of past musical styles, and one key example is "Yer Blues." As the title suggests, "Yer Blues" parodies the penchant among young white Englishmen for adopting the music of southern U.S. blacks. Despite the parodic title Lennon sounds fairly serious in his lyrics and vocal: the first two verses begin respectively, "Yes, I'm lonely, wanna die" and "In the morning, wanna die." And Lennon shrieks that he feels "suicidal" just like that lonely outsider Mr. Jones in Bob Dylan's "Bal-lad of a Thin Man." This could all sound unbearably self-involved but for one detail: instead of the usual 4/4 blues beat, most of the song lurches along in 12/8 time. Here, the music puts ironic quotation marks around the lyrics and vocal. Rather than being a revivalist take on the blues, the song parodies that revivalism yet still conveys Lennon's "blues."

Perhaps the most important example of musical borrowing occurs in the album's opening track, "Back in the U.S.S.R." In discussing this tune, critics invariably refer to it, in Riley's words, as a "Beach Boys parody," although the "more direct association is with Chuck Berry's 'Back in the U.S.A.'" (263). Berry's song concerns how "glad" he is when his plane touches down as he returns to the United States; McCartney takes this basic scenario and reverses it. Instead of returning to the United States, the singer joyously lands in his Soviet homeland: "Boy, you don't know how lucky you are / Back in the U.S.S.R." With the Beach Boys as intertext, the singer looks forward to seeing attractive women from all over Russia: in this parody of "California Girls," the Beatles sing (complete with falsetto back-up vocals), "the Ukraine girls really knock me out / they leave the West behind / And Moscow girls make me sing and shout / That Georgia's always on my mind." At the height of the cold war, McCartney appropriates the ultimate American middle-class music, and the ironic associations could hardly be more pointed.

"Back in the U.S.S.R." plays on stereotypical Western visions of both the United States and Soviet Union, and satirizes the absurdities in each. The song mocks the idealized fantasy of the United States as a vast beach populated with attractive women, a nation of sports cars and barbecues. At the same time, McCartney exposes how little the average listener knows of the real inhabitants of the communist empire (how many have been taught what a balalaika is by the Beatles?). The reference to "Georgia" seals the song's irony, as the name of the Soviet republic mirrors its U.S. twin and we confront our investment in the cold war fable of absolute good versus absolute evil. Such moral certainty must be upset by McCartney's lyrics, which question a firm sense of identity predicated on national pride. Listening to this song as it encapsulates the stylistic experiments on the *White Album*, have we entered a postmodern hall of mirrors, constructed through a multivalent irony that finally collapses on itself? Does the song reflect Jameson's notion of pastiche, which refuses any standard of judgment by which we can know what is normal? The irony here surely does go on unfolding, but we find political significance in having our identities troubled, in being asked to confront contradictions in the Western fantasy of purity and goodness as defined against an evil, Soviet Other.

The play of musical styles on the *White Album* ultimately reflects a complex response to conflicting pressures: from fans, reviewers, record companies, managers, girlfriends, and the political left. Seen in this context, the record offers a nuanced reply to cultural and political issues. True, the Beatles refuse to give explicit directives on the album, and they do not address the concerns that Landau, for example, thought were the urgencies of the moment. But that does not necessarily mean that Lennon's political career had not yet begun in 1968, nor must we buy Jon Wiener's suggestion that "Rock could become a real political force . . . when it was linked to real political organizing" (5). The *White Album* suggests, in fact, that politics is not singular, that there is not one "real" way of working for change. The album shows that parody and reflexivity can be used effectively to engage political and cultural issues; they can be used as the basis for a postmodern politics.

NOTE

1. Barbara Cartland was one of the leading progenitors of the romance novel as a popular literary genre.

PART III

"We can work it out"

The Beatles and Culture

CHAPTER 9

"The rest of you, if you'll just rattle your jewelry"

The Beatles and Questions of Mass and High Culture

PAUL GLEED

B Y THE TIME the Beatles took to the stage at the Prince of Wales Theatre for a televised Royal Command Performance in November 1963,
they had already become a genuine sensation. The lively set was punctuated with good-natured humor, and John famously prefaced "Twist and
Shout" with a typically endearing piece of wit: "Would the people in the
cheaper seats clap your hands, and the rest of you, if you'll just rattle your jewelry." The performance, of course, helped to cement the Beatles' success and
to define the kind of apt asides that would become a trademark. However, the
joke can also be seen as a lighthearted articulation of the issue of mass and
high culture, a theme that was important to the Beatles themselves and one
that has become increasingly important to those trying to understand the
band's continued success.

Mark Hertsgaard—in *A Day in the Life: The Music and Artistry of the Beatles* (1995), one of the best of many studies on the Beatles' musical achievement—remarks that "the music of the Beatles was, in short, high art for the
mass public" (317). This statement seems to represent the dominant way of
understanding the Beatles' position between "the people in the cheap seats"
and "the rest." And with a gentle nudge in this direction, "Roll Over
Beethoven" can today be ironically read less as a call for classical music to

make room for rock 'n' roll than for Ludwig to inch over and make room for the Beatles in the canon of Great Music History. Alternatively, however, the Beatles can be viewed as instrumental in challenging and dissolving such traditional and restrictive categories as "high art" and "mass culture." Indeed, even with the best of intentions, struggling to place the Beatles somewhere neatly between the hand-clappers and the jewelry-rattlers has for years obscured the true extent of their art and the impact that they exerted on how we understand culture at the beginning of the twenty-first century.

In 1964, the year that saw the Beatles first top the charts in the United States and enjoy great critical and popular success with their film *A Hard Day's Night*, Stuart Hall and Paddy Whannel published an important work in the history of cultural studies. *The Popular Arts*, an attempt to help educators usefully harness the appeal of contemporary culture in the classroom, saw its authors mark a distinction between "popular art" and "mass art." As Hall and Whannel suggest:

> Where popular art in its modern forms exist only through the medium of personal style, mass art has no personal quality but, instead, a high degree of personalization. Chaplin indelibly imprints his work with the whole pressure of his personality, which is fully translated into his art. By contrast, mass art often destroys all traces of individuality and idiosyncrasy which makes a work compelling and living, and assumes a sort of de-personalized quality, a non-style. (68)

Moreover, "for the popular artist stylization is necessary, and the conventions provide an agreed base from which true creative invention springs. In mass art, the formula is everything—an escape from, rather than a means to, originality" (69).

As the phenomenon of "Beatlemania" reaches its first great international peak, a new generation of cultural thinkers is beginning to carve up distinctions within the arena of pop culture, but no move is made to collapse the thick and high wall that separates pop culture from high culture. And as for the Beatles themselves, their appearances in *The Popular Arts* are somewhat fleeting. Aware that while they have been writing an important cultural force has been in the ascendancy, Hall and Whannel append a special note to the end of a chapter on "The Young Audience": "It is now clear that [the Beatles] represent a distinctive break with earlier patterns," the authors add. The Beatles have altered the focus from the individual singer to the group, but also the dominant mood has "given way to a much more affirmative, extrovert, uninhibited style." Yet although the Beatles clearly merited a last-minute addendum, Hall and Whannel seemingly had not had the distance required to make much more of the Liverpudlians than their sensation alone: "The fans 'play' at being worshippers as the Beatles 'play' at being idols" (312). For all the playfulness, however, or perhaps because of it, whether a few more months would have encouraged Hall and Whannel at that time to speak of the Beatles as popular artists rather than as mass artists is interesting to consider. Certainly, the group was more than qualified in terms of personality and inventiveness.

In 1970, scant months after the release of the *Abbey Road* album and the disbanding of the Beatles, Leslie Fiedler published his seminal essay "Cross the Border, Close the Gap." Primarily making a call for a new kind of literary criticism in the face of a new kind of literature, Fiedler's essay nonetheless has the broadest of cultural implications and marks an early moment in theorizing the postmodern:

> But to turn High Art into vaudeville and burlesque at the same moment that Mass Art is being irreverently introduced into museums and libraries is to perform an act which has political as well as aesthetic implications: an act which closes a class [gap], as well as a generation gap. . . . What the final intrusion of Pop into the citadels of High Art provides, therefore, for the critics is the exhilarating new possibility of making judgments about the "goodness" and "badness" of art quite separated from distinctions between "high" and "low" with their concealed class bias. (287)

Although beginning with novelists such as John Barth and Philip Roth, whose innovations in fiction had led them to appropriate such traditionally "low" genres as the western, science fiction, and pornography, Fiedler casts his net a little wider as he explores various crossings of cultural borders. Bob Dylan's "Pop surrealist poetry," for example, receives attention, but "even more spectacular, however, is . . . John Lennon, who coming into view first as merely one of the Beatles, then still just another rock group from Liverpool, has revealed himself stage by stage as novelist, playwright, movie maker, guru, sculptor, etc., etc." (288). Nobody but Fiedler, deliberately publishing his essay in *Playboy*, could have the bravado to write a line such as, "merely one of the Beatles," but in singling out Lennon's post-Beatles career and overlooking the previous decade, Fiedler misses the mark.

The point, of course, is not that the changes in cultural thinking, the dissolution of the boundaries between "high" and "mass" culture, are driven entirely by the Beatles, but that no one else can claim to have done more to create the environment that Fiedler theorized. In the years between 1964 and 1970, between Hall and Whannel's *The Popular Arts* and Fiedler's "Cross the Border," the Beatles made this new style of borderless art not simply widely visible but commercially very, very viable. In this and other ways, the Beatles achieved similar ends as Fiedler's fiction writers, but the band's trajectory marks their achievement as different. After all, the novelists sought to meld "high" and "low" from the privileged position of the high, while the Beatles worked upward and initiated the collapse of the distinction from the popular position. As important and notable as novels such as *The Sot-Weed Factor* and *Little Big Man* may be in bringing about the perception that boundaries between "high" and "low" art are porous, they do not convey that message as widely as, say, *Sgt. Pepper's Lonely Hearts Club Band*. And although this claim seems to emerge as a kind of reverse snobbery that continues to see differences between high and mass culture ("mass" is more powerful and "real," whereas "high" is aloof and cloistered), all these cultural texts broadly articulated related stylistic and cultural concerns.

Traditionally, disparity exists about exactly when the Beatles became the kind of artists (rather than entertainers or performers) deserving of praise usually reserved for "high" cultural texts. This debate is popularly formulated around the question, "when did the Beatles get all artsy?" Pub pundits and university scholars alike often point to the 1966 *Revolver* album, although we find almost equal precedence for selecting the preceding album, *Rubber Soul* (1965). Beyond this is usually agreement that the artistic growth culminates in the masterpiece of *Sgt. Pepper* (1967). All of this is by now time-honored, but it has the significant drawback of effacing many of the meaningful foundations laid during the time of the Quarry Men, the Hamburg years, and the Beatles' early albums.

Although we cannot claim that in these formative years the Beatles were already undermining great cultural distinctions, visible key characteristics are present that establish that potential: namely eclecticism and the desire to be "new" and different. The cultural roots of the Beatles, a spectrum that included skiffle music and Lonnie Donegan, the *Goon Show*, and American rock 'n' roll, has already been well documented, but nonetheless demonstrates that the intuition to put, say, a piccolo trumpet on "Penny Lane" or a string quartet on "Yesterday" was present from the beginning. Also present was a desire to be fresh and original, which, when combined with a genuine and passionate interest in eclecticism, is the very cornerstone of postmodern innovation. As Peter Eckhorn, manager of the Top Ten Club in Hamburg where the Beatles performed in 1962, observes, "The interesting thing about the Beatles was that people liked them more for their engaging personalities, their onstage antics, and smart remarks than for their music. Their music sounded very much like all the other English groups, but as performers they were unique" (qtd. in Pritchard and Lysaght 66). Although the Hamburg years saw sets mostly filled with covers and the perhaps indifferent sound of young men serving a hard musical apprenticeship, the creative energy of the band was visible. Soon that "uniqueness" would become something the Beatles sought in their music, too, even before the success of "Please Please Me." As Paul McCartney said of the Beatles' outlook in 1962, "We were very conscious of our image, and as you know, we wanted to be different from all the rest. We didn't want to be like Cliff Richard and everyone else in England, because it was all changing then, too. We felt we were the generation after Cliff" (qtd. in Pritchard and Lysaght

104). George Harrison would later undercut this way of seeing the Beatles' early years when he said, "We didn't believe our sound was different enough as a sound. As far as we were concerned, we began performing American rock-and-roll and rhythm-and-blues and our songs incorporated those elements." In this way, adjectives connoting newness, uniqueness, and difference characterize accounts of the Beatles in the early 1960s.

For the purposes of this chapter, such descriptions help to demonstrate how the Beatles' phenomenon became a space with the potential to confront entrenched cultural boundaries. But perhaps the strongest early evidence of the breakdown of "high" and "mass" art forms comes from the Beatles' first film, *A Hard Day's Night*. The film highlights the Beatles' playful but very genuine ability to straddle the cultural gap of "high" and "low" culture, not only in its universally positive critical reception or Richard Lester's innovative direction, but also in the situations and lines of the script itself and the lead performances. For example, as Paul delivers some mock theatrical lines to the mirror (Hamlet's first soliloquy), he spins to face the camera, hairdryer doubling as a ray gun, and gives a raucous "Zap!"—Shakespeare meets *Buck Rogers*. A number of interruptions occur, also, which can be seen as comic moments of rupture between "high" and "low" art forms: the fancy-footed duel between the boys and Lionel Blair and his dancers, and, most intrusively, Granddad's unwelcome operatic appearance via a trap door.

Moreover, the look of the film, borrowing aspects of its visual style from European avant-garde cinema, is similarly motivated. As well as popularizing a style of quick-cutting, which as many have suggested is the aesthetic parent of today's music videos, this stylistic move encouraged critics to see the film as much more than an opportunistic milking of celebrity. "Films are mirrors," observes Lester. "Films reflect the times. I had a marvelous image in front of me to reflect, and that is, or was, their energy and their originality. And whatever I had came because I was an enthusiast of Buster Keaton's work and of French cinema in the late 1950s" (qtd. in Pritchard and Lysaght 163). And if the look of the film and many of its moments reflected an exploration of "high" art forms and intelligent themes, then we should not be surprised that the Beatles themselves spent time offscreen engaged in a different kind of reflecting. "People have asked me what we spoke about on the set of the movies," says Victor Spinetti, an actor in *A Hard Day's Night* and *Help!* (1965), "and I tell them that we talked about everything from Proust to Picasso. You'd never have conversations like that on a normal movie set, but the Beatles were curious and wanted to learn everything. They weren't just interested in being the best group in the world. They also wanted to know what we were all about and why we were all here on this planet" (qtd. in Pritchard and Lysaght 165–66).

A Hard Day's Night is difficult to place within any preexisting notion of cultural hierarchies and in some instances foreshadows the feel and tone of

Sgt. Pepper. However, the notion that the Beatles were anything but a remarkably successful pop act was ebbing only slowly if at all. As if to bring this dilemma into sharp relief, the Beatles were awarded the honor of Member of the Order of the British Empire (MBE) in 1965 to the chagrin of some members of the MBE's elite. Some existing MBEs returned their medals at the news they would be sharing their titles with, as one particularly vexed Canadian put it, the "vulgar." Notably, however, when defending their right to the award, Lennon articulated the case of the Beatles not in terms of artistic worth or of cultural capital, but simply in the language of cool, hard business. "I reckon we got it for exports," Lennon told members of the media, "and the citation should have said that. Look, if someone had got an award for exporting millions of dollars' worth of fertilizer or machine tools, everyone would have applauded. So, why should they knock us?" (qtd. in Pritchard and Lysaght 191). The argument that they deserved the accolade on artistic merit seems to have been one that Lennon at least did not deem necessary or feel comfortable making. However, as Bernard Gendron revealed in his exemplary study of the gradual legitimization of rock and jazz music, *Between Montmartre and the Mudd Club*, 1965 witnessed a change in the reception of the Beatles that moved from a fascination with the social aspects of Beatlemania to positive value statements about the group members themselves. By 1965 the Beatles' music was enjoying significant praise, observes Gendron, but "the Beatles were not in any sense acquiring a formal highbrow certification, but rather a tenuous and somewhat patronizing endorsement, cavalierly doled out by highbrow agents outside their proper venues in lower arenas of accreditation" (184). Although "qualified" people were beginning to wax lyrical about the Beatles, they were guarding themselves from potential embarrassment by making the remarks appropriately informal and equivocal. Additionally, these "critics attributed the discovered high-culture compacts in [the Beatles'] music more to happenstance and cultural osmosis than to skill or creativity" (195).

Gradually, however, between *Rubber Soul* and the aftermath of *Sgt. Pepper*, Gendron observes yet another shift: "An adult Beatlemania was in effect replacing the apparently fading 'teenybopper' Beatlemania, supplanting the screams and rituals of worship with breathless reportage and grandiloquent praise. . . . The Beatles were being hailed as bona fide artists belonging in the same company as illustrious highbrow creators and not merely as pop cultural proxies or simulacra" (193–95). This shift represents an important change, but the plaudits, of course, function only to say that the doors of the cultural establishment are being opened to allow in some surprising but deserving young members to the fold. Little if any of the reams of contemporary responses to the Beatles suggest that the doors and walls separating "mass" from "high" culture were being razed. The language and conceptual approach of postmodernism was not yet in place to allow for this, but the Beatles continued to play a leading role in forcing the need to see culture through new eyes.

Most obviously, this process included the incorporation of classical instruments and techniques in popular music. George Martin, the Beatles' classically trained producer, encouraged and aided the band with his knowledge, but the Beatles embraced and became intricately involved in this musical conflation. On the preparatory work for McCartney's composition "Yesterday," Martin recalls one instance in which his background and the Beatles' desire for fresh sounds were in perfect harmony:

> I told him there was nothing else we could do, that we couldn't put heavy drums or even a heavy bass guitar on it. I said, "What about having a string accompaniment, you know, fairly tastefully done?" Paul said, "Yuk! I don't want any of that Mantovani rubbish. I don't want any of that syrupy stuff." Then I thought back to my classical days, and I said, "Well, what about a string quartet then?" He dug that. . . . So we sat down and together we wrote the score. I mean, obviously, I wrote it, but I had him with me when I was writing. He would say, "Can we have the cellos doing this bit?" And I'd say, "Sure, why not?" Or "No, that's out of their range." He devised the cello line, which I think is one of the best parts of it. So it was kind of a collaborative experience. (qtd. in Pritchard and Lysaght 192)

Similarly, when arranging the music for "In My Life," Martin believed that "it would be rather nice to have something fairly quaint or fairly Baroque . . . like a Bach invention" (qtd. in Pritchard and Lysaght 200). These were just several of the tracks that found either Martin or classical session musicians putting in hours at Abbey Road Studios on harpsichord, strings, brass, and so on. In these recordings, the Beatles are employing what Charles Jencks, writing a decade later, would call "double-coding." This important piece of terminology, coined for use in architectural criticism, describes the breakdown of binaries such as elite/popular, accommodating/subversive, and new/old (30). And, if as Jencks writes, "Postmodernism always carries the injunction to cross territories, break down modernist specialization, hybridize discourses, [and] attack false boundaries" (32), then the Beatles' musical double-coding truly stands out in the cultural skyline of the 1960s and beyond.

Thus, with this classical/pop double-coding, as well as East/West (Harrison's sitar, for example) and other dichotomies, the Beatles show that the eclecticism of the early days had continued, albeit in more mature directions. Alongside this aspect of the Beatles' music, however, was their thirst for innovation, which persisted with equal vigor. If the group, with Martin's guidance, had connected themselves with the practices of classical music, they also reached across to more obscure regions of the musical establishment; as the Beatles welcomed the reverberations of centuries past into their music, they embraced too the electronic techniques that created never-before-heard sounds. "I had an idea to use something I had been experimenting with at home on my tape player where I would put a piece of tape over the record head and saturate the tape with all kinds of sounds," McCartney remembers. "I was listening to [Karlheinz] Stockhausen, the experimental modern composer, at the time, and these saturated loops were inspired by his work. So I brought some of these recordings into the studio" (qtd. in Pritchard and Lysaght 209). One can certainly add Lennon and McCartney's powerful lyricism to these parallel drives of eclecticism and newness, qualities that characterized a collective literary talent that compared favorably to almost any poet of their generation. As Hertsgaard explains in his discussion of "Penny Lane," "McCartney's lyrical touch proves that the sophistication of 'Eleanor Rigby' earlier that year had been no fluke. Like a painter in full command of his canvas, Paul captures entire personalities with single strokes. His character sketches are specific enough that the individuals spring to life instantly in our mind's eye, yet archetypal enough to summon up an entire social reality" (209).

Of course, other aspects of the Beatles' work are left unconsidered here, which contribute to their unique career and the cultural changes they forged. However, the patterns outlined herein grew steadily together, creating what Martin calls "a new kind of art form" (qtd. in Pritchard and Lysaght 234). Although Martin specifically had "Strawberry Fields" in mind, the statement can be appropriately applied to numerous Beatles texts from *A Hard Day's Night* on and finally to their canon as a whole. And with this "new kind of art form" came the need to develop a new kind of artistic assessment, one that recognized the difficulties involved in categories such as "high" and "mass" art. Few descriptions of how this happened carry as much metaphorical weight as McCartney's description of his songwriting process; the picture of a cultural nexus that he presents stands as much for the Beatles as a whole as for his mind alone:

> It's funny and awkward talking about the songwriting process. You don't sit around with people and discuss it. It just comes out of nowhere, sort of out of the blue. It comes through your own mindset and your musical background. From your basic children's melody to classical to ragtime to Tin Pan Alley and from jazz lines all the way to Chuck Berry and Little Richard. My brain will just filter out all that I don't like. (qtd. in Pritchard and Lysaght 193)

A lot may be "filtered out," but the process is as much one of condensation as it is of selection; for all that is rejected, the rest is transformed into something very different and special. After all, the Queen Mother—who was no doubt attired with jewelry that could produce a very lusty rattle that November night in 1963—was noticeably seen to be clapping in time with the cheap seats.

CHAPTER 10

A Universal Childhood

Tourism, Pilgrimage, and the Beatles

KEVIN McCARRON

> And smale foules maken melodie,
> That slepen alle night with open eye,
> So priketh hem nature in hir corages;
> Than longen folk to gon on pilgrimages.
> —Chaucer, *Canterbury Tales*

WHILE THE MEDIA increasingly tend to use the words *pilgrim* and *tourist*—and often interchangeably—much scholarly energy over many years has gone into maintaining a rigid distinction between the two terms.[1] Historically, the pilgrim has been seen as a religious traveler and the tourist as a vacationer; tourism and pilgrimage have long been identified as opposite endpoints on a continuum of travel, revolving about a polarity defined as secular (tourism) and sacred (pilgrimage). In an article on pilgrimages to the English town of Glastonbury, for example, Marion Bowman writes, "One volunteer helper considered three-quarters of visitors pilgrims, the others 'just tourists'" (33).

Much contemporary scholarly work from a range of disciplines, however, has queried the rigidity of this distinction. Ian Reader, for example, suggests:

> pilgrimage need not, at least in popular perspective, be limited solely to explicitly religious traditions. . . . Indeed, a general examination of the word

> and concept of pilgrimage indicates that its scope runs far beyond the
> boundaries of visitors to shrines and holy sites connected with official reli-
> gious traditions into areas far more concerned with the secular world. . . .
> (Introduction 5)

In what is perhaps the most famous single pronouncement on this subject,
the anthropologists Victor and Edith Turner write that "a tourist is half a pilgrim, if a pilgrim is half a tourist" (20). Increasingly, scholars are suggesting
that the distinction is a culturally constructed polarity that may not do justice to the motives of individual travelers. Anthropologists, sociologists, and
historians are the principal participants in this discussion, and although I am
a professor of English, I also wish to enter the debate, investigating differences between "official" and "unofficial" activities associated specifically with
the Beatles in England.

In striking contrast with the abundance of literary tours available
throughout the United Kingdom, and particularly in London, we find a
dearth of formally organized, official tours to places associated with English
popular music.[2] The only tours that are regularly offered are devoted to the
Beatles. Nineteen passengers, of mixed ages and nationalities, were onboard a
minibus tour I joined entitled "The Beatles London," which left from Mar-
leybone Station. The driver was not out of first gear when the tour guide
pointed out the first sight: the Marylebone Registry Office, where Paul married Linda on March 12, 1969. Over the next three hours, we drove across
London, passing many places associated with the Beatles and stopping at
those that the guide deemed particularly important. We walked down St.
Anne's Court, where the Beatles played their first London concert at the long-
gone Blue Gardenia club. Slightly further along the narrow street, the guide
pointed out the site of the equally defunct Trident Studios, where the band
recorded "Hey Jude" in 1968. As Ian MacDonald writes about the song in
Revolution in the Head, "Hey Jude" is punctuated by "the huge chords suggesting both Jude's personal revelation and, along with the accompanying
chorale, a vast communality" (243), an astute reading that, later in Liverpool,
would take on considerable significance for our purposes here.

Next, we drove down Green Street, Mayfair, where John, George, and
Ringo shared a flat in 1963; we drove past 13 Chapel Street, Belgravia, where
Brian Epstein had lived—and died; we motored past the site in Baker Street
where the Apple Boutique once stood, and we stopped outside the Wimpole
Street house where Paul stayed with the Asher family in 1965. The guide
pointed out Carnaby Street as we passed by, and we drove past the Wigmore
Street site of the Apple offices and past 3 Savile Row, its luxurious successor,
where the Beatles played their last concert together on the building's rooftop
on a blustery day in January 1969. We stopped outside Cavendish Avenue,
St. John's Wood, the location of Paul's permanent London residence.

Whereas John, George, and Ringo moved some distance from London to the privacy and affluence of Esher and Weybridge, Paul loved London and often lived there—and London loved him for it. After photos had been taken, we drove a short distance to what is certainly, along with the Sun studios in Memphis, the most famous recording studio in the world: Abbey Road Studios. In "London's Rock 'n' Roll Shrines," the editors of *Time Out* report that "since the Beatles released the album *Abbey Road* on September 26, 1969, the studio has been London's shrine to the Fab Four, [and] some fans make an annual pilgrimage to the studio" (16). "Is it a shrine?" I wondered, as I attempted to decipher some of the graffiti that covered the walls along the street. Are the people who come here—obviously from all over the world, and who leave flowers and jellybeans, and write, "Paul we love you," "John lives," and "Beatles Forever"—pilgrims and not fans or tourists? I noticed that nobody who got off our minibus carried aerosols or paintbrushes or gifts; they took photographs and left nothing. I wondered if suggesting that if people leave something behind—if only a scrawl on the wall—they qualify as pilgrims was tenable.

We were summoned back onto the minibus and gradually the ostensibly objective, factual commentary of the tour guide yielded its covert agenda, and it did so not only through its priorities, but also through its numerous omissions. When we drove past Epstein's flat in Wimpole Street, nothing was said about his addiction to prescription drugs or about his homosexuality; obviously no reference was made to the very strong possibility that Lennon and Epstein had been lovers.[3] Similarly, when we drove past the Belgravia flat where the Beatles' manager died, the word *suicide* was not mentioned nor was *overdose*; indeed, the implication the guide left us with was that Epstein had fatally exhausted himself in the service of his charges. In short, he had been a martyr to the great cause of the Beatles. The guide made no mention of the grim flat at 13 Emperor's Gate, where Epstein exiled Cynthia Lennon to protect the band's image and to allow John the freedom to take advantage of his fame. Perhaps most strikingly, although the minibus went within a few hundred yards of Mason's Yard in the West End, no mention was made of the Indica art gallery where John first met Yoko Ono. Ono's name was not mentioned once during the tour. Nor was the notorious Allen Klein's. Strikingly absent from this brief account of their split were any contributory factors such as excessive drug use, creative rivalry, or financial wrangling. The Beatles' London was a place and a time of good-natured partying, where every now and again the band would casually make a record, always an effortlessly produced work of incontestable value and enduring quality. The Beatles' London was a place of excitement, creativity, liberation, and infinite possibility. It was a world of such remarkable innocence that for the first time I considered the significance of the band using a quasi-Edenic apple as their emblem. The dominant impression I received from the tour was of an innocence so unspoiled that it was actually childlike, and this motif would be repeated, using similar narrative strategies, in Liverpool.

London's Rock Circus, which proclaims itself to be "Britain's premier rock attraction," is located on Shaftesbury Avenue in the heart of the West End. It opened in 1989 at a cost of more than £10 million and was owned at that time by the Pearson Group, which also controlled Chessington World of Adventure, Alton Towers, Madame Tussaud's renowned wax museum, and numerous other popular tourist attractions. Rock Circus's principal selling point is the use of "animatronics," which its glossy program describes as "life-like robots," a definition unlikely to be endorsed by many of the attraction's visitors. Rock Circus is predicated on essentialist notions of the "popular." The Beatles, clearly, are afforded the honor of being central to the "live" show, as well as having their own dedicated space, not for any unique musical contribution they made to English popular music, but because they sold more records than any other English band. As Caspar Smith writes, "It may have 700,000 visitors a year, but it remains a flawed archive, because not all the most important people are there, only the most popular ones" (11).[4]

The governing trope of the display is synecdoche. The metanarrative, which Rock Circus ceaselessly promotes, is the celebration of the individual, and when a group must be included, the best-known member emerges as the signifier for the entire band. Hence, Johnny Rotten *is* the Sex Pistols, and Sting *is* the Police. Admittedly, space is limited and animatronic models are expensive, but the overall impression Rock Circus generates is that popular music is created by supremely talented individuals who owe nothing to any other human being, let alone to the complex web of historical, socioeconomic circumstances that contributed to their success. The Beatles are represented at the Rock Circus as four individuals: cute Paul, sardonic George, amiable Ringo, and cheeky John. Visitors first see the band on display in the Cavern club, or rather, in a resoundingly unevocative representation of it, while the delighted grins on their faces and the gold records on the adjoining wall are evidence of the teleology that shapes so many Beatle narratives. The ensuing "live" show, in which the Beatles are the star turn, is an abomination; as Anthony Everitt notes, "it is an embarrassment, with animatronic copies of the Beatles jerking their way through *Sgt. Pepper*" (22). The display is also, of course, historically inaccurate because the Beatles never performed *Sgt. Pepper* live. Ironically, while staring in horror at the grotesque writhings of the robots, I receive my first intimation of the significance of time to the Beatles' extraordinary, universal appeal. It occurs to me that the teleological imposition in the Cavern that seemed incongruous only a short while earlier can now be seen to have the effect of denying time, rejecting its rigid separations into distinct periods, and allowing the viewer to, momentarily at least, perceive a temporal totality. Writing about *Sgt. Pepper* in *Rock: The Primary Text*, Allan F. Moore contends that the album represents "an early endeavor for rock to build a unity greater than that of the individual, self-contained utterance" (*Beatles* 84). Moore's comments regarding the album's achievement easily could be said about the Beatles themselves: four individuals who were transformed into something far greater than the sum of their individual selves—a band, a group, a cultural unity. Time, individuality, and the collective, these elements seem to lie at the heart of the Beatles' appeal, but perhaps in different ways for tourists and pilgrims.

By Rock Circus's own definition, animatronic models are "robots." Jean Baudrillard suggests crucial differences exist between the automaton and the robot. He notes whereas the automaton raises questions about the relationship between being and appearance—and that its very existence questions nature, making it an "optimistic mechanics"—this is not at all the case with the robot:

> The robot no longer questions appearances, its only truth is its mechanical efficiency. . . . Being and appearance are founded on a single substance of production and labor. No more semblance or dissemblance, no more God or Man, only an immanent logic of the principle of operativity. (54)

The much-vaunted animatronic models, which take center stage at Rock Circus, attest to the hegemony of the robot, of dead labor over living labor. As Theodor Adorno writes, "Through the total absorption of both musical production and consumption by the capitalist process, the alienation of music from man has become complete" (qtd. in Paddison 98). Perhaps this phenomenon can be read, then, as an attempt to reclaim God and humankind, as well as the connected desire to reject the "alienation of music from man," that distinguishes the tourist from the pilgrim.

The minibus tour and Rock Circus, both of which charge admission and both of which are "official" attractions, function as part of a larger "culture industry." Both entities offer entertainment along with the appearance of cultural education. Popular music is now the aural backdrop to global capitalism, and Rock Circus is a "shrine" only to consumerism, the cult of the individual, and the law of market forces. Anthropologist Colin Turnbull suggests that pilgrims gain "a sense of belonging to a religious or spiritual heritage rather than to a cultural one" (qtd. in Valene Smith 2). The tourist is unlikely to query the ideology that animates cultural attractions such as Rock Circus; yet that same pilgrim may travel to a shrine whose very appeal lies in its symbolic rejection of the pervading ethos of the culture. In "From Custer to Kent State: Heroes, Martyrs, and the Evolution of Popular Shrines in the USA," Richard West Sellars and Tony Walter describe the two principal ways in which shrines are created. "In some instances," they write, "a memorial to the deceased is built or the place of death is preserved, and then come the pilgrims, turning the memorial into a popular shrine. In others, the pilgrims come regardless, the place becomes sacred, and a memorial has to be erected in response" (179–80).

The pilgrims have "come regardless," in Sellars and Walter's words, to the sites of T. Rex vocalist Marc Bolan's fatal car crash and the house where Freddie Mercury, the lead singer of Queen, died. Although neither has been officially recognized, both sites function as England's most important rock music shrines. Neither Lennon's nor Harrison's bodies have been buried in England; if either had been, their graves or plots would have become instant shrines.[5] Lennon's grave would, undoubtedly, be the most visited rock shrine in the world. Given, however, that this is not the case, a visit to the two most popular rock music shrines in England might afford us with a sense of what constitutes a shrine in the world of popular culture.

Bolan was killed near Barnes Common on September 16, 1977, when his car crashed into a tree. Every year on this date, fans gather at the tree for a candle-lit vigil, leaving the site covered in flowers, candles, ribbons, and photographs. Although the site receives most visitors on September 16, people come throughout the year to leave similar offerings. Freddie Mercury died at his London home, 1 Logan Place, from bronchopneumonia brought on by AIDS on November 24, 1991. What links Bolan and Mercury, in addition to their status as rock stars, is the denominator of violent death (shared, of course, by Lennon) and the very rock 'n' roll nature of their respective deaths, brought about as they were by speed and sex. In addition to describing the complex rituals that some "primitive" societies have employed for dealing with their dead, Baudrillard observes:

> we, for our part, no longer have an effective rite for reabsorbing death and its rupturing energies; there remains the phantasm of sacrifice, the violent artifice of death. Hence, the intense and profoundly *collective* satisfaction of the automobile death. In the fatal accident, the artificiality of death fascinates us. Technical, non-natural, and therefore *willed* (ultimately by the victim him- or herself) death becomes interesting once again since *willed* death has a meaning. (165)

Mercury's death, like Bolan and Lennon's, is also "nonnatural," not part of the natural order; it appropriates to itself the "phantasm of sacrifice" and, as a result, it becomes the business of the group, demanding a collective and symbolic response.

Only three years after Mercury's death, the editors of *Time Out* report that "since Freddie's death ... the wall outside the house has become London's biggest rock 'n' roll shrine." This wall, complete with wire netting and video cameras, is totally covered in graffiti, as is the door built into the wall and its adjoining footpath. Much of the graffiti devoted to Mercury's memory is adolescently mawkish and self-consciously sentimentalized: "Your soul is painted like the wings of butterflies" and "Fairy tales of yesterday will grow but never die." One comment, in particularly large writing, reads: "I cry with nostalgia at your front door you beautiful angel. Part of me died with you." Once again, hyperbole is the governing trope, while religious terminology abounds: "Unique. Genius. Freddie, you are a God" and "Here you are Freddie. You are the Prince of the Universe." We find a striking number of references to Mercury still "living": "Freddie you will never die," "You will live with us always," "Freddie lives." As Ian Reader notes, such sentiments are characteristic of pilgrimage cults: "An extraordinary number of pilgrimage cults across a wide variety of cultures have revolved around death, the tombs of saints, and the images of heroes," he writes. "Often, too, these assert the belief that the hero or saintly figure remains alive, transcending at least on a spiritual plane the reality of physical death" (Introduction 18). Speculating that perhaps the widely circulated "Paul is dead" rumors that followed the release of *Abbey Road* were a variation on this theme is tempting: Paul was killed precisely so that he could be resurrected and subsequently enshrined.

At Logan Place I was particularly struck by two comments that were by no means consistent with the pervading devotional ethos to Mercury's life and legend. One of them read, "You are six feet under, you fudgepacker, but your music lives on," and the other said that "Freddie blew niggers for beer money." Paradoxically, both statements underscore Victor and Edith Turner's concept of *communitas*. The Turners' notions of pilgrimage draw on theories in Arnold van Gennep's *The Rites of Passage* (1908), and they suggest that, as with van Gennep's initiate, pilgrims occupy a "liminal" position outside the confines of ordinary society and that people who enter this space experience a bonding and a sense of communality that the Turners call *communitas*. For the Turners, "*Communitas* involves the creation of an egalitarian bonding between individuals outside of, or freed from, the normal structures of society, and the formation of a temporary community and field of social relations that appears as an alternative to the normal structures of society" (Reader, Introduction 11). Both of the sentiments attempt to undermine the prevailing cultural assumptions the large majority of visitors to the wall. Mercury is not really being attacked here, but rather an entire subculture, one to which racism and homophobia are anathema. Pilgrims to the wall, like those who come to Abbey Road, share a worldview that bonds them even when no other visitors are present. The two writers at Logan Place seem to have recognized this phenomenon at some level, and their statements, although attempts to subvert the shared worldview, actually affirm its existence.

Nothing is either "magical" or "mysterious" about Liverpool's "official" Magical Mystery Tour; in this, in fact, lies much of the experience's charm. The two-and-a-half-hour tour crosses the city, taking in Woolton, Childwall, and Wavertree, as well as relevant aspects of the city center. When I went on the tour, twenty-eight people were on the bus—again, as in London, of mixed ages and nationalities—and everybody seemed already well informed about the Beatles. Like children, we enjoyed a familiar and comfortable narrative, made even more pleasurable by the sight of the real houses and schools and pubs that feature so prominently in the Beatles' story. We stopped outside Paul's family home in Allerton, where many photos were taken, but John's family home, "Mendips," in Menlove Avenue, Woolton, was undoubtedly the most popular of the houses visited. We drove to George's childhood home in Upton Green, Speke, and, as we stood in front of the modest house, the guide informed us that until his death George had lived in "a luxury mansion in Henley-Upon-Thames, near London." The comparison was obvious, and it was a constant feature of the tour, evoked again as we stood outside Ringo's childhood home, in Admiral Grove, part of Liverpool's once-notorious Dingle district. Generically, the Beatles' story mirrors the "Ugly Duckling" narrative, driven, as it is, by the transformation of the protagonists from near the bottom of the class pyramid to the apex of popular music's aristocracy. The tour is an illustrated rags-to-riches narrative, and it is also consistently anti-individualist: again and again, we were told of parents, grandparents, aunts, and friends who had played significant roles in the personal and professional lives of the four young Beatles. The tour guide emphasized the singularity of Liverpool and the vital role it plays in the story, highlighting, in particular, its status as a port city that catered to an influx of U.S. soldiers on leave from Germany who created a strong local interest in rhythm and blues.

Of course, the guide's story evinced a by-now-familiar agenda. Particularly apparent was the absence of any mention of the early incarnations of the Beatles and the other purveyors of the Mersey sound. While the Silver Beetles were mentioned, no reference at all was made to the Quarry Men, Johnny and the Moondogs, or Rory Storm and the Hurricanes. Similarly, the guide's story depicted the Beatles returning from Hamburg, where they had been massively successful, to Liverpool's Cavern club, where they were even more successful. The guide gave no suggestion that the Beatles were a poor to average beat band when they first went to Germany and became a good, even a great, group by working extremely hard in front of a very demanding audience. The Cavern was the only club mentioned during the tour. The guide did not mention the church halls where the Quarry Men played, St. Peter's in Woolton, or St. Barnabas near Penny Lane. The guide did not mention the band performing in front of handfuls of uninterested old men at the Broadway Conservative Club or in front of no one at all in the aptly named Morgue club located in Old Roan. The guide did not mention the Jacaranda club in Slater Street, or the Casanova club, or the Grosvenor, or Berkeley Street's New Colony. Similarly, the trio of clubs in Hamburg—the Indra, the Kaiserkeller, and the Top Ten club—where the Beatles honed their professional chops as a rock 'n' roll band were also not mentioned.

Along with a strong sense of class consciousness, teleology governed the guide's talk: every boyhood incident, every place name, every book read or record heard was clearly destined to form part of the overarching narrative that would take the group to unimaginable fame and fortune. The overall impression the guide's narrative generated was of four immensely talented young men who had been "fated" to meet. As with the London guide's narration, the "Liverpool" Beatles consistently made records of casual brilliance, of effortless genius. In contrast with every other artist, they endured no arduous apprenticeship; the fierce demands the Kaiserkeller and the Cavern placed on them did not help develop their collective talent; such clubs—at least in the whitewashed narrative of Liverpool's Magical Mystery Tour—simply provided showcases for their innate genius. The virtual absence of work, coupled with the immense rewards achieved without effort, as espoused by both the London and the Liverpool tour narratives, easily shifts the Beatles' story into the realm of fairy tale or myth.

The Magical Mystery Tour is clearly a trip for tourists rather than pilgrims. The tour's participants were unequivocally enthralled by the experience: "It's so nostalgic," said Pam Taylor, age thirty-eight, from Aberdare, "I grew up listening to the Beatles and it's great to be able to associate real places with their words." In many ways, the concept of the tourist seems inappropriate in this context. We are given no sense of spontaneous bonding or community on the Magical Mystery Tour, even when all of us were singing along to "Help!" as the minibus ambled along. In his celebrated critique of popular music, Adorno writes of the popular song, "the refrain still always preserves the memory of the collective power of music, while the narrative verses undertake the expression of the individual, who in truth remains separate from this collectivity; in this way, the hit song form tries to create totality" (qtd. in Paddison 27). While our friendly sing-along united us in the chorus, it returned us to our individual selves in the narrative verses: we always remained "separate" from the song's guise of "collectivity." *Communitas* was not to be experienced here. It was inconceivable that all of us on the tour bus shared the same understanding of the world. We were linked only spuriously, connected by a media-driven mythologizing and by an individual and private "nostalgia" that actually separated us from one another; we were twenty-eight individuals, twenty-eight tourists with twenty-eight personal responses to the Beatles, not a community of pilgrims who were connected by an objective, shared understanding of the Beatles. Interestingly, when the guide pointed out Penny Lane, I again consulted MacDonald, who writes that although the song is "seemingly naturalistic, the lyric scene is actually kaleidoscopic. As well as raining and shining at the same time, it is simultaneously summer and winter" (179). Again, we experience the rejection of time in the Beatles' narrative of nostalgia. For Lennon, the song "Penny Lane" "was just reliving childhood" (qtd. in MacDonald 177). I wondered if "reliving childhood," in one way or another, was all any of us were doing on that bus: reliving either our own literal childhoods, if we were old enough, or, if not, reliving vicariously an overly mythologized and symbolic childhood the simulacra of rock tours established.

Our lengthiest stop was at Strawberry Field, about which Albert Goldman, Lennon's notorious biographer, writes: "John's delight in his childhood haunt is suggested by the verbal slip that converted Strawberry Field to Strawberry Fields, with its strong suggestion of Elysian Fields" (255). As with Abbey Road Studios, where "Strawberry Fields Forever" was recorded in 1966, Strawberry Field has emerged as a pilgrimage site. Graffiti was everywhere, as were scraps of paper, presumably carrying poems and messages, that had been forced into crevices in the wall. Several small bunches of flowers were propped against the wall. Such graffiti and gifts were not left by members of tour groups such as our own; they were left by individuals or small groups who make their own way to Strawberry Field—pilgrims, not tourists. The question that I posed during my visit to Abbey Road seemed relevant once more: given that this is a place to which pilgrims come and "speak," what is Strawberry Field a pilgrimage to? I was reminded of Hanif Kureishi's prescient remark, "Lennon knew that the source of his art was the past" (15).

Browsing among the graffiti, I saw an expectedly large number of references to Lennon being "alive." I saw no comments of the subversive kind that I had seen at Logan Place, but I did notice one statement that performed a similar function if more conventionally: "No to war in Iraq." The assumption here was that the Beatles themselves, alive or dead, as well as other pilgrims to the site, would be in agreement with the sentiment. Conversely, it occurred to me that not everybody on the tour bus could be guaranteed to support this utterance. The phrase is indexical; in five words, it encapsulates a liberal worldview that takes a predictable stance on a variety of issues such as pollution, race, and sexuality. I remembered MacDonald's analysis of "Hey Jude," especially his reference to the song's inherent dualism in both its "personal revelation" and its "vast communality" (243). Reader suggests that a constant goal of the pilgrimage is to recapture the past by reacquainting ourselves with "what appears to have been lost to the present, and [by] reconstituting that past in an idealized and romanticized way" (Conclusion 230).

In this sense, the pilgrimage is inevitably a journey to an ethos. Strawberry Field, like Abbey Road, Logan Place, and Barnes Common, is a place in which the pilgrim's shared worldview is an a priori condition of being present. But it also began to occur to me that such sites have much more to offer the pilgrim. As MacDonald writes in his discussion of "Strawberry Fields Forever," the song is, "on the one hand, a study in uncertain identity, tinged with the loneliness of the solitary rebel against all things institutional; on the other, an eerie longing for a wild childhood of hide-and-seek and tree climbing: the visionary strawberry fields of [Lennon's] imagination" (172). In this manner, the sites of Beatles' pilgrimages are both political and personal. One of the most important differences between the tourist and the pilgrim may find its origins in the ways in which retrospection is oriented. MacDonald suggests that "Strawberry Fields" inaugurates the English pop-pastoral mood of the late 1960s and then shrewdly notes, "More significant, though, was the song's child-eye view—for the true subject of English psychedelia was neither love nor drugs, but nostalgia for the innocent vision of the child" (173). Perhaps Lennon's renaming of the site was not a "slip," as Goldman suggests, but a conscious attempt to transform the personal into the universal. Onboard the tour bus, we apprehend the past solely as a private, personal space, although perhaps the pilgrim's nostalgia, unlike that of the tourist, is not solely centered on the self; it may be as much about a universal innocence that we have all lost. The pilgrim's nostalgia is for Eden. Perhaps the Beatles' shiny Granny Smith apple functions as the pilgrim's time-eclipsing beacon?

Moore contends that *Sgt. Pepper* was the Beatles' self-conscious attempt to align themselves with the hippie movement and its "concomitant infatuation with Eastern religions" (*Beatles* 84). Although as with many others in the 1960s the Beatles were attracted to the exotic accoutrements of Eastern religion, they had little interest in religion, Eastern or Western. If one accepts that the opening reference to "mother Mary" in "Let It Be" is McCartney's autobiographical tribute to his mother, rather than a reference to the Virgin Mary, "Eleanor Rigby" emerges as the Beatles' most explicitly religious song, and not endorsing MacDonald's suggestion that the track is deeply pessimistic about the survival of a communal religiosity is difficult: "Eleanor Rigby dies alone because [she remains] unable to tell anyone how she felt," MacDonald writes. "MacKenzie's sermon won't be heard—not that he cares very much about his parishioners—because religious faith has perished along with communal spirit ('No one was saved')" (163). What the Beatles offered in place of a religious eschatology was an unprecedented emphasis on the reality of the here and now. As Kureishi writes, "Without conscience, duty, or concern for the future, the Beatles spoke of enjoyment, abandon, and attention to the needs of the self" (123). Doubly ironic, then, is that the Beatles should be viewed as simultaneously symbolic of the past and as quasi-religious figures themselves.

By contrasting the official Beatles' attractions against the unofficial sites, the suggestion emerges that although contemporary theorists are eroding the rigid demarcation between tourism and pilgrimage, Beatles fans, who can easily be classified as either tourists or pilgrims, maintain this distinction in practice: those on the tour bus in London and in Liverpool are tourists; for them, the vast majority, the Beatles are at the heart of what has been referred to as the "mass autobiography," in the words of Bryan Appleyard, that popular music has become (16). In addition, the Beatles tourist may well be attracted to the band's rags-to-riches metanarrative. As with Elvis, a humble truck driver from one of the United States' poorer states, the Beatles surmounted their modest origins to act out the alluring and decidedly materialist prospect, not of spiritual transcendence, but of class transcendence.

The Beatles pilgrim, however, is attracted to other political and spiritual possibilities represented by the band. For the pilgrim, the group symbolizes a period of infinite political possibilities: time is suspended during the act of pilgrimage and all things again seem possible as they did in the 1960s. The pilgrim may also revisit a self who is not only younger, but also better, an idealistic (possibly idealized) and perpetually undefeated self. Spiritually, the sense of community and of unity the pilgrimage site generates serves to negate, if only temporarily, the strong sense of alienation from modern society and its fragmented, individualistic ethos that large numbers of people, by no means all young, in the West experienced. These pilgrims venture to Strawberry Field or Abbey Road Studios to find, in Victor and Edith Turner's words, "a route to a liminal world where the ideal is felt to be real, where the tainted social persona is cleansed and revivified" (qtd. in Bowman 57). Eric Cohen deftly notes that pilgrimage centers "tend to be peripheral and remote, often located beyond a stretch of wilderness or some other uninhabited territory, as it were, in the 'chaos' surrounding the ordered 'cosmic zed' social world" (34). Not surprisingly, Rock Circus is situated in London's West End, the London tour departs from central London, and the Magical Mystery Tour leaves from Liverpool's city center. In each instance, geography and ideology coincide. The values celebrated in each venue are those Cohen describes as the "mundane sociopolitical centers of society" (34). Yet Strawberry Field, Barnes Common, and Abbey Road Studios also remain geographically remote, a considerable distance from their respective city centers, whereas Logan Place, although in central London, is in Earls Court, a long-established center for Australasians and for gay men, thus rendering it eccentric to societies' prevailing norms. Each site provides a sense of focus for a system of shared values and beliefs, and each is, paradoxically, both remote yet simultaneously the center of the world, not just in England, but also for the pilgrims who visit them. Perhaps we also glimpse the Beatles—or at least our highly personalized constructions of them—in these ostensibly shared spaces as well.

NOTES

1. For accounts of the relationships between medieval pilgrims and tourists, see Alan Kendall's *Medieval Pilgrims*; for evaluations of the history of tourism, see Gilbert Sigaux's *History of Tourism*, and John Towner's "The Grand Tour: A Key Phase in the History of Tourism." For theoretical considerations regarding the nature of pilgrimage, see Émile Durkheim's *Elementary Forms of Religious Thought* and Mircea Eliade's *Images and Symbols*.

2. For a comprehensive account of this phenomenon, see Allison Lockwood's *The Passionate Pilgrims: The American Traveler in Great Britain, 1800–1814*.

3. For additional discussion regarding Lennon and Epstein's relationship, see Christopher Münch's film, *The Hours and Times* (1991), which offers a fictive reading of a Spanish vacation that they shared in 1963 prior to the global onset of Beatlemania.

4. As Clive Davis writes in the July 13, 1997, *Sunday Times*, "Each year, 700,000 people visit Graceland, Presley's Memphis mansion, which is now on the National Register of Historic Places" (9).

5. Both Lennon and Harrison were cremated. According to Albert Goldman, Lennon's ashes remain in Ono's possession at the Dakota apartment building in New York City (690–91). Allegedly, portions of his ashes are embedded in the Strawberry Fields memorial in Central Park. Harrison's family spread his ashes over India's holy Ganges River in December 2001. Portions of his ashes were also dispersed in Portio Allahabad and Brindavan, holy provinces in the northern Indian state of Uttar Pradesh.

CHAPTER 11

"Baby You're a Rich Man"

The Beatles, Ideology, and the Cultural Moment

JAMES M. DECKER

> Us, Communists? Why, we can't be Communists. We're the
> world's number-one capitalists. Imagine us Communists!
> —Paul McCartney, August 23, 1966
> (qtd. in Giuliano, *The Lost Beatles Interviews* 79)

I N 1991, THE BEATLES' reputation for cool ebbed low. Indeed, when
MTV's hippest VJ, Downtown Julie Brown, told an astonished Katie
Couric that she could not even name all four Beatles, the group's status as
a Paleozoic relic seemed all but confirmed. After all, Brown—at age thirty, a
mere four years younger than Couric—most probably feigned her ignorance
of the most influential rock band in history. Nine years old when the group's
well-publicized split occurred, Brown would hardly have been able to avoid
media coverage of the aftermath, would certainly have heard the solo efforts
of Paul McCartney and John Lennon on the radio, and would probably even
have been aware of George Harrison and Ringo Starr's output as well. Even
if one grants Brown a preternatural ability to ignore some of the most popular music of her teenage years, not to mention the spectacle of Lennon's assassination, her story still fails to ring true. After she joined MTV in 1986,

Brown was obliged to play "high rotation" videos, including those of McCartney and Harrison. Furthermore, as a professional in the music business, avoiding the media onslaught attending the release of the Beatles' catalog on compact disc would have been a feat worthy of an O. J. Simpson juror. More likely, Brown, hired by MTV executives who worried that the original VJs lacked youth appeal, sought to maintain her faux adolescent credibility by disavowing any knowledge of the Fab Four. Based on Brown's sheepish smile and shrugged shoulders, it appeared that for the younger-than-twenty set, the Beatles possessed all the cool of a Dodge Dart. The sluggish chart performance of the Beatles' 1980's releases only foreshadowed Brown's public dismissal of the band in 1991.[1]

In 2001, however, the Beatles' hip quotient reached the stratosphere once more. Literally number one in nineteen countries, the Beatles' latest greatest hits compilation, *1*, unseated the Backstreet Boys from the top spot on *Billboard*'s pop chart in December 2000. By the end of 2001, consumers in the United States alone had purchased more than eight million units, bolstering a sagging record industry and—much to Shaggy's chagrin—anointing *1* as the bestselling album of the year. Although a solid percentage of those buying *1* knew of the Beatles long before 2001, a surprising number of listeners had not even been alive when 1982's *Twenty Greatest Hits* album first reached the shelves. In an intriguing study, *Brandweek* determined that fully half of those who searched the Internet for information on the "newest" pop stars in the galaxy logged in younger than eighteen years of age, contradicting the belief that the CD's success owed more to baby boomers waxing nostalgic than to any fresh audience ("I Queried Paul" 22). Four decades after the Beatles rocked Hamburg, "She Loves You" and "Let It Be" wafted across campus quadrangles, and high-school-aged teens wore their "official" Beatles caps backward in detention hall. In addition to wowing listeners young enough to be their grandchildren, the Beatles reached the pinnacle of popular literary success when their "autobiography," *The Beatles Anthology*, debuted at number one on the *New York Times* bestseller list. The Internet and microwave popcorn might have confused a 1960's Rip Van Winkle, but he would have at least recognized the songs playing in the background. "I'll Be Back," indeed. The Beatles were certifiably hot (and multiplatinum!), and Rose Cooper dismissed Downtown Julie Brown, languishing on the E! network, as "the old school MTV jock most in need of a duct-tape-to-mouth operation" ("Bam's").

Given the Beatles' apparent metamorphosis from the arbiters of taste for a generation to a group more suited for the mildewed archives of VH1 than to MTV's multipierced audience, how can one explain the band's phoenix-like rise in the mid-1990s, an ascent culminating in 1, their very first year-end chart topper? How could what is essentially a repackaged oldies collection connect with an entirely new generation without a hint of irony—à la the Tony Bennett renaissance of the early 1990s—or retro chic, as with the resurgence of bell-bottoms? Paul McCartney, as the de facto keeper of the Beatles' legacy, has suggested, to paraphrase *Hamlet*, the music's the thing. Despite his pre-Renaissance comment (February 1990) that "in the main we released all our best material, so now you know, it's like memorabilia" (qtd. in Giuliano, *The Lost Beatles Interviews* 181), McCartney's current tack is to package every phase of the Beatles' development to provide a complete historical assessment. In essence, his line of reasoning holds that the Beatles' aesthetic quality transcends the traditional boundaries of age. "From Me to You" and "Yellow Submarine" are just that good, and any kid with $18.98 plus tax will recognize it. The music sells itself. Many critics agree with Sir Paul's assessment, and one might be tempted to declare with Rob Sheffield, "these boys kick ass" (28).[2] They certainly do, but is that enough? Three quarters of my U.S. literature class had never even heard of the Who, another band that indisputably "rocks out," but all of them knew the Beatles, and many of them commented that writing an essay on the Beatles would be positively cool. As the Beatles' failed *Twenty Greatest Hits* album proved, however, music alone cannot resurrect "cool."

John B. Thompson's concept of valorization provides a sharp corrective to McCartney and Sheffield's faith in musical integrity and timeless harmonies. In *Ideology and Modern Culture* (1990), Thompson defines cultural phenomena as "symbolic forms in structured contexts" (123). The success or failure of such forms depends largely on interpretations grounded in a set of ideologies stemming from the nexus between production, transmission, and consumption. For Thompson, the "mediazation of modern culture" (124) has resulted in "processes of valorization . . . by which and through which they [cultural phenomena] are ascribed certain kinds of value" (146). Thompson further distinguishes between symbolic value, which refers to the veneration either the producer or the consumer places on the object, and economic value, which refers to the object's status as commodity (154–55). Both types of valuation inevitably lead to tension and dispute. Observers might attribute a high degree of symbolic value, for example, to a band such as the Velvet Underground, which earned negligible economic value, whereas the same individuals might claim an economically valuable group such as 'N Sync to have slight long-term symbolic importance. Thompson labels attempts to adjust the polarity of symbolic and economic values "cross-valorization" (157). By exploiting one's symbolic value, one might increase one's economic value and vice versa. For Thompson, such cross-valorization lies at the heart of ideology, which he tentatively defines as "meaning in the service of power" (7).

Thompson's principle of cross-valorization speaks well to the Beatles' efforts to capitalize on the cultural moment and parlay their symbolic valuation into fiscal dominance. Although Antony Easthope refers to textuality as a "secondary effect" of ideology, in the mid-1990s, McCartney became obsessed with the idea of protecting the Beatles' textual legacy (129). Spearheading a massive revision of Beatles history that would include *Live at the BBC*, the three *Anthology* CDs (and videos), *1*, and *The Beatles Anthology* (documentary), McCartney actively sought to correct the "misperceptions" spawned by the more than 400 books and countless articles concerning the group. This project, McCartney maintained, would yield the "true" story of the Beatles, their music, and their rise to fame: "In looking at *Anthology*, I saw the standards the Beatles had reached" (qtd. in Duffy 1). Ostensibly motivated by a concern for symbolic value (the conspicuously redundant position that the Beatles really changed the course of music and social history), McCartney's strategies ultimately reveal a more pecuniary agenda, a point that failed to escape Harrison, who cynically commented, "It just happens, every time Paul needs some publicity he announces to the press that we're getting back together again" (qtd. in Giuliano, *The Lost Beatles Interviews* 187).[3] As Thompson notes, such cross-valorization is intricately linked with methods and moments of transmission (169). Arguably, had McCartney undertaken his scheme a mere five years earlier, he would have failed miserably. In launching his project in the mid-1990s, however, he virtually ensured its success.

In 1991 McCartney's most lucrative venue, the United States,[4] vanquished Saddam Hussein and became mired in an economic recession. Reaganite economic and social policies had been in place for nearly eleven years, and thousands of homeless poignantly reminded the nation that love is not all you need. In such a context, the Beatles' overt message of peace and love seemed positively naïve. The 1992 presidential election of Bill Clinton, however, marked an ideological shift that established a cultural milieu conducive to the Beatles' brand of philosophy. Nearly fifty, Clinton could hardly be confused with a Teddy Boy (hooligan), but the media universally fawned over his "youthful" character. Juxtaposed with the World War II generation, Clinton exuded a youthful aura, playing saxophone on *The Arsenio Hall Show* and discussing his undergarments on MTV. The baby boomers—weaned on the Beatles—had unequivocally achieved ultimate power. As the boomers "grayed," they had achieved a political and economic power that was starting to bear fruit, although their legacy hardly corresponded to the idealism present in their adolescent rhetoric. As the largest U.S. generation ever, the boomers could look forward to an unprecedented political hegemony. Mirroring this political cache was an insistence that the social productions of the 1960s dwarfed those of subsequent generations. By controlling what Thompson calls the "channels of selective diffusion"—the network of institutions through which a symbolic form must pass to be cross-valorized—the 1960s generation could generate renewed interest in the cultural productions of the past and make them appear both aesthetically transcendent and ideologically relevant (166). As Nick Gillespie writes in "The Long and Whining Road," the boomers' "supposed generational exceptionalism" constitutes "an attempt by aging boomers to colonize the youth of their children (and grandchildren!), to make all who come after them replicate the boomers' own sensibilities, tastes, and experiences." The advent of popular Internet service providers, MP3 technology, and the refinement of "hype," coupled with a vibrant economy, made such replication nearly pro forma, and McCartney, a sort of Ur-boomer himself, answered the call.

Like Borges's Pierre Menard, who sought to write *Don Quixote* verbatim, although in a new cultural context, McCartney attempted to create the simulacra of Beatlemania. By accentuating the band's textual corpus, McCartney established the illusion that the Beatles had yielded their position as subject and were now in a position to reminisce over their considerable output. After all, Lennon's death seemingly precluded a Beatles' reunion and ensured that the band would not transform into an oldies act, shamelessly parodying its once vital message at corn fests and county fairs. Lennon, as quoted by Yoko Ono, averred "the world would be so disappointed to see four rusty old men" ("Big Decision"). Thus, by avoiding both the countless "final tours" of contemporaries such as the Rolling Stones and the Who and the sentimental flaccidity of the Beach Boys' post-1960's work, the Beatles preserved a sense of musical integrity. In addition, the fallout from the labyrinthine litigation surrounding Apple Corps ensured that the Beatles controlled most of their own recordings, a phenomenon that forestalled them from being packaged in Ronco's *Super Sounds of the Sixties* along with the Archies and Peaches and Herb.[5] Nevertheless, whereas such reification held benefits for maintaining—indeed, for increasing—the symbolic valuation of the Beatles' canon, it could not function viably for augmenting the economic valuation. If the remaining Beatles had learned one lesson from their experiences with Brian Epstein, Dick James, EMI, and Capitol, it was that transferring one's subjectivity hurt one's bottom line. They no doubt recalled the question Stephen Maltz, one of the Beatles' more ethical accountants, asked of them: "After six years' work . . . what have you got to show for it? . . . Your personal finances are a mess. Apple is a mess" (qtd. in Brown and Gaines 329). For this crucial secondary (tertiary?) moment of production and reception to deliver tremendous profits, the Beatles would have to behave like Apple executives rather than inspired artists. Hordes of screaming teenagers no longer awaited the Beatles, but the largest economic expansion in U.S. history ensured them that adolescents with formidable disposable incomes mobbed the record stores eight days a week.

McCartney's primary economic weapon, of course, consisted of the Beatles' considerable oeuvre, including unreleased tracks that even the boomers did not have in their massive album, eight-track, cassette, and CD collections. Bootleg records existed, of course, but McCartney and the remaining Beatles would consistently remark that the production value of these songs failed to measure up to Beatles' standards. Tapping into the Boomers' seemingly unquenchable desire for more Beatles' material, the band released *Live at the BBC* (1994), whose crude recordings gave off a mock bootleg aura. The media attention coinciding with the CD's release seemed shockingly disproportionate with the quality of the songs. Finally, the media intimated, we have the Beatles singing "Clarabella" and "Soldier of Love"! *Live at the BBC* certainly failed to target a new audience of Beatles fans and sold only tolerably according to the group's high standard. Nevertheless, McCartney's decision led to a reassessment of the symbolic value of the Beatles' classic recordings. The CD provided a baseline against which to judge the Beatles' tremendous aesthetic progression from frenetic cover band to profound innovator. The CD also introduced the pattern of calculated commodification that would surround the Beatles' quest to set the record straight, for neatly tucked inside the CD, along with an informative forty-six-page booklet, was an order form for "Official Beatles Merchandise." The Beatles sleuths who discovered a telephone number on the cover of *Magical Mystery Tour* could find another number in *Live at the BBC*, only this time it did not belong to the Walrus. Taking advantage of the "revolution" in credit card purchases, Apple executives importuned fans to call 1–800–GO-BEATLES, where they could immediately gratify their desire for "commemorative offset lithographs," "authentic USA bomber jackets," and duffle bags, among other items, all emblazoned with the "official" Beatles logo. The Beatles, who initially made a poor marketing deal, would not be fools, at least not a second time.

With the groundwork in place, the Beatles could now belatedly attempt to introduce themselves to a new generation via television. Billed as a Beatles reunion of sorts, the *Anthology* project purported to tell the Beatles' story "in their own words." Interestingly, Apple charged ABC Television a reported $20 million for the rights to the "documentary." Aiding the project was a $30-million advertising blitz, which featured incessant spots on MTV and VH1, including a tagline on the former network that encouraged teens to "see what messed up your parents" (Chen). In addition, large supplies of Beatles' buttons, bumper stickers, and other miscellany were distributed free across the United States where Beatles' kiosks had invaded the local mall (Chen). Of course, the first *Anthology* CD, T-shirts, and other "official" merchandise were discretely available for purchase as well. "The Beatles for Sale?" Certainly. Of course, the whole project really concerned the Beatles' desire to share their tale with the world, to reinforce their spot in music history. The first installment of the three-part show garnered the best ratings, as did the first *Anthology* double CD, which included an order form for "Apple Organic" products, such as the $40 "hemp mini-backpack," which was manufactured with cotton "grown on land without the use of pesticides, herbicides, fungicides, fertilizers, and defoliants, and made with the environment in mind." The remaining Beatles themselves might have purchased the "hemp wallet" for $17.50. Predictably, Apple press officer Derek Taylor denied the band's financial motivation, arguing that the "new" music's symbolic value was "like Winston Churchill's papers" (qtd. in Chen).

Nevertheless, the television shows and the CDs quite obviously demonstrate cross-valorization at its fever-pitched best. Spanning the Beatles' career from the earliest days until their disbandment, they provide a testament to the group's creative genius. Based on extensive interviews with the three surviving Beatles, as well as vintage footage of Lennon, the documentary sought to give the final word on the band. Like Bill Clinton's much-maligned gathering of presidential historians, the Beatles' *Anthology* attempted to place boundaries around the reception of the group's oeuvre and historical contributions. Although the CDs sold well, the group clearly could not foment more than a slight interest from the youth market. Although adolescents certainly bought the hype concerning the Beatles' status as Best Band Ever, ditties such as "My Bonnie" and "Besame Mucho" hardly qualified as cool, and the "new" Beatles songs jerry-rigged from decades-old Lennon recordings failed to pass contemporary muster, although they did foster the illusion of the assassinated Beatle's stamp of approval. As McCartney disingenuously observes, "somehow we did [bring Lennon back]—he was in the studio" (qtd. in Burns 186).[6] However, despite the tepid youth reaction to *Anthology*, McCartney's plan was multistaged, and it was beginning to succeed, as the rerelease of *Yellow Submarine* and its concomitant product tie-ins—including children's toys—demonstrated.

Although McCartney had predicated his reevaluation of the Beatles' heritage on musical integrity in general and on aesthetic vision in particular, his efforts at cross-valorization ultimately compelled him to contradict such noble rhetoric. Although the Beatles—in the form of Robert Whitaker's grotesque "butcher boy" cover—famously lodged a protest over Capitol Records' policy of withholding songs from the EMI releases to create more "product" for the North American market, they were not above becoming their own butcher boys with regard to increasing their economic value.[7] In 1982, for example, the Beatles released *Twenty Greatest Hits*. Despite the wave of nostalgia in the wake of Lennon's death, in Beatles' terms, the record flopped, stalling at number fifty on the charts and failing to reach the gold record plateau until 1984. The album inched up to the platinum and multiplatinum marks by 1991 and 1997 respectively ("Beatles"). Remarkably, *Twenty Greatest Hits* contains a playlist virtually identical to the megaplatinum *1* released in late 2000, lacking only "From Me to You," "Day Tripper," "Yellow Submarine," "Eleanor Rigby," "Lady Madonna," "The Ballad of John and Yoko," and "Something." Why release *1* when a virtually identical compilation already existed and the so-called *Red* and *Blue* albums (*The Beatles, 1962–1966* and *The Beatles, 1967–1970*, respectively) still sold well? Despite arguing for the artistic integration of the Beatles' recordings, McCartney, Harrison, Starr, and Ono did not choose to release remastered versions of their original studio albums.[8] Instead, they opted on a gimmick designed to lure the youth market and produced what Jerry McCulley refers to as a "trophy case of commercial success"

("Essential Recording"). Having established the Beatles as the Best Band Ever in the minds of many North American adolescents, the Beatles could now deliver a monument to that greatness and parlay their symbolic value into economic power. Although cynics might question the compilation's title, with its reference to economic (rather than symbolic) prowess, how could one deny the eminence of a group that had an incredible twenty-seven number-one hits? That the compilation lacked even a single contribution from *Rubber Soul*, *Sgt. Pepper's Lonely Hearts Club Band*, and the *White Album*, and side two of *Abbey Road* apparently did not matter. That songs were wrenched from context, resulting in ridiculous juxtapositions such as "Yellow Submarine" and "Eleanor Rigby," appeared not to faze Sir Paul's sense of history. Perhaps a sequel, 2, could satisfy the critics. Assisted by a media whose leaders had come of age with the Beatles, the group conquered the youth market, albeit temporarily. Story after story told young consumers just how good the Beatles were and lamented the paucity of contemporary talent. How could J Lo compete in such an environment? The Beatles' symbolic value, in other words, was never higher, and their economic value received an "unexpected" boost, too.

Perhaps the most conspicuous attempt at cross-valorization, however, was the release of the *Anthology* book. Obscenely priced at $60, the folio-sized text suggests not Lennon's "All You Need Is Love," but the Bradford-Gordy composition, "Money (That's What I Want)."[9] An expanded, deluxe version of the interviews from which the *Anthology* documentary was produced, the book's packaging is quasi-biblical in nature. An aesthetically impressive book encased in shrink-wrap, Anthology's only jacket blurb solemnly announces, "The Beatles' story told for the first time IN THEIR OWN words and pictures." Once one deigns to burst the shrink-wrap and quietly enter the grotto, one learns that "many books have been written about the Beatles, but this is their own permanent record of events up until 1970." Although the cover declares that the book is "by the Beatles," the editorial note reveals that far from collating the hundreds of interviews or dirtying their hands with the text, the group allowed a team of Apple editors to assemble the narrative. An immediate number-one bestseller, the book gives an oddly placid account of the Beatles' career, and even the disagreements take on a nostalgic, even passionless, air. Interestingly, the predominant theme is financial, rather than musical, in nature. Indeed, at many points in the text, the music seems practically tangential, and the anecdotes reveal a near obsession with sales figures, contracts, and royalties.[10] The vitriol evident in the immediate post-Beatles' era is lacking, however. Given that the majority of the McCartney, Harrison, and Starr contributions date from the mid-1990s, when their net worths were measured in the hundreds of millions, it is easy to detect why only Lennon's interviews depict any tension at all. Harrison, for example, conveniently masks his pain regarding the Apple litigation by referring to the company's executives as "dopey accountants" (*Anthology* 339), a statement quite in contrast to his earlier characterization of the same events as "a horror story, a nightmare" (qtd in Giuliano 149). Similarly, regarding inquiries about whether he were "a millionaire yet," Paul wistfully remembers that "it was actually very difficult getting anything out of those people and the accountants never made you feel successful" (*Anthology* 337). The loquacious style, coupled with a subtle revisionism, reflects the calm of a group that has nothing to prove, has come to terms with its prior legal wrangling, and is intent on "sharing" its symbolic value with a turn-of-the-century audience.

Although Gary Burns suggests that the entire *Anthology* project "represents the ultimate domestication and feminization of the Beatles," one might also claim that cross-valorization functioned even at the height of the Beatles' supposed critique of the capitalist ethos (185). One need only recall Lennon, who earlier in 1967 had purchased an £11,000 Rolls Royce (Giuliano 97), remarking that money "wasn't all that good" (qtd. in Badman 322), yet desiring in 1968 to "build a wall to protect us from all the beggars and lepers in Britain" (349). The disconnect between the anticapitalist-militarist rhetoric (evident both in songs such as "Piggies" and in some interviews) and the conspicuous consumption and search for tax shelters (such as the "Beatles boutique") reflects the pervasiveness of the dominant ideology even within institutional apparatuses ostensibly designed to question those beliefs. Within its original context(s), the Beatles' music thus, paradoxically, functions both as a "radical" indictment of the power elite (including record industry executives) and as a sanitized reinforcement of the very ideals that group represented. The Beatles' late-1960s quest to use their songs as a bully pulpit is predicated on both the group's relative financial security and on the tacit approval of the record industry (and other allied industries), which profited from the "challenges" to their social authority. Crudely put, because adolescent rebellion was fashionable, naturally the music industry would allow its most visible artists to explore such profitable terrain. In fact, Burns astutely observes that the Beatles' "political" songs "sounded unequivocally radical, but were actually ambiguous in their sentiments" (177). No practical social alternatives stood behind the calls for change. In essence, the Beatles were domesticated from the moment Epstein—in Lennon's words—"literally fuckin' cleaned [them] up!" (qtd. in Badman 38). Epstein knew, of course, that the hopped-up, dirty, edgy young men were tremendously talented, but he also recognized that they, and not their later incarnations, represented the "real" threat to the social order. As the market changed, so did the Beatles. Although the Beatles of the late 1960s had more control over their images, they could never alter the underlying institution that had "created" them, a phenomenon clearly exemplified in the failure of Apple Corps and its vision of art for art's sake.

Economically, then, the Beatles' catalogue always coexisted uneasily with the symbolic or aesthetic value inherent in the songs. In particular, their output from *Rubber Soul* onward explored a musical realm that no previous artist had. Such experimentation, however, was tolerated for no other reason than the Beatles' early efforts were such a success and earned them more creative control from the studio than they had when promoters handed a dollar and a T-shirt to everyone willing to meet the Beatles at New York's Kennedy Airport in 1964 (Marshall 166). When asked of their thoughts on their early songs, John remarked, "I can't stand listening to most of our early stuff" (qtd. in Badman 247), while Paul curtly replied, "I hate it" (266). Most music critics agree that the Beatles' legacy rests in their later work because whereas the early releases strained at the boundaries of the love song formula, they nonetheless do not transcend it. The lasting symbolic value—that which also offers enduring economic value—rests squarely with their later recordings. The conditions from which the Beatles' astonishing musical growth stemmed, of course, are precisely those unavailable to less successful groups. Although the Beatles depict themselves as harried and beleaguered, once they quit touring (an unheard of maneuver for a commercially successful group regardless how talented) they enjoyed the luxury of self-reflection paralleled by few recording artists. Precisely during this period, their songs took on a more reflective, radical bent. At this juncture, long-term cross-valorization, as opposed to the fleeting cross-valorization open to most groups, became possible.

The turmoil following the group's disbandment, however, coupled with shifts in political outlook, prevented this cross-valorization from realizing itself fully from the economic standpoint until the mid-1990s. Lennon's death in particular devastated the group's core following and problematized any overt marketing campaign on the part of the surviving Beatles, and the legal problems associated with Apple Corps rendered large-scale cooperation among the parties moot. Whereas the Beatles' corpus, however startling in its aesthetic innovation, remained essentially static, its symbolic import could not attract new listeners on a scale comparable to that achieved by artists of considerably less long-term symbolic value (for example, M. C. Hammer, Paula Abdul). Were the "music itself" able to enrapture audiences and transcend generational boundaries, certainly Capitol and EMI would have pressed top forty—rather than classic rock—stations to play the Beatles incessantly, thereby eliminating some of the expense needed to produce new talent. Obviously, a belief in the music itself reveals an exaggerated, sentimental notion of symbolic value within the arena of popular culture. One thinks, for instance, of an early 1960's cartoon that depicts two teens commenting disparagingly of another's age because she "remembers the Beatles." The cartoon's message speaks to the core of the pop-culture ideology: change and ostensible difference, especially from the tastes of older generations. The music of Frank Sinatra and Billie Holiday, of Bob Dylan and John Coltrane, is unquestionably innovative, influential, and "powerful," yet it cannot, of itself, replicate its previous economic success. Such a renaissance could only arise from a vigorous effort that manipulated the available outlets for cultural transmission and created conditions ripe for duplicating the consumable symbolic value (as opposed to the historical symbolic value academics and critics advance) that results in a burst of economic profit. As Chris Stephenson, a major advertising executive, argues about the Beatles' millennial success, "It was a great exercise in music marketing—what a great way of leveraging your catalog" (qtd. in Friedman 1). Quite consciously, Apple managing director Neil Aspinall produced a marketing plan "aimed at young teens and kids who, while familiar with the Beatles, had never bought a release" (qtd. in Friedman 1). Of course, such a strategy is dependent on the possession of a genuinely vibrant commodity that subtly reflects aesthetic qualities present in the current popular mode. The Beatles' widely acknowledged influence on virtually every sphere of popular music readily supplies both conditions in a way that a campaign to valorize Herman's Hermits would not.

Ultimately, the Beatles' successes in 2000 and 2001 arose not from the power of the music itself, but from a well-crafted, timely strategy of cross-valorization. Contrary to Kit R. Roane's assertion that "the simple answer [to the Beatles' popularity] lies in the music" (43), one must hold with Ira Robbins that "this is essentially a marketing moment" (qtd. in Grace 50). By seizing on the tremendous economic prosperity of the Clinton-era United States, the Beatles carefully manipulated their symbolic valuation to augment the economic value of their canon, particularly in terms of the youth market. Their keen awareness of the cultural moment suggests that their combined efforts to guide and shape their historical reception were both symbolically redundant and economically fruitful. While in "speaking out," the surviving Beatles alleged a concern for protecting their legacy and annotating their achievements; even the most cursory examination suggests that disputes over their symbolic value were negligible and that most observers of popular culture ranked them as the undisputed champions of rock 'n' roll from the view of both aesthetic experimentalism and listenability. Indeed, one might conceivably interpret their actions as betraying a cynical indifference to their musical integrity and as constituting a calculated business plan quite in opposition to the love they made. One can only imagine what McCartney will try after he's sixty-four.

NOTES

1. When I delivered a version of this piece at the Popular Culture Association's (PCA) annual meeting in March 2002, an audience member astutely suggested that the nostalgic kitsch of Broadway's *Beatlemania* heavily contributed to the band's diminished authenticity, particularly among teens.

2. The music-is-supreme argument was also offered by a PCA audience member who was visibly offended at any mention of the Beatles using marketing to build a new audience. Such loyalty, however, cannot speak to the failure of the Beatles' 1980's releases, and it refuses to face the Beatles' long history of market manipulation. Michael Bryan Kelly, for instance, reminds us that "when [the Beatles'] first British single failed to make the charts in 1962 . . . Brian [Epstein] bought 10,000 copies himself with his own money, simply to get them on the charts" (125). The young McCartney avidly studied Epstein's techniques and was tremendously interested in the band's image as well as its music. Indeed, as early as 1964, Paul reprimanded Lennon for not polishing his comments to the media, declaring "You're bad for my image" (qtd. in Badman 130).

3. Perhaps not coincidentally, McCartney's renewed interest in the Beatles' legacy paralleled his own demise as a major solo artist. Although his solo CDs inevitably went platinum, they no longer represented the pop juggernaut of his earlier efforts. His core audience comprised grandparents, not the younger-than-twenty demographic industry marketers apotheosized.

4. In the televised *Beatles Anthology* documentary, McCartney refers to the United States as the "biggest showbiz town ever."

5. Nike's infamous "Revolution" commercial, brought about by Michael Jackson's purchase of part of the Beatles' catalogue, infuriated surviving band members, who resisted the image of corporate "shill."

6. Technology thus aided a pseudoreunion that avoided the oft-mentioned "solution" of enlisting Julian Lennon as a surrogate for his father. The illusion helped create the aura that Lennon would have approved of the undertaking and that a new spirit of camaraderie and artistic collaboration had replaced the "former" bitterness between John and Paul. As Gary Burns asserts, the Beatles' "quasi-religious" (176) "story would not be complete without a reunion or without Lennon's resurrection by one means or another" (178).

7. See Kenneth Womack's "Editing the Beatles" for additional discussion of the ways in which Capitol Records reassembled the band's pre-1967 releases to increase U.S. consumption.

8. Rereleases of newly mastered Beatles' CDs will almost certainly reach the market within a few years, however.

9. The more "modestly" priced paperback retailed at $35.

10. An examination of the Beatles' interviews indicates a fascination with sales figures from the start of their career. Even if one accounts for the Beatles' flippant attitude toward the legions of reporters who questioned them, the focus on money is remarkable.

11. Wolfe and Haefner speculate that the Beatles' popularity (specifically that of the song "All You Need Is Love") might be explained because the current college-aged

generation may be seen as "the counterpart of an older social group which first propelled the song to its initial popularity" (136). Although the song is indeed still popular, Wolfe and Haefner's suggestion seems problematic because it bases its assumption
entirely on age and neglects other variables, such as the influence of 1960s-generation
program directors or the change in political climate. One must remember that the initial "social group" rejected the popular culture of its forebears and that the second group
represents a distinct minority—most of the students in the latter group were not listening to the Beatles in 1992.

CHAPTER 12

Spinning the Historical Record

Lennon, McCartney, and Museum Politics

JOHN KIMSEY

"**A**HHH," READS THE TEASER, "it seems like old times—Paul McCartney and Yoko Ono feuding again" (McMullen). It is mid-December 2002, and news leads such as this appear frequently in the popular media, as reporters document McCartney's decision to reverse the traditional Lennon-McCartney credit line on the nineteen Beatles songs included in his recent live-in-concert recording, *Back in the U.S.* In the track listings for the release, "Yesterday," "Hey Jude," "We Can Work It Out," and sixteen other songs from the Beatles catalog are credited to "Paul McCartney and John Lennon," a reversal that has Yoko Ono contemplating legal action and that McCartney spokesman Geoff Baker attributes to McCartney's concern about his "place in history." Ono's spokesman Elliot Mintz has labeled McCartney's decision a misguided "act of Beatle[s] revisionism" and "an attempt to rewrite history" ("Paul").[1]

This move by McCartney can be read as merely the latest in a series of actions undertaken by various parties, all of whom are engaged in a struggle over the meaning of, and the power to frame, the Beatles' historical legacy. Whereas McCartney has recently busied himself with an array of projects that seem designed both to reaffirm his iconic status and to reframe his work as that of a high *artiste*, numerous end-of-the-century retrospectives have marked the huge impact of the Beatles on postwar Western culture. Moreover, several such retrospectives have celebrated Lennon as the Beatles' heart and soul, as well as a culture hero who ventured beyond megastardom into uncharted (for celebrity culture) realms of self-examination, social enlightenment, and political engagement. This view of Lennon as culture hero is crystallized in the recent exhibition, *Lennon: His Life and Work*, mounted by the Rock and Roll Hall of Fame and Museum. This powerful, multilayered exhibition can be seen as working to confirm Lennon's status as icon and martyr while rewriting the conventional narrative that depicts Lennon's Beatles work as the finest of his career. Most pointedly, the exhibit frames McCartney not as Lennon's greatest collaborator/rival, but as a relatively marginal figure.

In the pages that follow, I trace some current outlines of this struggle by examining recent statements from McCartney and by providing a close, critical reading of *Lennon: His Life and Work*. I suggest that the concerns, noted herein, about "history"—McCartney's insistence about his "place," Mintz's disparagement of "revisionism"—represent more than rhetorical gestures. As we move into the twenty-first century, Western culture of the mid- to late 1900s recedes from immediate consciousness to become the object of memory. At the public level, that memory takes the form not only of popular nostalgia or media spectacle, but also "official" history—a shift signaled by the entry into the process of figures such as museum curators and, yes, academic scholars. These figures can be seen as culture brokers working at the level of institutions—museums, universities—generally thought to be removed from the commercial/pop cultural fray. Such institutions have the clout to powerfully influence, if not control, what is included and excluded from the historical record. Given this, the concerns McCartney and Mintz registered are apt. For anyone interested not just in the Beatles, but in the history and politics of culture itself, the stakes in this struggle are real and rising.

THE GUY WHO CAME FIRST

"So," Paul McCartney told radio host Terri Gross in an April 2001 interview, "you've hit on a sore point of mine there." The sore point in question was McCartney's sense that songs in the Lennon-McCartney catalog should be "better credited," a remark indicating that the youthful agreement John Lennon and he made (that is, that they both be credited as authors of songs written by either one of them and that the credit line should read "words and music by John Lennon and Paul McCartney") has become for McCartney problematic. As illustrations, McCartney pointed to his song "Blackbird," which has been anthologized as the work of Lennon and McCartney, an erroneous listing because "John hadn't anything to do with that," and "Give Peace a Chance," which credits McCartney as cowriter despite the song's being strictly "John's stuff." Citing "Yesterday" as another composition in which Lennon had no hand, McCartney went on to recount his request (ultimately vetoed by the other living Beatles) that, in the recent *Anthology* release, he be allowed to place his own name "in front of John's" in the credit line for the song. As a rationale for such actions, McCartney noted "the way that computers often knock off the ends of sentences" and speculated that "with the computer generation coming in and data being stored . . . there probably is a scenario in the future where someone will think that 'Hey Jude,' 'Let It Be,' 'The Long and Winding Road' . . . were written by the guy who came first." To underscore the point, McCartney related an encounter with an Italian pianist's fake book that credited "Hey Jude" to John Lennon "just because his name came first."

Coming from Sir Paul McCartney (to whom Larry King, in a contemporaneous interview said, "There's no one who doesn't know you"), such statements sound both petty and bizarre. However, their insistent tone and melodramatic hypotheses can be read as signs of deep anxiety on McCartney's part concerning his "place" in relation to both Lennon and history. Although expressed with vehemence in 2001, this anxiety was first voiced in May 1981, less than six months after Lennon's murder. In a conversation with Beatles biographer Hunter Davies, McCartney complained that, since John's death, Paul's former partner (a great "debunker") had become "Martin Luther Lennon" (qtd. in Davies 370). In recounting this exchange, Davies recalls McCartney's "strange" affect, attributing this "upset" tone to the fact that Lennon's death had produced a "cult," such that "many people, in praising John, were at the same time putting down Paul" (368). In the same conversation, McCartney complained about erroneous songwriting attributions and claimed that, although he initially "idolized John," they "grew to be equals" as his own writing developed (qtd. in Davies 371). But, with Lennon having become "some sort of holy saint," this truth was most likely to be forgotten: "People are printing *facts* about me and John. They're *not* facts. This will go down in the records. It will become part of history. It will be there for always. People will believe it all" (qtd. in Davies 372).

In the late 1990s, McCartney returned to such concerns, cooperating closely with biographer Barry Miles on *Paul McCartney: Many Years from Now* (1997), a book that sets out to correct popular "bias" (ix) and to redress what its author sees as an imbalance in the historical record: "From 1968 onwards . . . John and Yoko did as many as ten interviews a day," whereas "the other Beatles rarely spoke to the press at all." Through this great quantity of interviews Lennon "has already covered much of the contentious ground," and, in effect, assumed first place once again. Thus, the biography will attempt "to sort out . . . attributions, dispel . . . inaccuracies," and provide a "close-focus portrait of Paul" and his heretofore unpublicized involvement with the avant-garde arts community of 1960s London. Miles goes on to suggest that this task is burdensome because since his murder Lennon "has become St. John" and "any attempt at an objective assessment" of his role in the Beatles "inevitably becomes iconoclastic" (x).

Regarding the notion of a Lennon "cult," Anthony Elliott has written that "since his tragic death in 1980 at the age of 40, John Lennon has become . . . an object of mourning, of fantasy, of intense feelings of hope and dread" (1), such that, as "a transcendent hero, Lennon haunts our culture" (4). McCartney noted this phenomenon in another 2001 interview (with television host Larry King), explicitly linking it to his concerns about "credit":

> KING: Do you ever think that he got more credit than you?
>
> McCARTNEY: No, I—what's happened since he died is that. . . .
>
> KING: There's a martyrdom.
>
> McCARTNEY: You can't blame people. You know, there's a lot of sympathy. It was such a shocking way to go that you want to try and give him everything. But the trouble is that there is . . . revisionism, where certain people were saying, "Well . . . the only thing Paul ever did was book the studio."

The implication: by losing his life and becoming the object of the intense feelings that Elliott describes, Lennon gains more ("you want to . . . give him everything") than McCartney can ever hope to possess. In this light, McCartney's recent flurry of public activities—including record-setting concert tours; well-publicized forays into poetry and painting; the composition and presentation of several orchestral works; the release of three pop albums in three years; much-hyped star turns at the Queen's Jubilee, the Concert for New York City, and the Super Bowl; and his celebrated marriage to Heather Mills—begin to resemble the desperate efforts of a man chasing a ghost.

At the conclusion of the Miles biography, McCartney again insists that "the truth of the matter is, John and I were kind of equal" (595), a claim that, if made about Beatles creativity, is arguably the case, as analysts such as Walter Everett, Ian MacDonald, and Allan Moore have suggested. But in terms of cultural iconicity, Lennon "the transcendent hero" appears, in Elliott's terms, to be "always already there"—the guy who came first by losing most.

IN HIS LIFE

This complex of themes and concerns is thrown into high relief by *Lennon: His Life and Work*, an exhibition mounted by the Rock and Roll Hall of Fame and Museum and unveiled on October 19, 2000, to commemorate the sixtieth anniversary of John Lennon's birth and the twentieth anniversary of his death. More than three floors of Cleveland's I. M. Pei–designed structure were devoted to the exhibition, which has remained the central attraction at the museum well into 2002, drawing thousands of visitors.[2] Billed as "the first major exhibit in America to celebrate John Lennon" and "the largest exhibit the Hall of Fame has ever devoted to one artist," it features a broad and striking array of artifacts grouped into the categories "Belongings," "Works on Paper," "Lyrics," and "Photographs." These range from the expected (a piano, pieces of wardrobe); to the little seen (complete "editions" of schoolboy Lennon's *Daily Howl*; surrealistic collage art from the 1970s); to the shocking (eyeglasses stained with the dying Lennon's blood). In addition, the exhibit includes audio, video, and interactive modules with all of these elements framed by "minimalist" installation work of the "thoughtful and studious" Abbot Miller of Pentagram Design (Henke, "Story" 1–2).

In his introduction to the exhibit catalog, curator James Henke proclaims Lennon a unique figure in modern cultural history. Yes, Lennon was "the leader of the biggest rock group ever," "a superb singer and stellar songwriter" who "consistently pushed the boundaries of what was considered rock and roll." Moreover, writes Henke, the influence of Lennon:

> extended well beyond rock and roll. He excelled as a poet, a writer, a filmmaker and artist. He was a political activist. He had a huge social conscience, and an enormous wit. Though it may sound like a cliché, he was, truly, a spokesman for a generation. And perhaps more than anything else, he was a seeker of the truth, a person whose life reflected the values and beliefs he spoke of. (*Lennon* 9)

Henke concludes with the hope that the exhibit will help keep Lennon's "legacy alive for generations to come" (9).

This tone of high seriousness infuses much of the exhibit, as does the sense that, in both his artistic endeavors and the contour of his life, Lennon is an epochal figure; thus, the totalizing display that introduces the exhibit—a sort of walk-in triptych with a large bed (against a white backdrop) on the right, a rectangular, orange-and-white panel featuring the numeral "60" in the center, and an orange column on the left, each of these items (or their backdrops) towering roughly ten to twelve feet high. The white-and-orange color scheme deployed in this initial display alludes to that of *Milk and Honey*, the last album that Lennon and Ono recorded together. The bed on the right is the one in which the couple slept while living at the Dakota. It is suspended here, as it was there, between two church pews facing each other, as if to say the union of John and Yoko is both a delicate balance and a sacred thing. The central panel, with its larger-than-life-sized numeral "60" marking Lennon's birthday, is itself dotted with circular, face-sized portals (sixty in all) through which one may peer at artifacts of everyday life at the Dakota, including snapshots of Lennon, Ono, and their son Sean. The column on the left features portals too, although only a few (as if to make viewing, particularly in a large crowd, difficult) and through these one can glimpse artifacts of Lennon's murder—the bloodstained eyeglasses (as pictured on the cover of Ono's *Season of Glass*), along with a brown paper bag (turned over to Ono by the police) containing the clothes Lennon was wearing when he died. Rich with metaphoric overtones, the three parts of this display juxtapose a symbol of peace (the bed-in for peace having been invented by John and Yoko) with images of prosperity (the family photos) and trappings of violence (the bloodstained belongings). They also evoke the triad of birth, life, and death.

But if a bell tolls at this initial stage of the exhibit, it tolls not for Lennon alone. The central rectangle presents its circular portals in six rows of ten each (that is, in literal decades). Combined with the large "60" in the center, this arrangement suggests not just the number of years since Lennon's birth, but also the historical period with which Lennon and the Beatles have come to be synonymous, the decade of the 1960s. Moreover, the entire display is located at a kind of crossroads, on a mezzanine where two escalators, one moving up and the other down, intersect. Whether entering or leaving the exhibit, one passes this display on one's way. Thus, the three transitions figured by the display—passage into, through, and out of the world—are reproduced on a pedestrian level for visitors moving through the exhibit. The implication is that those transitions are not just Lennon's, but ours as well; the number "60" looms large not only in his biography but also in ours. Like some world-historical individual—a saint or a messiah—Lennon embodies, at the level of the microcosm or individual life, the universal experience of the macrocosm (that is, the 1960's generation for which he is supposed to be "the spokesman."

Similar design points characterize the rest of the exhibit. The numerals "40" (Lennon's age when murdered), "20" (the number of years since his death), "00" (a cipher for emptiness? a cry of mourning? the millennial complement to the number 20?), hang in prominent places. The orange-and-white color scheme is maintained with particular emphasis on the "white-on-white that John and Yoko used in much of their work" (Henke, "Story" 2). An array of artifacts from Lennon's artistic and personal life (for example, guitars, Beatles outfits, kimonos, passports, watercolors, love notes) are displayed, many of them in glass cases. Numerous photographs, most of them depicting Lennon and Ono together, are on view as well. As with the initial display, the exhibit designers make artful use, in hanging these pieces, of the convoluted windings of the Rock Hall's upper floors.

Moreover, the tone of solemnity is reproduced. Writing for the online Lennon fanzine *Instant Karma*, Marsha Ewing recounts her trip to the exhibit's culminating display:

> The third floor . . . of the exhibit was, for me, the most emotionally charged.
> A carpeted spiral staircase winds up and around into a smaller space where

the white walls are covered with framed lyrics from John's songs. What was so striking about this room is the hushed reverence we felt when we arrived there. One reporter wrote that some people were taking their shoes off to walk up the staircase. Just down the stairs, a band was playing ear-splittingly loud rock and roll music, but with each step into this Song Sanctuary, the sound faded until it was completely silenced.

Such worshipful silence may seem appropriate for memorializing a culture hero of the sort Henke hailed. Yet this same quality of "hushed reverence" makes the exhibit (despite the inclusion of some interactive installations) very much a one-way communication, a monological affair.[3] In the exhibit commentary and catalogue, Henke simply asserts Lennon's exceptional greatness. He neither moves beyond generalities in supporting this assertion, nor does he acknowledge, let alone engage, other assessments of Lennon. The same posture is reflected in the exhibit itself, which presents a wealth of artifacts but little in the way of context or background. There is no serious overview of Lennon's career, and certainly no criticism of it. The catalog makes what seems a timid gesture in this direction, concluding with a two-page piece by journalist Parke Puterbaugh that reads like a celebrity bio, followed by a chronology of events in Lennon's life. Lennon's greatness is simply assumed; never detailed, dramatized or debated. Perhaps this lack of depth and analysis is attributable to the fact that the exhibit focuses on an iconic celebrity from mass media culture. Icons speak, if at all, not through words, but through images and emotions; and celebrities, some suggest, are mysterious, mythic figures whose inscrutable appeal is an index of their numinous power. Moreover, in a society saturated in electronic communications, celebrities take on, through the mass dissemination of their images, a quality of intimate familiarity for their followers.

But should a museum, even one devoted to popular culture, simply accept such notions or, for that matter, endeavor to enhance such effects? A naïve question, that; the Rock and Roll Hall of Fame functions, among other things, as a "tourist magnet" (Strausbaugh 179). Besides, major museums of all sorts have today adopted "the strategies of . . . the mass media: the emphasis on spectacle, cult of celebrity, the whole masterpiece-and-treasure syndrome" (Hughes; qtd. in Luke 225), such that "curators are trying to promote their show as well as the allure of associated consumer packages" (Luke 225). Given this, one can understand the Hall of Fame staff not wanting to complicate matters with analysis, critique, or even too much contextual information. Better to simply invoke the Lennon image, capitalize on its popularity, and put on a diverting spectacle. So, despite the catalogue's salutes to Lennon as "complicated man" (Puterbaugh 168) and boundary-pushing artist/activist, the exhibit offers little to disturb the light trance of the consumerist museumgoer (Strausbaugh 180) and nothing to disrupt the vague notion of

Lennon-as-culture-hero. The most "edgy" items on display are the aforementioned belongings from the murder scene. But within the framework of reverent awe Ewing noted, even these seem more like martyr's relics than instances of boundary-crossing transgression.

Linked to this sense of placidity is the exhibit's emphasis on John and Yoko as ideal couple. As noted herein, the design style takes its cue from the late work of Lennon and Ono, a period when the duo had given up political provocation, instead making an artistic and public relations theme of their loving relationship and "well-upholstered" family life (Widgery 74). Contentwise, the prime focus of the exhibit—as indicated by quantity of artifacts and photographs, the selection of audiovisual material (primarily the film *Imagine*) and the posting of Lennon quotes such as "I only believe in me, Yoko and me, that's reality"—is on the hyphenated entity John-and-Yoko. This can be seen as fitting for at least a few reasons. Foremost among these must be Lennon's own assessment of his partnership with Ono, a relationship that Lennon hailed, until the day he died, as the most significant of his personal and working life. Then there is the body of work the two produced together, which is highly varied (encompassing audio recordings, films, performance art, and media activism) and groundbreaking in the way it plays at the borders of the popular, the avant-garde, and the politically engaged while exploiting the power of the spectacle in the process. Moreover, much of this work was influenced by Ono's own singular career in the art world, such that, among other things, it lends itself well to the milieu of gallery and exhibition.[4]

But regarding the question of emphasis, we should note that *Lennon: His Life and Work* developed out of Ono's concerns and initiative. Curator Henke notes that Ono has been a supporter of the Rock and Roll Hall of Fame since its inception and that it was "her idea to celebrate John's sixtieth birthday with a major exhibition" (*Lennon* 7). Henke writes that Ono contacted him in spring 2000 to propose the idea, because she felt that the anniversary year "would be a fitting time to share much of her personal collection of artifacts with John's fans" ("Story" 1). According to a note at the end of the exhibit catalog, all the artifacts on display come "from the collection of Yoko Ono" (*Lennon* 176). In addition to Ono and her companion Sam Havadtoy, the other major supporter to whom Henke extends thanks is Jann Wenner of *Rolling Stone*, whose long career in mass media has focused, at crucial junctures, on "The Ballad of John and Yoko," a borrowing Wenner employs for the title of an essay composed for a contemporaneous exhibition of Ono's own work (58).

An online posting recounting this initiative describes Ono as "ever-mindful of her husband's place in history" (King). And despite "the uncritical admiration of an entire generation of Americans" (Widgery 75), Lennon's image, as well as that of Ono herself, has come under strenuous attack in recent years. These attacks have tended to take the form of purported exposes of the "dark side" of John Lennon and have emphasized allegations about Lennon's last years, a period that he and Ono spent largely out of the public eye. Albert Goldman's lengthy *The Lives of John Lennon* (1988) depicted its subject as a "rock 'n' roll Howard Hughes" (Wiener xxiv), unable to function autonomously and utterly in thrall to a domineering, manipulative Ono. In the voice of an omniscient narrator, Goldman retailed lurid (and often unverifiable) tales of dreary dysfunction and casual depravity; in addition, he at times resorted to racist and misogynistic stereotypes when referring to Ono. Although widely denounced—friends and admirers of the couple, including McCartney, called on consumers to boycott its purchase—the book became a bestseller. It has been described as "the second assassination" of John Lennon (Elliott 26) .

One of Goldman's key sources was Fred Seaman, a disgruntled former employee of Lennon and Ono's who was convicted of stealing personal belongings (including Lennon's diaries) after his employer's death. Seaman went on to write *The Last Days of John Lennon*, another book offering sensational gossip and unflattering, seemingly vindictive, portraits of Lennon and Ono. And then there is May Pang's *Loving John*, which focuses on the author's affair with Lennon and which depicts the Lennon-Ono relationship as again based on dependence and control. So it seems plausible that Ono would see *Lennon: His Life and Work* not just as an occasion to share her "personal collection . . . with John's fans," but as an opportunity to impart, through the sharing of that collection, her own narrative of Lennon's life and work. That narrative depicts Lennon not as codependent recluse, but as what Henke calls a "seeker of the truth" who integrated into his life the values he proclaimed; moreover, it places the Lennon-Ono relationship/partnership at the center of that life and that truth-quest.

According to museum studies scholar Eilean Hooper-Greenhill, "the establishment of collections is a form of symbolic conquest" (18). Furthermore, argues political scientist Timothy Luke, the artifacts shown in museums "are products of an ongoing struggle by individuals and groups to establish what is real, to organize collective interests and to gain command over what is regarded as having authority" (xxiv). In this light, *Lennon: His Life and Work* can be seen as an instance of what Luke calls "power plays at the exhibition" (that is, as an attempt to establish "what is real" about Lennon and Ono), motivated at least in part by Ono's concern about her husband's (and her own) place in history, a concern perhaps exacerbated by recent attacks on the couple's reputation. If well-publicized gossipmongering has besmirched the dignity of Lennon and Ono, then a major museum exhibition is one means by which that dignity might be restored. Moreover, suggests Hooper-Greenhill, museum exhibitions lend themselves to the production of narratives of concord and integrity: "The power of display as a method of visual communication lies in its capacity to produce visual narratives that are apparently harmonious, unified and complete." And, for parties engaged in rhetorical struggle, the harmonious visual narratives the museum display produced have one additional advantage: "These holistic and apparently inevitable visual narratives" are "generally presented with anonymous authority"; thus, they have the effect of legitimizing "specific attitudes and opinions" to give them "the status of truth" (151).

IN WHOSE LIFE?

But if *Lennon: His Life and Work* intends to affirm, or reaffirm, John-and-Yoko, it pursues this goal in part by minimizing the role of the Beatles in Lennon's development and by presenting what is a shallow, one-sided account of the Lennon-McCartney collaboration.[5] This is not to say that references to the Beatles are absent from the exhibit. Out of seventy-two artifacts itemized in the catalogue, eighteen refer to the Beatles. But the references that do appear have a perfunctory tone, much like the passage in Henke's introduction where he first identifies Lennon as leader of "the biggest rock group ever" (locating the Beatles firmly within the bounds of "rock and roll history") and then goes on to claim that Lennon's significance lies in the way his influence and achievements transcended rock. The Beatles are thus reduced to an impressive line on Lennon's resume. Of course, such a view is supportable, although many critics and musicologists agree that Lennon's solo activities compare feebly to his work with the Beatles (something that can be said of McCartney as well). But the problem lies in the exhibition's failure to acknowledge that it is propagating a particular view—and a controversial one at that.

Regarding the exhibit's treatment of McCartney and his collaboration with Lennon, looking at references to songs and songwriting is helpful. In the aforementioned introduction to the catalogue, Henke follows his summary of Lennon's musical achievements by remarking that "His song, 'In My Life,' was recently named 'the greatest song of all time' by Britain's *Mojo* magazine" (*Lennon* 9). As if to underscore this point, "In My Life" is listed first in "Lyrics," the section of the catalogue that reproduces artifacts (mostly lyric sheets written in Lennon's hand) on display in the top-floor space Ewing dubbed the "Song Sanctuary." The lyrics to "In My Life" are accompanied by the longest curatorial entry in the exhibit, a 222–word essay framing the song as a signal breakthrough, "the one that Lennon felt elevated his work to another level of songwriting" (*Lennon* 98). Indeed, Lennon often pointed to "In My Life" as the first real sign of his move from pop artificiality (writing jinglelike lyrics, as would a mere "craftsman" [*All We Are Saying* 8]) to personal authenticity (writing songs that were "true to . . . *me*," and that placed self-expression ahead of entertainment value [Wenner 9]). The curatorial commentary concludes by repeating, and fleshing out, the *Mojo* anecdote:

Mojo, a British music magazine, recently ranked "In My Life" the "Greatest Song of All Time," beating out the Rolling Stones' "Satisfaction," at Number Two, "Over the Rainbow" . . . at Number Three, and another Beatles' tune, the McCartney composition "Here, There, and Everywhere" at Number Four. (Henke, *Lennon* 98)

The entire discussion implies that the song "In My Life" is the work of John Lennon and John Lennon alone. Indeed, the closing reference to its "beating out" a "McCartney composition" puts a very fine point on that implication, invoking, as it does, the songwriting collaboration/competition that lay at the heart of Beatle music-making.[6]

At issue here is not whether Lennon or McCartney ever composed complete songs separately (while crediting these to "John Lennon and Paul McCartney"). As is well known, they composed numerous songs in this fashion, just as with certain songs they collaborated "fifty-fifty" on both words and music and, in the case of others, split up the songwriting chores less evenly.[7] In the case of "In My Life," Lennon himself acknowledged that McCartney had a hand in its composition, telling interviewer David Sheff that "Paul helped with the middle eight musically" (*All We Are Saying* 178), while going on to claim all credit for the lyric (and implying that he wrote the rest of the music). But, as MacDonald notes, "In My Life" has no middle eight section; moreover, McCartney recalls "taking the words over to a keyboard . . . and setting them to music from start to finish" (151). Surveying the range of comments made over the years by both composers, McCartney biographer Barry Miles concludes that, out of hundreds of songs credited to Lennon and McCartney, "there are only two that are the subject of contention": "Eleanor Rigby" (where Lennon claimed credit for most of the lyric, whereas McCartney says his partner contributed little) and "In My Life" (276). In *Many Years from Now*, McCartney tells Miles that he recalls "writing the whole melody" of "In My Life": "The melody structure's very me" (277).

On this point—that the melody of "In My Life" is "very McCartney"—MacDonald concurs (151), as does musicologist Walter Everett (*Quarry Men* 319). Both base their assessments on analysis of the respective melodic/harmonic styles of Lennon and McCartney. In MacDonald's terms, Lennon favors "horizontal" melodies that do not skip around much and that derive their character from the movement of the harmonies supporting them. (Consider, for example, "Lucy in the Sky with Diamonds," with its melody that hovers around one note while the chords and bass line change beneath, or "I Am the Walrus," where a melody consisting of two chromatically adjacent tones is suspended over a similar descending figure in the bass.) Horizontal melodies are common in blues, and Lennon saw himself as being more blues-influenced than McCartney. MacDonald suggests that the horizontal quality of many Lennon tunes reflects a desire to confine melody to the (relatively narrow) pitch-range of the human speaking voice, a touchstone for the verbally oriented Lennon. By contrast, McCartney's melodies tend to have a vertical quality, meaning that they include wide interval skips and range frequently beyond an octave (11). (Think, for example, of McCartney tunes such as "Fixing a Hole," or "The Fool on the Hill.") Vertical melodies derive less of their character from accompanying harmonies than do horizontal ones, partly because they tend to outline chordal arpeggios as they arc their way along. Concerning the melody of "In My Life," MacDonald observes that its "angular verticality, spanning an octave in typically wide—and difficult—leaps, certainly shows more" of McCartney's touch than Lennon's "despite fitting the latter's voice snugly" (151). But, as Everett remarks, even though McCartney "is correct in claiming" that the melody's structure reflects his own style, "the two composers' individual harmonic languages are so tightly intertwined that it is difficult to make a firm determination as to whose music graces 'In My Life'" (*Quarry Men* 319). Although each has a characteristic approach to melody and harmony, "John and Paul had such a history of writing 'into each other's noses' that the origins of such Beatle-marking can't be securely placed with one or the other" (320).

In sum, "In My Life" is one of the few songs about which the dispute between Lennon and McCartney is over the question of authorship. While both agree that Lennon composed the lyric, they disagree about who wrote—or who wrote how much of—the music to the song. Lennon stated that McCartney wrote a portion of the music, whereas McCartney claims full credit for the melody and chords. Musicological analysis suggests that McCartney's claim that the melody is "very me" is valid, although ultimately we have no way to decide the question objectively. Moreover, Lennon could have simply written, on this occasion, a McCartneyesque tune because the two composers worked so closely together for such a long period that each seems to have internalized, to some extent, the style of the other. Thus, "Who wrote 'In My Life'?" is a difficult and unsettled question, serious probing of which leads one to consider—and perhaps appreciate more deeply—the complexities, both musical and interpersonal, of the Lennon-McCartney collaboration. However, none of this rich complexity is addressed, or even acknowledged, in the exhibit commentary for "In My Life." Rather, the song is presented as if no dispute about its invention exists and we have nothing to learn from it about the Lennon-McCartney interaction. And, although "In My Life" is presented in the "Lyrics" section of *Lennon: His Life and Work*, from the repeated references by the curator to its having been voted "the greatest song"—not lyric—"of all time," the emphasis is clearly on the music as well as the words and on Lennon as the author of both. This point is further reinforced by the rhetorical move that seeks to enhance the status of this supposed Lennon-only creation by contrasting it with the lower-rated "Here, There, and Everywhere," a "McCartney composition" (Henke, *Lennon* 98).

THE BAD GUY

Through such emphases and omissions, the exhibit makes McCartney Lennon's foil, constructing an implied opposition in which Lennon's success, as artist and collaborator, will be measured by difference from McCartney. Moreover, as its treatment of "In My Life" suggests, the exhibit will strain, where necessary, to establish this difference. The exhibit catalogue follows "In My Life" with the thoroughly Lennon-composed "Run for Your Life," another selection from the same album *(Rubber Soul)* and period. The commentary notes that Lennon considered the song among his "worst work" and repeats Lennon's admission that the opening lines ("I'd rather see you dead, little girl / Than to be with another man") were lifted from an Elvis song. Such songs, the entry points out, were written under deadline pressure, for in this period of their career the Beatles were "churning out" an album and a single every six months. Lennon's dislike for the song is attributed to the "rush," "plagiarism," and hackwork conditions of its composition (101). In this context, "Run for Your Life" poses a striking contrast to "In My Life": Whereas the latter song represents Lennon's breakthrough to authenticity as a songwriter, "Run For Your Life" exemplifies the derivative, formulaic, assembly-line composing style from which he escaped with the shift to personally expressive writing. The binary implicit here—authenticity versus artifice—will structure the "Lyrics" section as it tracks eighteen additional selections in roughly chronological order, from the Beatles years through the end of Lennon's solo career. In the course of this presentation, Beatles material will be linked not only to Lennon's writerly beginnings, but also with an oppressive sense of other-directedness, whereas the solo work will be made to tell the story of Lennon finding his own voice and truth.

Unlike "Run for Your Life," the next lyric, "We Can Work It Out," is discussed quite closely in relation to its author's private life. However, the author in question is Paul McCartney, this song having been composed in large part by him. The commentary explains that the song "was inspired by a disagreement between . . . McCartney and his then-girlfriend Jane Asher." Asher, we are told, had a thriving acting career; when she took a position with the Bristol Old Vic company, far from London, this "upset McCartney's notions of how a proper girlfriend should behave." The song is thus McCartney's "plea to his girlfriend to see things (his) way, get it straight or say good night" (102). In making this point, the commentary quotes McCartney's lyric, substituting the pronoun "his" for the original "my" (that is, see things "my way"). The same point could have been made without changing the pronoun; however, changing it draws more attention to "him"; and "he," it has been made clear, is not an everyman figure or poetic persona, but the real-life individual Paul McCartney, who, it appears, was quite the controlling male chauvinist. Of course, Lennon's lyric to "Run For Your Life" might also have been discussed in terms of sexist attitudes, for its content ("Let this be a sermon, I mean everything I said / Baby I'm determined and I'd rather see you dead") is decidedly misogynistic. Indeed, Lennon later admitted that, during this period of his life, he "fought men and hit women" (*All We Are Saying* 182).[8] But whereas the "I" of "We Can Work It Out" is identified with its author, the "I" of "Run for Your Life" is not. By placing "Run for Your Life" under the sign of artifice/inauthenticity, the exhibit exempts the lyric from being read as a piece of personal expression. McCartney's lyric, on the other hand, is framed as providing a window into its author's disagreeable personality—a legitimate reading, perhaps, but also a narrow one, for other writers have assessed "We Can Work It Out" differently. Thus, Mark Hertsgaard has praised the song's words as "a triumph because they work on so many different levels" (152), articulating concern about a romantic "relationship" as well as a "plea for reconciliation" on the "global scale of defusing wars" (152).

Less generous than Hertsgaard was to "We Can Work It Out," the Lennon exhibit reinvokes the theme of personal expression while unhooking it from the theme of writerly authenticity. Thus, after noting that Lennon wrote the words and music to the song's middle eight, the commentary concludes with Lennon's remark that "We Can Work It Out" illustrates the different outlooks of the two songwriters, "with Paul optimistic" and "me, impatient" (102), an appraisal that, according to MacDonald, misreads the song (152) and that plays to stereotypes of McCartney as naïve lightweight and Lennon as tough-minded realist.[9] In this context, to be authentic means to be true not just to one's personal feelings, but to "reality" itself, and in that undertaking, McCartney is found wanting while Lennon gets high marks. Perhaps most important, with its discussion of this song, the exhibit rearticulates the theme of relationship/partnership, albeit in a negative register. Through "We Can Work It Out," the McCartney-Asher pairing is posed, implicitly, as the opposite of John-and-Yoko: where one is a relationship undermined by male chauvinism and the urge to dominate, the other, celebrated throughout the exhibit, is a meeting of enlightened equals.[10]

And so it goes: the lyrics to "Drive My Car" (another song composed largely by McCartney) are similarly framed, opposing McCartney's ostensible lyrical vapidity to Lennon's incisive wit. Emphasizing Lennon's assessment of his partner's original words as "crap" (a view with which McCartney concurred), the commentary depicts Lennon (who put a fine, ironic point on the lyric) as the song's savior (Henke, *Lennon* 106). The point may be apt in this case, but outside the larger context of the team's collaborative record, it is misleading. Among the catalogue's seven Beatles selections, we find no parallel reference to, say, a Lennon song for which McCartney supplied the compositional coup de grace, although in fact several such cases exist.[11] Indeed, the song displayed next to "Drive My Car" ("Tomorrow Never Knows") should raise this point, but is not allowed to do so. Although the exhibit hails the song as a landmark for Lennon and the Beatles and acknowledges the lyrics' extraordinary sources (the LSD experience and Timothy Leary's adaptation of the *Tibetan Book of the Dead*), it makes no mention of McCartney's role in the creation of the song's astonishing soundscape. But it was McCartney who conceived of and created the piece's most innovative and distinctive feature, the otherworldly tape loop array that swirls throughout its "seething dazzle" (MacDonald 170; Everett, *Revolver* 37–38).[12]

Following two other selections ("When I Get Home" and "Lucy in the Sky with Diamonds"), the Beatles portion of "Lyrics" concludes with "Glass Onion," a song that Everett labels "mystifying" (*Revolver* 181) and MacDonald a string of "misleading self-quotations" (275), and both writers note a tone of sneering sarcasm on Lennon's part. The exhibit, however, places this lyric in the context of the Beatles' 1968 retreat in Rishikesh to reprise the theme of authenticity: "Lennon's "songs from India were . . . simpler, more direct and less-self-conscious than . . . his previous work, and 'Glass Onion' is an example of that newfound lyrical candor" (Henke, *Lennon* 113). The question of candor aside, the lyrics can safely be said to associate Beatles fandom, music, and, arguably, McCartney himself, with mass foolishness. Thus, the Beatles section of "Lyrics" ends not with the bang, say, of "A Day in the Life" (a song often called the duo's masterpiece and that might have been used to show Lennon—who wrote all but the middle—at his poetic best and the team at a collaborative peak), but the relative whimper of "The walrus was Paul."[13] By such effort, "Glass Onion" serves the exhibit's emphasis on the quest for authenticity as well as its association of the Beatles with the other-directed artifice that Lennon struggled to overcome. The "Lyrics" section then segues into thirteen selections from Lennon's career as a solo artist and collaborator with Ono. His riveting denunciation, "God," is discussed primarily in terms of its attack on the Beatles myth and its singular affirmation that "I only believe in me / Yoko and me / That's reality" (118), a premise that apparently justifies the inclusion, alongside a stinging jeremiad such as "Working Class Hero" or a visionary collaboration such as "Imagine," relative trifles such as "Crippled Inside," "Dear Yoko," and "(Just Like) Starting Over," each of which, whatever its artistic weaknesses, works well as a chapter in the story of John-and-Yoko. In the words of the catalogue's biography, Lennon's artistry is finally beside the point. As Puterbaugh observes:

> Much of what lingers in the public memory goes beyond musical legacy. Rather, it has to do with leading by example. The relationship between John and Yoko endured challenges from within and without to become one of the most touching and celebrated of twentieth-century romances. (169)

But "what lingers in the public mind" is precisely the issue; and the suggestion here—that *Lennon: His Life and Work* is merely reflecting, and not actively

working to shape, "public memory"—is disingenuous. Moreover, in constructing this narrative—of Lennon as exemplary individual and John-and-Yoko as
ideal partnership, the exhibit relies on dubious omissions, questionable
emphases, and unexamined binaries such as authenticity/artifice, in the
process of which it casts the Beatles, and McCartney in particular, as the inau-
thentic others of Lennon's noble quest.

This is, of course, the spin that Lennon himself began to put on his career
as early as the 1970 *Rolling Stone* interviews. But in a museum exhibit, or at least
one of this sort, that spin is not ascribed to Lennon or, indeed, any particular
source; nor is it acknowledged to be one among many possible constructions of
the meaning of Lennon's (or the Beatles') oeuvre. Rather, this narrative is mate-
rialized through the selection and presentation of certain objects (as well as the
omission of others) and put forth with "anonymous authority" (Hooper-Greenhill 151). According to Luke, such "sophisticated narrative indirection" steers
"inclinations tacitly or implicitly through amusing diversion," a veiled form of
persuasion that is much more powerful than gestures (such as, say, the realign-
ment of author's credits), which attempt to "impose order from above through
coercive acts" (220). One does not have to hold a brief for McCartney to be dis-
turbed by this exhibit's uncritical inscription of the narrative of Lennon as culture hero. Arguably both Lennon's legacy and the public's memory of his life
and work are ill served by grandiose mythmaking, particularly when that myth-
making is reproduced by establishment institutions and passed off as truth.
Moreover, we all have a stake in the project of historical inscription and cultural
remembrance. In the words of Timothy Luke, "Any astute reading of the
museum recognizes that its modes of remembering are also necessarily always
modes of forgetting" (224). In working to "remember" its subject in this fashion,
Lennon: His Life and Work has had a lot to forget.

NOTES

1. I am indebted to James Kimsey for drawing my attention to this news story
and for help in gathering sources for this chapter.

2. I visited the Rock and Roll Hall of Fame and viewed *Lennon: His Life and
Work* during July 2001. On that occasion I presented a guest lecture to the Rock Hall's
summer program for academics, "So You Want to Be a Rock and Roll Teacher"; my
topic was titled, "The Beatles and the Creative Process."

3. The interactive installations include a white phone on which Yoko occasionally
rings in, and a "wish tree" stationed on the ground floor so that visitors can write down
wishes on slips of paper and attach them to the tree. "*Wish Tree* is a splendid machine
of and for desiring" and "the title of a generic series of works created by Ono in the
1990s using actual trees as the primary . . . pillar of her conceptual project" (Rico 266).

4. For a comprehensive overview of Ono's artistic oeuvre and career, see *Yes: Yoko Ono*, edited by Alexandra Munroe and John Hendricks.

5. One could argue that the Beatles are a separate topic, best treated elsewhere, but the exhibit neither raises the point nor makes the case.

6. Regarding "Here, There, and Everywhere," no dispute exists about its having been composed solely by McCartney.

7. For comprehensive musical analyses of all Beatles songs and the specific roles of Lennon, McCartney, Harrison, and Starr in their creation and performance, see Everett (1999, 2001) and MacDonald.

8. Discussing "Run for Your Life" in this context could have provided (a) an opportunity to present Lennon in a less idealized light, and (b) an illustration of his unsparing honesty as well as his commitment (lionized only in vague terms by the exhibit) to acknowledging the worst about himself while working toward, and affecting, real change.

9. There is another sense in which "We Can Work It Out" can be said to highlight the differing approaches of the two writers. As MacDonald notes, the song, with its horizontal melody, "tense suspensions, and irregular phrase-lengths," shows McCartney at his "most Lennonish" (152).

10. The only reference to rockiness in the Lennon-Ono relationship is found in the Chronology: "Fall 1973: John and Yoko begin an 18–month separation" and "January 1975: John and Yoko are reunited" (Henke, *Lennon* 174). No mention is made of Lennon's drunken misadventures during this period or his affair with May Pang.

11. For example, see "A Day in the Life," where McCartney supplied the pivotal bridge section, or "Norwegian Wood (This Bird Has Flown)," where Lennon gave McCartney credit for the middle eight (Wenner 85); whereas McCartney claims credit, as well, for the song's pivotal closing image: "So, I lit a fire" (Miles 270–71).

12. Everett (1999) describes this Beatles songwriting phenomenon as McCartney applying "his magic" (36). For a sense of what the song sounded like when Lennon first presented it to the group, see *Anthology 2*.

13. McCartney is even made to play the heavy regarding the breakup of the group (Henke, *Lennon* 173). No mention is made of Lennon's having been the first to announce (to the inner circle) that he was leaving the band (Wenner 31–32), an action in which he took great pride.

Afterword

I Want to Hold Your Hand

JANE TOMPKINS

I N 1963, I WAS LIVING in an apartment in New Haven, Connecticut, with my first husband. The apartment, formerly the New Haven draft board, lacked both amenities and charm. It looked across to the freshmen dorms at Yale University, where I imagined the hungry eyes of freshmen looking at me as I undressed at night. I was prudish and afraid of many things, especially sex and everything related to it, which made young marriage difficult, although it was also tender and sweet. My prudery was part of a more general condition of being colossally unhip. I took everything seriously; I tried so hard to be good it hurts me to even think about it now. An earnest English graduate student, I was a stranger to television, to fashion, to popular music, to drugs, and to myself. I smoked, but that was before anyone knew it was bad for you. Having been introduced to alcohol carefully by my parents, I drank socially with no ill effects.

All my life I'd been a "brain" in school, not part of the clique that ran things, struggling to look and sound right, but without a shred of interest in the things that interested the people I was imitating. When the girls who hung around Kavner's drugstore in eighth grade played songs on the jukebox, I didn't even like most of them. I'd taken piano lessons for practically my whole life and liked Bach and Mozart pretty well. When Elvis came on the scene, he did not just leave me cold, he left me squirming; I could not stand, and did not understand, the raw sex. I liked the occasional song, the occasional singer, but I did not listen to music on the radio, except now and then, and I did not buy records. Popular music belonged to the masses of people I felt myself mysteriously divided from. I would never make it on their terms: being self-confident, having a sexy figure, liking to dance, and looking like either Marilyn Monroe or Doris Day (which one you were supposed to be like, the apron-wearer or the sexpot, was not clear). Because I knew I could be like neither one—among other reasons, my breasts were too small—I was all the more determined to *be* a brain and to succeed in a world where brains counted: graduate school.

And so it was with incredulous delight that one day I found myself in Brothers Coffee Shop on Chapel Street in New Haven listening to a popular song that made me happy: it was called "I Want to Hold Your Hand." My husband of a few months and I sat across from each other nodding our heads to the music. I could not believe it was happening—a song was playing on a jukebox that I really liked. It made me want to jump up and down. And it was by this popular new group called the Beatles, a misspelling which offended my English major's sensibilities, but never mind. For the first time in my life I felt the possibility of being connected to the rest of the world in a certain way. The possibility of normalcy. Of liking what other people liked, enjoying what they enjoyed. I felt the connection immediately, like an injection straight to the vein.

The promise of belonging contained in that first song was true. Song after song came out and they were all wonderful. The Beatles sang about loners like me ("Eleanor Rigby"); they sang about having troubles ("Yesterday"); about a girl misunderstood by her parents ("She's Leaving Home"); about needing friends ("I get by 'With a Little Help from My Friends'"). In short, they seemed human.

Most of the popular songs I had heard were not human in this sense. They had no range of topic or of feeling. They were about "love." I love you. Or, I love you but you do not love me. Or sometimes, I love you but you are far away. That is what it boiled down to. But the Beatles seemed to have compassion for people other than themselves. They told stories about things that had happened. They could express pain, or neediness, and have it not just be the same old "you did me wrong" kind of thing.

I did not think any of this consciously at the time; I just responded to the human pathos of their music. Besides their story lines, I loved their melodies and their harmonies, and the effects they tried—using bits of classical music, singing falsetto, playing around with the sounds of instruments, just being playful. Something about their music was innocent and appealing, it had a childlike quality and it affirmed that quality, rather than being world-weary and knowing. I think that was what I loved about them the most. They did not protect themselves with sophistication or righteousness or sheer masculinity; they tried vulnerability and it worked, so they tried it some more.

What a relief! Their voices did not have that authoritarian baritone of a lot of male singers who declared, with every note, the supremacy of the male point of view. And though young, they were not empty-headed *vitelloni* with tans, white teeth, and tight bathing suits who had never had a thought and never would have one. There was something new about the Beatles. The newness was not only generational; it had to do with gender, authority, showing your feelings, being vulnerable, and wanting to change the world. They believed in love. Not the "love" that was sold in romance comics and most popular music, the thing that went on between men and women over and over again. No, it was more the "though I speak with the tongues of men and of angels" kind of love. They had compassion, and wonder, and delight.

It was the 1960s, of course. It was the 1960s that was happening in the Beatles' songs, but in 1963 and 1964, we did not know that yet. All I knew was that they convinced me—against all odds—that their universe was the same as mine. They knew more about getting high and had had more sexual experience than I had, but that did not matter. What mattered was that they had human hearts. With their soft suits and long, floppy hair and soft voices, they blurred the line between female and male just enough to let women feel comfortable with them. The Beatles were not out to lay you; and they did not seem to feel that women were from some other planet. After they arrived on the scene, being like Marilyn Monroe or Doris Day—either of whom would have made a ludicrous object of romantic love in a Beatles song anyway—was no longer necessary.

Because the Beatles themselves were somewhat androgynous, they gave women permission to be more androgynous, too. No need for those huge breasts, that cinched waist, those curler-produced curls. You could relax a little. Because none of the Beatles was big or rugged like Gregory Peck or Rock Hudson (no one knew he was gay then), and because none of them was aggressively male, like Elvis, or, in his way, John Wayne, women did not have to work so hard to look feminine, or rather, opposite. We did not have to be the "opposite" sex.

For a woman like me, the Beatles changed sexuality in our culture, at least for a while, into something less terrifying, less overtly marked. They partook of beauty and not so much of the beast. They took sexuality out of the realm of that opposition and made of it something more malleable, more imaginative, less hidden ("Why Don't We Do It in the Road?"), and infinitely less scary. If it had a certain Peter Pan quality, well, that was better than the stupidities foisted on us in the name of sex by the movies of the 1950s and the early 1960s—in the impossible figures of Raquel Welch and Anita Ekberg, the overheated passions of Jennifer Jones in *Duel in the Sun*, the caricatures of maleness in *Shaft* and *Hud*, and the endless worship of toughness in Westerns and gangster movies.

At the same time that they played with androgyny and (in the media goings-on of John and Yoko) tried both to demystify and re-sacralize sex, the Beatles embraced Eastern spirituality in their songs and in their public association with the Maharishi Mahesh Yogi—a double blow to the secular, xenophobic world of John Wayne and Doris Day. I did not quite know what the Eastern stuff meant because it would be another twenty-five years before I would go that route myself, but I felt vaguely comforted at seeing pictures of the four of them with flowers around their necks, getting off a plane that had brought them home from India. They were exploring, they were open to new things, they were not buying the bill of goods their parents had accepted, they were questioning everything—gently, without harming anyone. And then they began to take on the world.

With *Sgt. Pepper* and subsequent albums, the scope of their vision broadened to include history, politics, the justice system. The music got bigger—cosmic, chaotic, unbelievably original. The psychic pain deepened and became existential as well as personal. At first I did not understand it, and I wanted them to go back to holding hands and longing for "Michelle," but that did not last. Listening to some of their later songs, full of cacophony and weird effects, I felt in touch with strange enormous states of being and with a largeness of view I had not encountered before. The Beatles were socially conscious and they were also kind. They were shocked at World War II and they appreciated the performers in a small-time circus, Mr. Kite and Harry the Horse. As for "I'd love to turn you on," what that meant was that they were sensitive enough to the world to feel its pain, not just their own, and they had discovered this wonderful way to escape suffering for a while, so why not share it?

Who would not want to go along with them to Strawberry Fields? Who did not share that longing for nirvana? There was something so invitational about the Beatles' music. I had never done drugs in my life, except for a couple of puffs on a marijuana cigarette, but drugs looked graceful on the Beatles, sort of like the leis they were receiving after deplaning from India. Instead of treating their drug experiences with in-your-face defiance, they asked you to join them, and they made you feel that their experience of life as a whole was, if not the same as yours, then so close as to be virtually indistinguishable. Even when I did not know what they were singing about (at least, not until somebody told me, as in "Lucy in the Sky with Diamonds") whatever it was had a familiar feel.

This familiar, invitational quality made them completely different, in my eyes, from a band such as the Rolling Stones. The Stones scared me. I got the feeling they were angry most of the time, and their sexuality was menacing. The Rolling Stones, I suspected, did not like people like me and never would, so what was the point? I knew what all that aggressive rolling of the pelvis was about, and I wanted no part of it. But the Beatles made me feel, not safe, exactly, because their world was full of loneliness and disappointment, but welcome, befriended. Mowgli's words to the animals in *The Jungle Book*—"we be of one blood, thou and I"—might have been their motto. They did not bully you, they did not shout, they did not threaten, or whine—they reached out through their music and touched a part of your soul that was tender and vulnerable and needed befriending.

The Beatles gave me a sense that the world was a larger place than I had thought. They let me know that kindness, fantasy, creativity, and vulnerability could go together and were not necessarily unmarketable traits. This knowledge did not make much difference in how I conducted my life, but it comforted me and made me feel better about myself; it comforted me to know that some of the sensitivities and longings I had were shared, and it made me feel better because these attitudes and feelings were being expressed in a way that joined me to millions of other people by virtue of the Beatles' popularity. "Oh yeah, I-I'll . . . tell you so-omething . . . da da da da dum, I think you'll understand, when I-I'll say that so-omething, da da da da dum, I want to hold your hand, I want to hold your ha-a-a-a-and, dum dum, I want to hold your hand." I still feel warmed by those words and that music. They bestowed on me a precious gift. While listening to the Beatles, back in 1963, '64, '65, '66, and for some time afterward, I did not feel so separate from the human race.

BIBLIOGRAPHY

"100 Classic Album Covers." *Rolling Stone* 14 November 1991: 91–154.

Appleyard, Bryan. "Megastars March into History with the Rock of Ages." *Sunday Times* 24 June 1990: 16–17.

Attali, Jacques. *Noise: The Political Economy of Music.* Trans. Brian Massumi. Minneapolis: U of Minnesota P, 1985.

Babiuk, Andy. *Beatles Gear: All the Fab Four's Instruments, from Stage to Studio.* San Francisco: Backbeat, 2001.

Badman, Keith, ed. *The Beatles: Off the Record.* New York: Omnibus, 2000.

Baker, Geoff. Interview by Katie Couric. *Today Show.* NBC. 16 December 2002.

Bakhtin, Mikhail. "Epic and Novel: Toward a Methodology for the Study of the Novel." *The Dialogic Imagination: Four Essays.* Ed. Michael Holquist. Trans. Caryl Emerson and Michael Holquist. Austin: U of Texas P, 1981. 3–40.

———. "Forms of Time and of the Chronotope in the Novel: Notes toward a Historical Poetics." *The Dialogic Imagination: Four Essays.* Ed. Michael Holquist. Trans. Caryl Emerson and Michael Holquist. Austin: U of Texas P, 1981. 84–258.

Bannister, Matthew. "Ladies and Gentlemen, the Beatelles!: The Influence of Sixties Girl Groups on the Beatles." Heinonen, Heuger, Nurmesjärvi, and Whiteley 170–79.

Barlow, Hugh. "George Not So Quiet." *Wairarapa Times* [New Zealand]. 3 December 2001. <times-age.co.nz/news2001/011203b.html>.

Barrow, Tony. "The Story behind *A Hard Day's Night.*" *Beatles Monthly Book* 204 (September 1993): 5–11.

———. "The Story behind *Yellow Submarine.*" *Beatles Monthly Book* 204 (April 1993): 8–13.

Barth, John. *The Sot-Weed Factor.* 1960, 1967. Garden City: Anchor, 1987.

Baudrillard, Jean. *Symbolic Exchange and Death*. Trans. Iain Hamilton Grant. London: Sage, 1993.

BBC Third Programme. *The Tragedy of King Lear*. 29 September 1967.

The Beatles. *1*. Capitol, 2000.

———. *5.1 Degrees of Separation*. Blue Meanie Records, 2000.

———. *Abbey Road*. 1969. Parlophone, 1987.

———. *Anthology 1*. Capitol, 1995.

———. *Anthology 2*. Capitol, 1996.

———. *Anthology 3*. Capitol, 1996.

———. *Beatles for Sale*. 1964. Parlophone, 1987.

———. *The Beatles* [*The White Album*]. 1968. Parlophone, 1987.

———. *The Beatles, 1962–1966*. 1973. EMI, 1993.

———. *The Beatles, 1967–1970*. 1973. EMI, 1993.

———. *The Beatles Anthology*. DVD. EMI, 2003.

———. *The Beatles Anthology*. Television documentary. ABC, 1995.

———. *The Beatles Anthology*. Video cassette. EMI, 1995.

———. *The Beatles Anthology*. San Francisco: Chronicle, 2000.

———. *The Compleat Beatles*. Delilah Films, 1981.

———. *A Hard Day's Night*. 1964. Parlophone, 1987.

———. *Help!* 1965. Parlophone, 1987.

———. *Let It Be*. 1970. Parlophone, 1987.

———. *Let It Be . . . Naked*. Capitol, 2003.

———. *Live at the BBC*. Apple, 1994.

———, dir. *Magical Mystery Tour*. Apple Films, 1967.

———. *Magical Mystery Tour*. 1967. Parlophone, 1987.

———. *Please Please Me*. 1963. Parlophone, 1987.

———. *Revolver*. 1966. Parlophone, 1987.

———. *Rubber Soul*. 1965. Parlophone, 1987.

———. *Sgt. Pepper's Lonely Hearts Club Band*. 1967. Parlophone, 1987.

———. *Twenty Greatest Hits*. Capitol, 1982.

———. *With the Beatles*. 1963. Parlophone, 1987.

———. *Yellow Submarine*. 1969. Parlophone, 1987.

———. *Yellow Submarine Songtrack*. Capitol, 1999.

——— . *Yesterday . . . and Today*. Capitol, 1966.

"The Beatles." *Recording Industry Association of America*. 2002. <riaa.org>.

Benjamin, Walter. "The Work of Art in the Age of Mechanical Reproduction." *Illuminations*. New York: Schocher, 1955. 217–51.

Berger, Thomas. *Little Big Man*. 1964. New York: Delta, 1989.

"Big Decision to Allow Beatles Reunion." Reuters. 13 November 1995. <www.eskimo.com/~bpentium/antholog.html.>.

Blake, Peter. Liner notes. *Sgt. Pepper's Lonely Hearts Club Band*, by the Beatles. 1967. Parlophone, 1987.

Bonzo Dog Band. *The Doughnut in Granny's Greenhouse*. 1968. Edsel, 1987.

Bowman, Marion. "Drawn to Glastonbury." Reader and Walter 29–61.

Breines, Wini. "'Of This Generation': The New Left and the Student Movement." *Long Time Gone: Sixties America Then and Now*. Ed. Alexander Bloom. Oxford: Oxford UP, 2001. 23–45.

Brocken, Michael. "Some Other Guys! Theories about Signification: Beatles Cover Versions." *Popular Music and Society* 20.4 (1996): 5–40.

Brown, Peter, and Steven Gaines. *The Love You Make: An Insider's Story of the Beatles*. New York: McGraw-Hill, 1983.

Burke, John. *The Beatles in 'A Hard Day's Night.'* New York: Dell, 1964.

Burns, Gary. "Rehab Four: Beatles for Sale in the Age of Music Video." Inglis, *Beatles* 176–88.

Burroughs, William S., and Allen Ginsberg. *The Yagé Letters*. San Francisco: City Lights, 1963.

Chen, Ed. "The Beatles Anthology." 2001. <beatles.cselt.it/rmb/anthFAQ.html>.

Cohen, Eric. "Pilgrimage Centers: Concentric and Eccentric." *Annals of Tourism Research* 19.1 (1992): 33–50.

Connolly, Ray. *The Beatles Complete*. London: Wise, 1983.

Cooper, Rose. "Bam's Review of *The Homeboy*." 2001. <www.3blackchicks.com/bamshomeboy.html>.

Cott, Jonathan, and Christina Doudna, eds. *The Ballad of John and Yoko*. Garden City: Rolling Stone, 1982.

Covach, John. "Form in Rock Music: A Primer." *Engaging Music: Essays in Musical Analysis*. Ed. Deborah Stein. Oxford: Oxford UP, 2005. 65–76.

Davies, Hunter. *The Beatles: The Authorized Biography*. 2nd ed. New York: Norton, 1996.

Davis, Clive. "The Presley Phenomenon." *Sunday Times* 13 July 1997: 9.

Debord, Guy. *La Société du Spectacle*. 1967. Paris: Gallimard, 1992.

Douglas, Susan. *Where the Girls Are: Growing Up Female with the Mass Media*. New York: Times, 1994.

Dowlding, William J. *Beatlesongs*. New York: Simon and Schuster, 1989.

Duffy, Thom. "McCartney 'Falls In' with Ringo, Miller on New Set." *Billboard* 12 April 1997: 1–2.

Dunning, George, dir. *Yellow Submarine*. United Artists, 1968.

Durkheim, Émile. *Elementary Forms of Religious Thought*. London: Allen and Unwin, 1912.

Dylan, Bob. "Ballad of a Thin Man." *Highway 61 Revisited*. Columbia, 1965.

Easthope, Antony. *Literary into Cultural Studies*. London: Routledge, 1991.

Eco, Umberto. "Postmodernism, Irony, the Enjoyable." *Postscript to the Name of the Rose*. New York: Harcourt, Brace, Jovanovich, 1984. 65–72.

Ehrenreich, Barbara, Elizabeth Hess, and Gloria Jacobs. "Beatlemania: Girls Just Want to Have Fun." *The Adoring Audience: Fan Culture and Popular Media*. Ed. Lisa Lewis. London: Routledge, 1992. 93–119.

Eliade, Mircea. *Images and Symbols*. New York: Sheed and Ward, 1969.

Elliott, Anthony. *The Mourning of John Lennon*. Berkeley: U of California P, 1999.

Everett, Walter. "The Beatles as Composers: The Genesis of *Abbey Road*, Side Two." *Concert Music, Rock, and Jazz since 1945: Essays and Analytical Studies*. Ed. Elizabeth West Marvin and Richard Hermann. Rochester: U of Rochester P, 1995. 172–228.

———. *The Beatles as Musicians: The Quarry Men through* Rubber Soul. Oxford: Oxford UP, 2001.

———. *The Beatles as Musicians:* Revolver *through the* Anthology. Oxford: Oxford UP, 1999.

Everitt, Anthony. "All the Fun of the Fair." *Guardian* 16 September 1994: 22.

Ewing, Marsha. "John Lennon: His Life and Work—Shaking Up the House that Rock Built." *Instant Karma*. 21 October 2000/3 November 2002. <www.instantkarma.com>.

Fiedler, Leslie. "Cross the Border, Close the Gap." *The Fiedler Reader*. New York: Stein and Day, 1977.

Fitzgerald, Jon. "Lennon-McCartney and the 'Middle Eight.'" *Popular Music and Society* 20.4 (1996): 41–52.

Forte, Allen. *The American Popular Ballad of the Golden Era, 1924–1950*. Princeton: Princeton UP, 1995.

Friedman, Wayne. "Via 1, Beatles Reborn as Ultimate Boy Band." *Advertising Age* 26 March 2001: 1–2.

Frith, Simon, and Angela McRobbie. "Rock and Sexuality." *On Record: Rock, Pop, and the Written Word.* Ed. Simon Frith and Andrew Goodwin. London: Routledge, 1990. 371–89.

Gendron, Bernard. *Between Montmartre and the Mudd Club.* Chicago: U of Chicago P, 2002.

Gennep, Arnold van. *The Rites of Passage.* 1908. Chicago: U of Chicago P, 1960.

Gillespie, Nick. "The Long and Whining Road: The Beatles, the Boomers, and Boredom." *Reason* June 2001. <reason.com/0106/cr.ng.long.shtml>.

Gilmore, Mikal. "The Sixties." *Rolling Stone: The Decades of Rock and Roll.* Ed. Holly George-Warren. San Francisco: Chronicle, 2001. 65–77.

Giuliano, Geoffrey, ed. *The Lost Beatles Interviews.* New York: Dutton, 1994.

———. *Two of Us: John Lennon and Paul McCartney—Behind the Myth.* New York: Penguin, 1999.

Goldman, Albert. *The Lives of John Lennon.* New York: Morrow, 1988.

Goldstein, Richard. "On *Revolver.*" *Village Voice* 11.45 (1966): 23–26.

Grace, Kevin Michael. "Beatles Forever." *Report/Newsmagazine* 1 January 2001: 50.

Gunderson, Edna. "The Beatles: The Magical Mystery Lure." *USA Today* 30 March 2001: E1.

Hall, Stuart, and Paddy Whannel. *The Popular Arts.* New York: Pantheon, 1965.

Harrison, Daniel. "After Sundown: The Beach Boys' Experimental Music." *Understanding Rock: Essays in Musical Analysis.* Ed. John Covach and Graeme Boone. Oxford: Oxford UP, 1997. 33–58.

Harrison, George. *I Me Mine.* New York: Simon and Schuster, 1980.

Heinonen, Yrjö, Markus Heuger, Terhi Nurmesjärvi, and Sheila Whiteley, eds. *Beatlestudies 3.* Jyväskylä: U of Jyväskylä Department of Music Research Reports, 2000.

Henke, James, ed. *Lennon: His Life and Work.* Cleveland: Rock and Roll Hall of Fame and Museum, 2000.

———. "The Story behind the Exhibit: Lennon: His Life and Work." Rock and Roll Hall of Fame and Museum. 3 November 2002. <www.rockhall.com/exhibitions/curator>.

Hertsgaard, Mark. *A Day in the Life: The Music and Artistry of the Beatles.* New York: Delacorte, 1995.

Hieronimus, Robert R. *Inside the Yellow Submarine: The Making of the Beatles' Animated Classic.* Iola: Krause, 2002.

"A History of Egyptian Tarot Decks." 2001. <www.spiritone.com/~filipas/Masquerade/Reviews/-historye.html>.

Hooper-Greenhill, Eilean. *Museums and the Interpretation of Visual Culture*. London: Routledge, 2000.

"I Queried Paul." *Brandweek* 5 February 2001: 22.

Inglis, Ian, ed. *The Beatles, Popular Music, and Society: A Thousand Voices*. New York: St. Martin's, 2000.

———. "'Nothing You Can See that Isn't Shown': The Album Covers of the Beatles." *Popular Music* 20.1 (2001): 83–97.

Jameson, Fredric. *The Political Unconscious: Narrative as a Socially Symbolic Act*. Ithaca: Cornell UP, 1981.

———. "Postmodernism and Consumer Society." *Anti-Aesthetic: Essays on Postmodern Culture*. Ed. Hal Foster. Port Townsend: Bay, 1984. 111–25.

———. *Postmodernism or, The Cultural Logic of Late Capitalism*. Durham: Duke UP, 1992.

Jencks, Charles. *What Is Postmodernism?* New York: Wiley, 1996.

Kelly, Michael Bryan. *The Beatle Myth: The British Invasion of American Popular Music, 1956–1969*. Jefferson: McFarland, 1991.

Kendall, Alan. *Medieval Pilgrims*. London: Wayland, 1970.

King, Dominique. "Imagine—Lennon: His Life and Work." 3 November 2002. <www.practical-prose.com/Imagine.html>.

Kozinn, Allan. *The Beatles*. Singapore: Phaidon, 1995.

Kuhn, Annette. *The Power of the Image: Essays on Representation and Sexuality*. London: Routledge, 1985.

Kureishi, Hanif. *London Kills Me: Three Screenplays and Four Essays*. London: Faber and Faber, 1991.

Leary, Timothy. *High Priest*. Berkeley: Ronin, 1968.

Leary, Timothy, Ralph Alpert, and Ralph Metzner. *The Psychedelic Experience: A Manual Based on the Tibetan Book of the Dead*. 1964. New York: Citadel, 1995.

Lee, Martin, and Bruce Shlain. *Acid Dreams: The Complete Social History of LSD—The CIA, the Sixties, and Beyond*. New York: Grove, 1985.

Lennon, John. *In His Own Write*. London: Cape, 1964.

———. *Lennon Remembers*. Interview by Jann Wenner. 1970. New York: Verso, 2000.

———. *A Spaniard in the Works*. London: Cape, 1965.

Lennon, John, and Yoko Ono. Interview by David Sheff. *All We Are Saying: The Last Major Interview with John Lennon and Yoko Ono*. New York: Griffin, 2000. 197.

Lester, Richard, dir. *A Hard Day's Night*. United Artists, 1964.

———, dir. *Help!* United Artists, 1965.

Lewisohn, Mark. *The Beatles: Recording Sessions*. New York: Harmony, 1988.

———. *The Complete Beatles Chronicle*. London: Pyramid, 1995.

Lindsay-Hogg, Michael, dir. *Let It Be*. United Artists, 1970.

Lockwood, Allison. *The Passionate Pilgrims: The American Traveler in Great Britain, 1800–1814*. Oxford: Oxford UP, 1981.

"London's Rock 'n' Roll Shrines." *Time Out* 2–9 November 1994: 16.

Luke, Timothy. *Museum Politics: Power Plays at the Exhibition*. Minneapolis: U of Minnesota P, 2002.

MacDonald, Ian. *Revolution in the Head: The Beatles' Records and the Sixties*. New York: Henry Holt, 1994.

Marshall, P. David. "The Celebrity Legacy of the Beatles." Inglis 163–75.

Martin, George, prod. "The Making of *Sgt. Pepper*." Television documentary. ATV, 1992.

———, with Jeremy Hornsby. *All You Need Is Ears*. New York: St. Martin's, 1979.

———, with William Pearson. *With a Little Help from My Friends: The Making of "Sgt. Pepper."* Boston: Little, Brown, 1994.

Masters, R. E. L., and Jean Houston. *The Varieties of Psychedelic Experience*. New York: Holt, Rinehart, and Winston, 1966.

McCartney, Paul. Interview by Mark Lewisohn. *The Beatles: Recording Sessions*. 6–15.

———. Interview by Terri Gross. *Fresh Air*. NPR. 30 April 2001.

———. "Paul McCartney Discusses *Blackbird Singing*." Interview by Larry King. *Larry King Live*. CNN. 12 June 2001.

———. *Back in the U.S.: Live 2002*. Capitol, 2002.

McCartney, Paul, and Wings. *Band on the Run*. Apple, 1973.

McCulley, Jerry. "Amazon.com Essential Recording." 2001. <www.amazon.com>.

McMullen, Randy. "McCartney, Ono at It again over Songwriting Credits." *BayArea.com*. 17 December 2002. <www.bayarea.com/mld/cctimes4753>.

Mellers, Wilfred. *Twilight of the Gods: The Music of the Beatles*. New York: Schirmer, 1973.

Middleton, Richard. *Studying Popular Music*. Milton Keynes: Open UP, 1990.

Miles, Barry. *Paul McCartney: Many Years from Now*. New York: Holt, 1997.

Miller, James. *Flowers in the Dustbin: The Rise of Rock and Roll, 1947–1977*. New York: Fireside, 1999.

Moore, Allan F. *The Beatles: Sgt. Pepper's Lonely Hearts Club Band*. Cambridge: Cambridge UP, 1997.

——— . *Rock: The Primary Text*. Milton Keynes: Open UP, 1993.

Morris, David B. "Burns and Heteroglossia." *The Eighteenth Century: Theory and Interpretation* 28.1 (1987): 3–27.

Münch, Christopher, dir. *The Hours and Times*. Fox Lorber, 1991.

Munroe, Alexandra, and John Hendricks, eds. *Yes: Yoko Ono*. New York: Japan Society and Abrams, 2000.

Murphy, Patrick D. "Reclaiming the Power: Robinson Jeffers's Verse Novels." *Western American Literature* 22.2 (1987): 125–48.

Neaverson, Bob. *The Beatles Movies*. London: Cassell, 1997.

——— . "Tell Me What You See: The Influence and Impact of the Beatles' Movies." Inglis 150–62.

Norman, Philip. *Shout!: The Beatles in Their Generation*. New York: Simon and Schuster, 1981.

O'Grady, Terence. *The Beatles: A Musical Evolution*. Boston: Twayne, 1983.

Paddison, Max. *Adorno's Aesthetics of Music*. Cambridge: Cambridge UP, 1993.

Pang, May, and Henry Edwards. *Loving John: The Untold Story*. Los Angeles: Warner, 1983.

"Paul McCartney Defends Songwriting Credit Switch." *Salon Magazine* 19 December 2002. <www.salon.com/ent/wire/2002/12/18/mccartney>.

Poirier, Richard. *The Performing Self: Compositions and Decompositions in the Languages of Contemporary Life*. Oxford: Oxford UP, 1971.

Price, Charles Gower. "American with a Liverpudlian Accent: The First Two Beatles' EMI Singles." Heinonen, Heuger, Nurmesjärvi, and Whiteley 181–88.

Pritchard, David, and Alan Lysaght, eds. *The Beatles: An Oral History*. New York: Hyperion, 1998.

Puterbaugh, Parke. "John Lennon, 1940–1980." Henke 168–69.

Reader, Ian. Conclusion. Reader and Walter 220–46.

——— . Introduction. Reader and Walter 1–25.

Reader, Ian, and Tony Walter, eds. *Pilgrimage in Popular Culture*. London: Macmillan, 1993.

Reising, Russell, ed. *"Every Sound There Is": The Beatles' "Revolver" and the Transformation of Rock and Roll*. Aldershot: Ashgate, 2002.

——— . "Introduction: 'Of the Beginning.'" Reising 1–14.

——— . "'It is not dying': *Revolver* and the Birth of Psychedelic Sound." Reising 234–53.

Rice, Tim, Paul Gambaccini, and Mike Read. *Guinness British Hit Singles*. 5th ed. Enfield: Guinness, 1985.

Rico, Pablo. "Seduction of the Gaze and Life Experience in the Work of Yoko Ono." Munroe and Hendricks 265–67.

Riley, Tim. *Tell Me Why: A Beatles Commentary*. New York: Knopf, 1988.

Roane, Kit R. "We Love Them Yeah, Yeah, Yeah, and Yeah!" *U.S. News and World Report* 15 January 2001: 43.

Sambhava, Padma. *The Tibetan Book of the Dead: The Great Book of Liberation through Understanding in the Between*. Trans. Robert Thurman. New York: Bantam, 1994.

Savage, Jon. "100 Greatest Psychedelic Classics." *Mojo* 43 (1997): 56–67.

Schaffner, Nicholas. *The Beatles Forever*. Harrisburg: Cameron, 1977.

Scheurer, Timothy E. "The Beatles, the Brill Building, and the Persistence of Tin Pan Alley in the Age of Rock." *Popular Music and Society* 20.4 (1996): 89–102.

Scott, Derek. "What's the Copy?: The Beatles and Oasis." Heinonen, Heuger, Nurmesjärvi, and Whiteley 201–11.

Seaman, Fred. *The Last Days of John Lennon*. New York: Birch Lane, 1991.

Sellars, Richard West, and Tony Walter. "From Custer to Kent State: Heroes, Martyrs, and the Evolution of Popular Shrines in the U.S.A." Reader and Walter 179–200.

Sheffield, Rob. "Beatles Save World for Second Time." *Rolling Stone* 15 February 2001: 28.

Siegel, Jules. "Requiescat in Pace: That's Where It's At." *Village Voice* 11.46 (1966): 7, 14.

Sigaux, Gilbert. *History of Tourism*. London: Leisure Arts, 1966.

Smith, Caspar. "Bastion of the Politically Incorrect." *Daily Telegraph* 2 September 1995: 11.

Smith, Valene. "The Quest in Guest." *Annals of Tourism Research* 19.1 (1992): 1–17.

Sontag, Susan. "Amerikas dotre." *Henne* 10 (September–October 2000): 118.

Strausbaugh, John. "The Hall of Lame: Why There Shouldn't be Rock Museums." *Rock 'Til You Drop: The Decline from Rebellion to Nostalgia*. New York: Verso, 2001. 173–89.

Sulpy, Doug, and Ray Schweighardt. *Get Back: The Unauthorized Chronicle of the Beatles' Let It Be Disaster*. New York: Griffin, 1997.

Thompson, John B. *Ideology and Modern Culture: Critical Social Theory in the Era of Mass Communication*. Stanford: Stanford UP, 1990.

Tillekens, Ger. "A Flood of Flat-Sevenths." Reising 121–38.

Tong, Rosemarie. *Feminist Thought: A Comprehensive Introduction*. London: Routledge, 1998.

Towner, John. "The Grand Tour: A Key Phase in the History of Tourism." *Annals of Tourism Research* 12 (1985): 297–334.

Turner, Steve. *A Hard Day's Write: The Stories behind Every Beatles Song*. London: Carlton, 2000.

Turner, Victor, and Edith Turner. *Image and Pilgrimage in Christian Culture*. Oxford: Blackwell, 1978.

Valdez, Stephen. "*Revolver* as a Pivotal Art Work: Structure, Harmony, and Vocal Harmonization." Reising 89–108.

———. "Vocal Harmony as a Structural Device in the Commercial Recordings of the Beatles, 1962–1970." Heinonen, Heuger, Nurmesjärvi, and Whiteley 243–54.

Wagner, Naphtali. "Tonal Family Resemblance in *Revolver*." Reising 109–20.

Warwick, Jacqueline. "You're Going to Lose That Girl: The Beatles and the Girl Groups." Heinonen, Heuger, Nurmesjärvi, and Whiteley 161–68.

Wenner, Jann S. "Notes on the Ballad of John and Yoko." Munroe and Hendricks 58–61.

Whiteley, Sheila. "'Love is all and love is everyone': A Discussion of Four Musical Portraits." Reising 209–21.

———. "No Fixed Agenda: The Position of the Beatles within Popular/Rock Music." Heinonen, Heuger, Nurmesjärvi, and Whiteley 3–13.

———, ed. *Sexing the Groove: Popular Music and Gender*. London: Routledge, 1998.

———. *The Space between the Notes: Rock and the Counter-Culture*. London: Routledge, 1992.

———. *Women and Popular Music: Sexuality, Identity, and Subjectivity*. London: Routledge, 2000.

Whitley, Ed. "The Postmodern *White Album*." Inglis 105–25.

Widgery, David. "Lennonism." *Preserving Disorder*. London: Pluto, 1989. 69–75.

Wiener, Jon. *Come Together: John Lennon in His Time*. 1984. London: Faber and Faber, 1995.

Wolfe, Arnold, and Margaret Haefner. "Taste Cultures, Affective Alliances, and Popular Music Reception: Theory, Methodology, and an Application to a Beatles Song." *Popular Music and Society* 20.4 (1996): 127–55.

Womack, Kenneth. "Editing the Beatles: Addressing the Roles of Authority and Editorial Theory in the Creation of Popular Music's Most Valuable Canon." *TEXT: An Interdisciplinary Annual of Textual Studies* 11 (1998): 189–205.

You Can't Do That: The Making of "A Hard Day's Night." MPI Home Video, 1994.

Yule, Andrew. *The Man Who "Framed" the Beatles: A Biography of Richard Lester.* New York: Fine, 1994.

Zappa, Frank, and the Mothers of Invention. *We're Only in It for the Money.* 1968. Ryko, 1995.

CONTRIBUTORS

John Covach is professor of music at the University of Rochester. He has written widely on twelve-tone music, the philosophy and aesthetics of music, and rock music. He is the coeditor (with Walter Everett) of *Understanding Rock: Essays in Musical Analysis* (1997). He recently coedited two special issues of *Contemporary Music Review* on "American Rock and the Classical Music Tradition" and "Traditions, Institutions, and American Popular Music." He currently serves as coeditor of the journal *In Theory Only*.

Todd F. Davis is assistant professor of English at Penn State University's Altoona College. In addition to publishing numerous articles and reviews in journals such as *Critique, College Literature, Western American Literature, Literature/Film Quarterly, Studies in Short Fiction, Mississippi Quarterly,* and *Yeats/Eliot Review,* among others, Davis is the author of *Ripe,* a collection of poetry published by Bottom Dog Press. He is the coeditor (with Kenneth Womack) of *Mapping the Ethical Turn: A Reader in Ethics, Culture, and Literary Theory* (2001) and the author (with Womack) of *Formalist Criticism and Reader-Response Theory* (2002).

James M. Decker is assistant professor of English at Illinois Central College, where he specializes in twentieth-century literature and culture. His articles have appeared in journals such as *Deus Loci, George Eliot-George Henry Lewes Studies, Paintbrush,* and *College Literature.* He is the author of *Ideology* (2003).

Walter Everett is associate professor of music in music theory at the University of Michigan. He is the author of *The Beatles as Musicians,* a two-volume study that includes *Revolver through the Anthology* (1999) and *The Quarry Men through Rubber Soul* (2001). He is also the editor of *Expression in Pop-Rock Music: A Collection of Critical and Analytical Essays* (2000), which includes his essay, "Confessions from Blueberry Hell, or, Pitch Can Be a Sticky Substance."

Paul Gleed is a doctoral candidate at the State University of New York at Buffalo. His research interests include literary theory as well as early modern and contemporary British literature and culture. His favorite (and first) Beatles album is *Rubber Soul*.

John Kimsey is assistant professor in DePaul University's School for New Learning. He teaches and writes about modern literature and popular culture and has worked as a professional musician. His essay, "How the Beatles Invented the A-Bomb," appeared in the spring 2001 issue of *Proteus*.

Ian Marshall is professor of English at Penn State University's Altoona College. He is the author of *Story Line: Exploring the Literature of the Appalachian Trail* (1998) and *Peak Experiences: Walking Meditations on Literature, Nature, and Need* (2003). Marshall has published numerous essays in journals such as *Modern Language Studies*, *Legacy*, *Interdisciplinary Studies in Literature and Environment*, *Papers on Language and Literature*, *Western American Literature*, and *Mississippi Quarterly* among others.

Kevin McCarron is reader in American literature at the University of Surrey Roehampton. He is the author of *William Golding* (1995), *The Coincidence of Opposites: William Golding's Later Fiction* (1997), and the coauthor of *Frightening Fiction: Contemporary Classics of Children's Literature* (2001). He is currently working on a book about drug addiction, alcoholism, and recidivism.

William M. Northcutt teaches literature, grammar, and cultural studies at the University of Wuppertal in Germany. In addition to publishing articles on Pound and Yeats, he is currently working on a book titled *Rocking the Culture/Popping the Lit*, a study of contemporary American novels and their generic use of popular culture and its iconography.

Russell Reising is professor of American literature and culture at the University of Toledo. He is the author of *The Unusable Past: Theory and the Study of American Literature* (1986), *Loose Ends: Closure and Crisis in the American Social Text* (1996), and the editor of *"Every Sound There Is": The Beatles' Revolver and the Transformation of Rock and Roll* (2002). He is currently editing a collection of essays on Pink Floyd's *Dark Side of the Moon*, as well as working on book-length manuscripts on cold war popular music and on Anglo-American psychedelia.

Jeffrey Roessner is assistant professor of English at Mercyhurst College in Erie, Pennsylvania. His scholarly interests include cultural studies and contemporary British historiographic fiction, and he has published essays on the work of John Fowles, Angela Carter, and Jeanette Winterson among others. A longtime Beatles fan and a musician, he plays guitar in a band that once opened for Bo Diddley.

Jane Tompkins is professor of education at the University of Illinois at Chicago. She is the author and editor of a number of volumes devoted to literary theory and culture, including *Reader-Response Criticism: From Formalism to Poststructuralism* (1980), *Sensational Designs: The Cultural Work of American Fiction, 1790–1870* (1985), *West of Everything: The Inner Life of Westerns* (1992), and *A Life in School: What the Teacher Learned* (1996).

Sheila Whiteley is professor of popular music at the University of Salford. She is the author of *The Space between the Notes: Rock and the Counter-Culture* (1992), *Women and Popular Music: Sexuality, Identity, and Subjectivity* (2000), and *Too Much Too Young: Popular Music, Age, and Gender* (2003). She is also the editor of *Sexing the Groove: Popular Music and Gender* (1998).

Kenneth Womack is associate professor of English and head of the Division of Arts and Humanities at Penn State University's Altoona College. He serves as editor of *Interdisciplinary Literary Studies: A Journal of Criticism and Theory* and as coeditor (with William Baker) of Oxford University Press's *Year's Work in English Studies*. He is the author of *Postwar Academic Fiction: Satire, Ethics, Community* (2001), the coauthor (with Ruth Robbins and Julian Wolfreys) of *Key Concepts in Literary Theory* (2002), and the coeditor (with John V. Knapp) of *Reading the Family Dance: Family Systems Therapy and Literary Study* (2003).

INDEX

Abbey Road, 1, 3, 10, 17, 25, 28, 34, 46, 50, 84, 92, 107, 163, 171, 175

Abbey Road Medley, 3, 25, 46, 49, 53n13, 93n2, 94n17, 190

Abbey Road Studios, 29, 107, 133, 167, 171, 175, 177, 180

ABC Television, 101, 105, 188

Abdul, Paula, 192

"Across the Universe," 91

"Act Naturally," 79

Adorno, Theodor, 173, 177

"Ain't No Sunshine," 120

Ali, Mohammad, 137

Alice's Adventures in Wonderland, 17, 142, 144, 156

Alice's Adventures through the Looking-Glass, 17

"All I Have to Do Is Dream," 40

"All I've Got to Do," 74, 75

"All My Loving," 73, 105

"All You Need Is Love," 61, 68, 91, 105, 119, 149, 190, 194n11

Alpert, Richard, 112, 114

"And I Love Her," 74, 75, 76

"And Your Bird Can Sing," 66, 118, 124

Angels, The, 62

"Anna (Go to Him)," 73, 74, 81

"Another Girl," 64, 78

"Any Time at All," 76

Apple Corps, 98, 105, 151, 165, 187, 188, 190, 191, 192, 193

Appleyard, Bryan, 179

Aqualung, 112

Archies, The, 187

"Are You Lonesome Tonight?," 58

Arsenio Hall Show, The, 186

Asher, Jane, 165, 209, 210

"Ask Me Why," 44, 73

Aspinall, Neil, 193

Attali, Jacques, 99

Auden, W. H., 19

Babiuk, Andy, 86, 93n3, 93n6, 94n7, 94n8, 94n13

"Baby It's You," 60, 68n7, 72, 73

"Baby You're a Rich Man," 88

"Baby's in Black," 76, 77, 79

Bach, Johann Sebastian, 113, 167, 215

Bacharach, Burt, 57

"Bachelor Boy," 58

Back in the U.S., 197

"Back in the U.S.A.," 15, 157

"Back in the U.S.S.R.," 3, 15, 19, 79, 89–90, 91, 157

Backstreet Boys, The, 1, 184

"Bad Boy," 79

Badman, Keith, 191, 192, 194n2

Baez, Joan, 15

Baker, Geoff, 197

Bakhtin, Mikhail M., 4, 9–35, 156

"Ballad of John and Yoko, The," 89, 92, 94n9, 189

Banana Splits, The, 102

Band on the Run, 146n7

Bannister, Matthew, 69n9

Barlow, Hugh, 108n4

Barrow, Tony, 99, 105

Baudrillard, Jean, 173, 174

BBC, 18, 37, 105

Beach Boys, The, 15, 19, 51, 53, 85, 137, 143, 151, 154, 157, 187

Beatlemania, 1, 4, 26, 97, 98, 102, 108n1, 109n7, 131, 132, 133, 138, 162, 166, 180n3

Beatlemania [Broadway show], 193n1

Beatles, 1962–1966, The, 189

Beatles, 1969–1970, The, 189

Beatles, The [The White Album], 3, 4, 5, 15, 16, 17, 24, 25, 28, 31, 67, 84, 89, 91, 92, 101, 105, 107, 126, 127, 147–58, 190

Beatles Anthology, The [albums], 186, 189, 199, 213n12

Beatles Anthology, The [book], 1, 14, 17, 18, 21, 22, 23, 28, 29, 32, 34n1, 107, 130, 135, 136, 139, 144, 146n2, 184, 190, 191

Beatles Anthology, The [documentary], 52n5, 108, 186, 188, 189, 190, 194n4

Beatles for Sale, 76, 91, 108n1

Beethoven, Ludwig van, 113

"Because," 3, 31, 89, 94n13

Beck, 91

Beggar's Banquet, 126

"Being for the Benefit of Mr. Kite," 17, 27, 85, 86, 143, 145, 218

Berry, Chuck, 15, 38, 40, 57, 58, 150, 151, 154, 157, 168

"Besame Mucho," 189

Best, Pete, 68n6

Bhagavadgita, 139

"Bike," 119

"Birthday," 31, 91, 148, 155

Björk, 91

"Blackbird," 15, 89, 153, 198

Blackboard Jungle, 98

Blair, Lionel, 165

Blake, Peter, 104, 137

Blue Gardenia Club, 170

"Blue Jay Way," 50, 88, 105

"Blueberry Hill," 40

Bolan, Marc, 174

Bonzo Dog Band, 128n5

Bootles, The, 62

Borges, Jorge Luis, 187

Bowman, Marion, 169, 180

"Boys," 60

Bradford, Janie, 190

Brahms, Johannes, 113

Brando, Marlon, 27, 104

Breines, Wini, 148

Bricolage, 15

Brill Building, 37, 38, 39, 40, 52n9

Brodax, Al, 105

Brocken, Michael, 51n2

Brown, Julie, 183, 184, 187

Brown, Peter, 108n2, 108n5

Browne, Tara, 145

Bruce, Lenny, 27, 137

Buck Rogers, 165

Burke, John, 108n3

Burns, Gary, 191, 194n6

Burns, Robert, 11

Burroughs, William, 27, 124–25

Butthole Surfers, The, 129

Byrds, The, 51

"California Girls," 157

Californication, 113

Canterbury Tales, 169

"Can't Buy Me Love," 43, 52n10

Capitol Records, 100, 103, 109n6, 187, 189, 192, 194n7

Carnival, 25–28

Carroll, Lewis, 17, 86
"Carry That Weight," 92
Cartland, Barbara, 156, 158n1
"Cathy's Clown," 60
Cavern Club, 98, 109n7, 172, 176, 177
"Chains," 10, 60, 68n7, 73
Channel, Bruce, 59
Character Zones, 10, 13, 30–32
Chaucer, Geoffrey, 160
Chen, Ed, 188
Christ, Jesus, 103, 130, 137
Chronotope, 13, 28–30
Churchill, Winston, 188
Clapton, Eric, 91
"Clarabella," 188
Clash, The, 127
Cleave, Maureen, 130
Clinton, Bill, 186, 189, 193
Cohen, Eric, 180
Coltrane, John, 125, 192
Columbia Records, 151
"Come Together," 28, 79, 89, 90, 92
Connolly, Ray, 65
"Continuing Story of Bungalow Bill,
    The," 2, 15, 89, 91
Cookies, The, 60
Copeland, Stewart, 15
Costello, Elvis, 127
Couric, Katie, 183
Covach, John, 4, 37–53, 52n7
Cream, 91
"Crippled Inside," 211
Cross, Mike, 12
Crowley, Aleister, 27
"Cry Baby Cry," 89

Daily Howl, 201
Dakota, 181n5, 201
Dalai Lama, 82, 103
Dark Side of the Moon, 113
David, Hal, 57
Davies, Hunter, 94n12, 152–53, 199
Davis, Clive, 181n4

Davis, Todd F., 1–6, 97–110
Day, Doris, 216, 217, 218
"Day in the Life, A," 18, 21, 24, 25, 29,
    48–49, 85, 86, 114, 138, 140, 141,
    142, 144–45, 211, 213n11
"Day Tripper," 81, 91, 189
Days of Future Passed, 146n5
"Dear Boy," 34
"Dear Prudence," 24, 67, 89
"Dear Yoko," 211
Debord, Guy, 135, 146n6
Decca Records, 2
Decker, James M., 5, 183–95
Dekker, Thomas, 17
"Devil in Her Heart," 61, 73, 74
"Devil in His Heart," 93n5
Dialogism, 10, 11, 12
"Dig a Pony," 91, 94n9
"Dig It," 90
"Directive," 114
"Dizzy Miss Lizzie," 79
"Do You Want to Know a Secret?," 74
"Doctor Robert," 26, 112, 115, 118, 122
"Doctrine of Kabalism, The," 94n12
Domino, Fats, 40
Don Quixote, 187
Donays, The, 61, 93n5
Donegan, Lonnie, 58, 164
Donne, John, 113
"Don't Bother Me," 12, 50, 74, 75, 76
"Don't Ever Change," 73
"Don't Let Me Down," 91
"Don't Pass Me By," 92, 148
"Double-Coding," 5, 167
Douglas, Susan, 62
Dowlding, William, 130, 135
Driscoll, Julie, 67
"Drive My Car," 3, 20, 45, 80, 81, 82,
    210
Duel in the Sun, 217
Duffy, Thom, 186
Dunning, George, 105
Durkheim, Émile, 180n1

Dvořák, Antonín, 126
Dylan, Bob, 13, 15, 19, 24, 27, 64,
    69n10, 134, 156, 163, 192

E! Network, 184
Eastern Music Circle of London, 14
Easthope, Antony, 185
Ebert, Roger, 102
Eckberg, Peter, 164
Eco, Umberto, 156
Ed Sullivan Show, 9, 37, 51n1, 56, 75,
    98, 100, 102, 108, 151
Ehrenreich, Barbara, 56
Eight Arms to Hold You, 102
"Eight Days a Week," 29, 42–43, 77, 138
Einstein, Albert, 27
Ekberg, Anita, 217
"Eleanor Rigby," 2, 21, 26, 61, 66, 83,
    84, 112, 115, 116, 119, 120, 124, 129,
    132, 168, 179, 189, 190, 207, 216
Eliade, Mircea, 180n1
Elliott, Anthony, 200, 205
Emerick, Geoff, 134
Emerson, Lake, and Palmer, 127
Emerson, Ralph Waldo, 118
EMI, 57, 74, 86, 93n3, 187, 189, 192
"End, The," 12, 25, 34, 90
Epstein, Brian, 57, 93n3, 98, 99, 102,
    106, 108n1, 108n2, 108n5, 109n9,
    109n10, 136, 171, 187, 191, 194n2
Eric Burdon and the Animals, 119, 127
Evans, Mal, 80, 85, 86
Everett, Walter, 4, 17, 25, 51n2, 53n13,
    71–94, 93n2, 93n3, 93n5, 94n17,
    116, 134, 139, 200, 207, 208, 211,
    213n7, 213n12
Everitt, Anthony, 172
Everly Brothers, The, 40, 58, 60
Everly, Don, 73
Everly, Phil, 73
"Every Little Thing," 45, 77
"Everybody's Trying to Be My Baby," 73
Ewing, Marcia, 202–03

Faith, Adam, 57, 58
Faithful, Marianne, 67, 144
Fiedler, Leslie, 163
Fields, W. C., 27
Fitzgerald, Jon, 52n9
5.1 Degrees of Separation, 94n10
"Fixing a Hole," 19, 85, 129, 140, 208
"Flying," 88
Fonda, Peter, 21
"Fool on the Hill, The," 19, 28, 31, 88,
    93n1, 105, 155, 208
"For No One," 66, 82, 112, 116, 117,
    119, 120, 121, 123, 124
"For You Blue," 90
Forte, Allen, 52n8
Friedman, Wayne, 193
Frith, Simon, 61
"From Me to You," 4, 41, 56, 61, 73, 74,
    185, 189
From the New World, 126
Frost, Robert, 114
Fun in Acapulco, 98

Gaines, Steven, 187
Gambaccini, Paul, 69n8
Gandhi, Mahatma, 137
Gang of Four, 127
Gendron, Bernard, 166
Genesis, 113
Gennep, Arnold van, 175
Genre Blending, 13–16
Gerry and the Pacemakers," 58
Get Back, 107, 110n11, 110n12
"Get Back," 90, 168
"Getting Better," 85, 87, 127n3, 134,
    138
Ghost of Tom Joad, The, 113
G.I. Blues, 98
Gillespie, Nick, 186
Gilmore, Mikal, 51n1
Ginsberg, Allen, 124
"Girl," 80
Girl Can't Help It, The, 101

"Girl Named Sandoz, A," 119
Girls! Girls! Girls!, 98
Giuliano, Geoffrey, 14, 15, 17, 21, 31, 183, 185, 186, 191
"Give Peace a Chance," 198
"Glass Onion," 19–20, 49, 92, 155, 211
Gleed, Paul, 5, 161–68
"God," 211
"God Only Knows," 85
Goffin, Gerry, 38, 39, 57, 68n7
"Golden Slumbers," 17
Goldman, Albert, 177, 179, 181n5, 205
Goldstein, Richard, 113
"Good Day Sunshine," 29, 81, 82, 83, 84, 116, 120, 123, 124
"Good Morning Good Morning," 29, 143, 145
"Good Night," 15, 89, 148
Goon Show, 164
Gordy, Berry, 190
"Got to Get You into My Life," 82, 112, 116, 118, 121, 123, 124
Grace, Kevin Michael, 193
Graceland, 181n4
"Great Balls of Fire," 40
Gross, Terri, 198
Gundersen, Edna, 1
Guthrie, Woody, 113
Guzman, Abimael, 111

Haefner, Margaret, 194n11
Hall, Stuart, 162, 163
Hamilton, Richard, 154
Hamlet, 165, 185
Hammer, M. C., 192
Handel, George Frideric, 82
"Happiness Is a Warm Gun," 15, 18, 24, 49, 90, 91, 93n1
Hard Day's Night, A [album], 15, 75, 108n1, 168
Hard Day's Night, A [film], 1, 4, 97, 98, 99–102, 104, 105, 108, 108n1, 108n3, 109n9, 162, 165

"Hard Day's Night, A," 29, 41–42, 73, 76, 109n7
Harris, Paul, 51
Harrison, Daniel, 51, 53
Havadtoy, Sam, 204
Hayward, Justin, 146n5
"Heartbreak Hotel," 40
Hedley, David, 108n4
"Hello Goodbye," 88
Help! [album], 13, 15, 61, 63, 76, 78, 81, 108n1
Help! [film], 4, 13, 97, 102–04, 105, 108, 108n1, 109n7, 165
"Help!," 13, 30, 43, 77, 79, 177
"Helter Skelter," 24, 25, 30
Hendricks, John, 213n4
Hendrix, Jimi, 112, 137
Henke, James, 201–06, 207, 208, 210, 211, 213n10, 213n13
"Her Majesty," 25
"Here Comes the Sun," 50, 80, 89
"Here, There, and Everywhere," 66, 112, 116, 119, 120, 121, 123, 124, 207, 208, 213n6
Herman's Hermits, 193
Hertsgaard, Mark, 161, 210
Hess, Elizabeth, 56
"Hey Baby," 59
"Hey Bulldog," 91
"Hey Jude," 25, 32, 66, 89, 90, 170, 178, 197, 199
Hieronimus, Robert R., 109n10
Hitler, Adolph, 137
"Hold Me Tight," 12, 75
Holiday, Billie, 192
Holly, Buddy, 38, 40, 57, 150
"Honey Don't," 76
"Honey Pie," 81, 91–92, 148, 155
Hooper-Greenhill, Eilean, 205, 212
Hopkins, Nicky, 89
Hornsby, Jeremy, 52n10
"Hound Dog," 40
Houston, Jean, 125

"How Do You Do It?," 58
"How Do You Sleep?," 34
Hud, 217
Hudson, Rock, 217
Hussein, Saddam, 186
Huxley, Aldous, 27

"I Am the Walrus," 17, 18, 19, 24,
    27–28, 86, 88, 91, 105, 155, 207
"I Call Your Name," 76
I Ching, 17
"I Don't Want to Spoil the Party," 23, 76
"I Feel Fine," 32, 76
"I Me Mine," 29, 89
"I Need You," 50, 79
"I Saw Her Standing There," 60, 73
"I Should Have Known Better," 76
"I Wanna Be Your Man," 72
"I Want to Hold Your Hand," 2, 4, 41,
    42, 75, 216, 219
"I Want to Tell You," 115, 121, 123, 124
"I Want You (She's So Heavy)," 25, 67,
    90
"I Will," 90, 92
"If I Fell," 76, 77
"If I Needed Someone," 50, 64, 80
Ifield, Frank, 58
"I'll Be Back," 44, 76, 184
"I'll Follow the Sun," 76
"I'll Get You," 77
"I'll Let You Hold My Hand," 62
"I'm a Loser," 13, 30, 43, 76
"I'm Down," 45, 79
"I'm Looking through You," 45, 81
"I'm Only Sleeping," 26, 83, 114, 116,
    119, 120, 121, 122, 123
"I'm So Tired," 24
"I'm Sure to Fall," 59
Imagine [film], 204
"Imagine," 211
In His Own Write, 17, 21
"In My Life," 30, 81, 132, 167, 206–09
Indica Gallery, 171

Indra Club, 57, 176
Inglis, Ian, 153
"Inner Light, The," 88, 92, 93n1, 114,
    118
"Interstellar Overdrive," 119
Intertextuality, 13, 16–20
Isley Brothers, The, 60
"It Won't Be Long," 44
"It's All Too Much," 76, 88, 93n1
"It's My Life," 127
"It's Only Love," 79
"I've Got a Feeling," 89
"I've Just Seen a Face," 79

Jackson, Chuck, 68n7
Jackson, Michael, 194n5
Jacobs, Gloria, 56
Jagger, Mick, 144
James, Dick, 187
Jameson, Fredric, 131, 134, 135, 148,
    149, 150, 157
Jeffers, Robinson, 11
Jefferson Airplane, 119–20
Jencks, Charles, 167
Jethro Tull, 112
Johnny and the Moondogs, 68n6, 136,
    176
"Johnny B. Goode," 40
Jones, Jennifer, 217
"Julia," 17, 31, 66, 89
Jungle Book, The, 218
"(Just Like) Starting Over," 211

Kaiserkeller Club, 57, 176, 177
"Kama Sutra," 128n5
Kandinsky, Wassily, 92
"Kansas City," 72, 109n7
Keaton, Buster, 165
Kelly, Michael Brian, 194n2
Kendall, Alan, 180n1
Kennedy, John F., 2
Kennedy, Robert F., 149
Kimsey, James, 212n1

Kimsey, John, 6, 197–213
King, Ben E., 68n7
King, Carole, 38, 39, 57, 68n7
King, Dominique, 204
King, Larry, 199, 200
King Lear, 18, 88
King, Martin Luther, Jr., 149
Kirschherr, Astrid, 57
Klein, Allen, 171
Knots, 116
"Kon Tiki," 58
Koschminder, Bruno, 57
Kozinn, Allan, 15
Ku Klux Klan, 131
Kuhn, Annette, 67
Kureishi, Hanif, 178, 179

"Lady Madonna," 19, 49, 67, 89, 91,
    155, 189
Laing, R. D., 116
Lamb Lies Down on Broadway, The, 113
Landau, Jon, 149, 150, 158
Last DJ, The, 113
"Last Train to Liverpool," 62
Laurel and Hardy, 27
Leander, Mike, 35n2, 86
Leary, Timothy, 17, 112, 114, 117, 132,
    134, 139, 142, 146n3, 211
LeBlanc, Jim, 128n4
Led Zeppelin, 91
Lee, Martin, 125
Leiber, Jerry, 38, 57
Lennon: His Life and Work [exhibition],
    200–12, 212n2
Lennon, Julian, 94n11, 94n12, 108n5,
    194n6
Lennon, Sean, 201
Lester, Richard, 101, 102, 109n9, 165
Let It Be [album], 28, 32–33, 82, 91, 92,
    110n11, 110n12
Let It Be [film], 4, 28, 46, 97, 106–08,
    109n7, 110n11
"Let It Be," 66, 89, 90, 179, 184, 199

Let It Be . . . Naked, 110n12
"Let Me Roll It," 34
Lewis, Jerry Lee, 40
Lewisohn, Mark, 61, 133, 143
Lindsay-Hogg, Michael, 28, 107
Liston, Sonny, 27, 104
"Little Beatle Boy," 62
Little Big Man, 164
"Little Child," 72
Little Richard, 57, 151, 168
Live at the BBC, 51n3, 186, 187, 188
Lockwood, Allison, 180n2
"Long and Winding Road, The," 89, 90,
    199
"Long Long Long," 89, 92
Lopez, Jennifer, 190
"Love Me Do," 12, 56, 57, 58, 59, 60,
    61, 74
Love Story, 105
"Love You To," 66, 84, 112, 114, 115,
    117, 119, 120, 124, 139
"Lovely Rita," 18, 27, 67, 85, 86, 127, 139
LSD, 26, 33, 114, 115, 117, 118, 119,
    122, 125, 132, 141–42, 211
"Lucy in the Sky with Diamonds," 14,
    17, 66, 85, 86, 88, 93n1, 94n13,
    94n15, 115, 119, 134, 140, 141, 142,
    146n1, 207, 211, 218
Luke, Timothy, 203, 205, 212
Lyotard, Jean-François, 15
Lysaght, Alan, 164, 165, 166, 167

MacDonald, Ian, 3, 124, 131, 134, 138,
    139, 142, 145, 146n3, 170, 177, 178,
    200, 207, 208, 210, 211, 213n7,
    213n9
Madame Tussaud's Wax Museum, 152,
    172
"Maggie Mae," 90
"Magic Bus, The," 119
"Magic Carpet Ride," 119
Magical Mystery Tour [album], 16, 27,
    28, 39, 46, 49, 88, 188

Magical Mystery Tour [film], 4, 39, 46, 49, 97, 104–06
"Magical Mystery Tour," 88, 94n9
Maharishi Mahesh Yogi, 14–15, 67, 217
"Make Love Flying," 119–20
Maltz, Stephen, 187
Mantovani, Annunzio Paolo, 167
Mao Tse-Tung, 111
Marshall, Ian, 4, 9–35
Marshall, P. David, 192
"Martha My Dear," 15, 67, 89, 91
Martin, George, 2, 21, 35n2, 52n10, 57, 58, 59, 78, 79, 80, 83, 86, 89, 94n9, 94n13, 133, 134, 137, 144, 146n4, 155, 167, 168
Marvelletes, The, 60
Marx, Karl, 27
Marylebone Registry Office, 170
Mason, Bonnie Jo [Cher], 62
Masters, R. E. L., 125
"Matchbox," 72, 73
"Maxwell's Silver Hammer," 89, 92
MBE, 166
McCarron, Kevin, 5, 169–81
McCartney, James, 138, 146n9
McCartney, Linda, 170
McCartney, Mary, 179
McCulley, Jerry, 189
McMullen, Randy, 197
McRobbie, Angela, 61
"Mean Mr. Mustard," 2, 89
Mellers, Wilfrid, 52n6, 147, 152
Melville, Herman, 120
Mercury, Freddie, 174, 175
"Michelle," 20, 44, 45, 65, 80, 81, 218
Middle Eight, 14, 40, 52n9, 207, 210, 213n11
Middleton, Richard, 56, 57
Miles, Barry, 132, 136, 141, 145, 146n9, 199, 200, 207, 213n11
Milk and Honey, 201
Miller, Abbot, 201
Miller, James, 130

Mills, Heather, 200
Milton, John, 113
Minoff, Lee, 105
Mintz, Elliott, 197, 198
"Misery," 39, 72
"Misty," 39
Möbius, August Ferdinand, 123
"Money (That's I Want)," 72, 190
Monkees, The, 102
Monologism, 10, 11, 12, 13, 32–34
Monroe, Marilyn, 216, 217
Moody Blues, The, 119, 146n5
Moore, Allan F., 136, 137, 172, 200
Morris, David B., 11
Moses, 146n9
"Mother Nature's Son," 15, 93n1
Mozart, Wolfgang, Amadeus, 215
"Mr. Moonlight," 73, 77, 82
MTV, 183, 184, 186, 188
Münch, Christopher, 180n3
Munroe, Alexandra, 213n4
Murphy, Patrick, 11
"Musée des Beaux Artes," 19
Musique concrète, 15
Mussorgsky, Modest Petrovich, 127
"My Bonnie," 189
"My Generation," 127
"My Ole Man's a Dustman," 58

'N Sync, 1, 185
Neaverson, Bob, 98, 101, 102
Nelson, Willie, 113
"Next Time, The," 58
"Night Before, The," 78, 79
"Nights in White Satin," 146n5
Nike, 194n5
"No Reply," 73, 77
Norman, Philip, 99, 154–55
Northcutt, William M., 5, 129–46
"Norwegian Wood (This Bird Has Flown)," 14, 20–21, 23, 44, 45, 50, 65, 72, 80, 213n11
Nostalgia, 150

"Not a Second Time," 72, 77
Novelization, 13, 20–23, 34
"Nowhere Man," 13, 44, 45, 80, 81, 82
Nurk Twins, The, 136

O'Grady, Terence, 60, 64
Oasis, 55, 68n2
"Ob-La-Di, Ob-La-Da," 15, 89, 156
"Oh! Darling," 91
"Old Brown Shoe," 90
On the Waterfront, 104
1 [album], 186, 189
"One after 909, The," 90
"Only a Northern Song," 139
"Only the Lonely," 60
Ono, Yoko, 5, 67, 141, 146n10, 171,
    181n5, 187, 189, 197, 199, 201, 202,
    204, 205, 210, 211, 212, 212n3,
    213n4, 213n10, 217
Open-Endedness, 4, 13, 23–25
Orbison, Roy, 60
Osmond, Donny, 61
Oswald, Lee Harvey, 137
"Over the Rainbow," 39, 207

Pacey, Ann, 102
Paddison, Max, 173, 177
Pang, May, 205, 213n10
"Paperback Writer," 83
Parlophone, 57, 101
Pastiche, 148, 150, 157
Peaches and Herb, 187
Peck, Gregory, 217
Pei, I. M., 200
Penny Lane, 29, 176, 177
"Penny Lane," 29, 46–47, 85, 86, 133,
    134, 137, 144, 164, 168, 177
Perkins, Carl, 57, 59, 73
Perkins, Jay, 73
Pet Sounds, 143
Peter and Gordon, 136
Peyton, Dori, 62
Picasso, Pablo, 153

Pictures at an Exhibition, 127
"Piggies," 15, 31, 83, 89, 191
Pilgrimage, 5, 169–81
Pink Floyd, 112–13, 119
Please Please Me, 3, 10, 60
"Please Please Me," 2, 12, 56, 59, 60, 61,
    74, 88, 164
"Please Mr. Postman," 60
Plummons, The, 62
Poe, Edgar Allan, 18, 27
Poirier, Richard, 113
Police, The, 15
"Polythene Pam," 2, 25
"Poor Me," 58
Porter, Cole, 15
Portishead, 91
Powell, Cynthia, 102, 108n5, 171
Presley, Elvis, 38, 40, 57, 58, 98, 101,
    102, 150, 151, 179, 181n4, 215, 217
Preston, Billy, 89, 91
Price, Charles Gower, 58
Pritchard, David, 164, 165, 166, 167
Private Eye, 63
Profumo Affair, 63
"P.S. I Love You," 74
Psychedelia, 84–88
Puterbaugh, Parke, 203, 211

Quadrophenia, 112
Quarry Bank, 28
Quarry Men, The, 68, 136, 164, 176
Queen, 174
Queen Mother, 168

"Rain," 83, 84, 85, 115, 116
Ramones, The, 127
Read, Mike, 69n8
Reader, Ian, 169, 175
Red Headed Stranger, 113
Red Hot Chili Peppers, 113
Reising, Alma, 128n4
Reising, Russell, 4–5, 68n1, 111–28,
    119, 124, 127n1

Reliant Shirt Corporation, 108n2

"Revolution," 23, 49, 89, 111, 126, 127, 147, 149, 155, 194n5

"Revolution 1," 92, 109n8, 126, 127, 149

"Revolution 9," 15, 29, 79, 88, 91, 92, 148, 155

Revolver, 3, 4–5, 17, 21, 26, 32, 55, 61, 65, 66, 68n1, 69, 72, 82–84, 101, 111–28, 139, 141, 151, 164, 211

Rice, Tim, 69n8

Richard, Cliff, 58, 151, 164

"Richard Cory," 19

Rico, Pablo, 212n3

Riley, Tim, 3, 155, 157

"Ringo Boy," 62

"Ringo, I Love You," 62

"Rip It Up," 109n7

Roane, Kit R., 193

Robbins, Ira, 193

Robinson, Edgar Arlington, 19

Rock and Roll Hall of Fame and Museum, 198, 200–12

"Rock and Roll Music," 40, 72, 73

Rock Around the Clock, 101

"Rock Around the Clock," 40

Rock Circus, 172–73, 180

Rock 'n' Roll Circus, 28

"Rocky Raccoon," 2–3, 15, 148

Roessner, Jeffrey, 5, 109n8, 147–58

"Roll Over Beethoven," 161

Rolling Stones, The, 52n4, 61, 126, 127, 187, 207, 218

Ronco, 187

Rooftop Concert, 1, 28, 107, 170

Rory Storm and the Hurricanes, 176

Rubber Soul, 3, 13, 15, 16, 20, 45, 63, 65, 76, 78, 80, 82, 84, 101, 108n1, 127n3, 151, 164, 166, 190, 191, 209

Ruby, Jack, 137

"Run for Your Life," 20–21, 81, 127n3, 209, 210, 213n8

Ryko, 146n8

"Satisfaction," 207

Savage, Jon, 113

"Savoy Truffle," 90, 92, 93n1, 156

Schaffner, Nicholas, 15, 109n6

Scheurer, Timothy E., 52n9

"School Day," 40

Schweighardt, Ray, 107, 110n11

Scott, Derek, 68n2

Seagal, Erich, 105

Seaman, Fred, 205

Season of Glass, 202

"See Saw," 119

Sellars, Richard West, 173

Sex Pistols, The, 127

"Sexy Sadie," 14–15, 25, 28, 49, 67

Sgt. Pepper's Lonely Hearts Club Band, 3, 4, 5, 9, 14, 15, 16, 21, 24, 27, 28, 33, 38, 46, 48, 51, 55, 61, 65, 66, 69n14, 84, 85, 87, 88, 91, 94n14, 104, 114, 127, 127n3, 129–46, 148, 151, 152, 153, 154, 155, 164, 166, 179, 190, 218

"Sgt. Pepper's Lonely Hearts Club Band," 47–48, 85, 86, 88, 134, 136, 137, 140, 144, 146n11, 172

"Sgt. Pepper's Lonely Hearts Club Band (Reprise)," 134

Shadows, The, 58

Shaft, 217

"Shake, Rattle, and Roll," 40, 109n7

Shakespeare, William, 16, 18, 113, 165

Shapiro, Helen, 58

Shatner, William, 129, 146n1

"She Loves You," 2, 11–12, 42, 43, 52n10, 56, 60, 61, 63, 68, 73, 74, 105, 152, 184

"She Said She Said," 21, 84, 112, 115, 116, 120, 121–22, 123, 124

Sheff, David, 149, 207

Sheffield, Rob, 185

Shenson, Walter, 99

"She's a Woman," 77

"She's Leaving Home," 2, 21, 22–23, 35n2, 61, 85, 127, 138, 139, 143, 216

Shirelles, The, 60, 68n7
Shlain, Bruce, 125
Siegel, Jules, 113
Sigaux, Gilbert, 180n1
Silver Beatles, The, 136
Silver Beatles, The, 68n6, 136, 176
Simpson, O. J., 184
Simpsons, The, 129
Sinatra, Frank, 192
"Slow Down," 72
Sly and the Family Stone, 114, 126
Smith, Caspar, 172
Smith, Norman, 93n3
Smith, Valene, 173
Smokey Robinson and the Miracles, 68n7
"Soldier of Love," 188
"Something," 31, 50, 90, 189
Sontag, Susan, 66
Sot-Weed Factor, The, 164
Spaniard in the Works, A, 17, 21, 144
Spector, Phil, 38, 92
Spinetti, Victor, 165
Springsteen, Bruce, 113
Star Club, 57
Steele, Tommy, 57
Stephenson, Chris, 193
Steppenwolf, 119
Stockhausen, Karlheinz, 168
Stoller, Mike, 38, 57
Strausbaugh, John, 203
Strawberry Field, 29, 177, 180
"Strawberry Fields Forever," 19, 28, 48,
    84, 86, 87, 88, 133, 134, 140, 141,
    142, 144, 155, 168, 218
Strawberry Fields Memorial, 181n5
"Street Fighting Man," 127
Students for a Democratic Society, 148
"Sue Me, Sue You Blues," 34
Sulpy, Doug, 107, 110n11
Summer of Love, 130, 131
"Sun King," 83, 89
Sun Studios, 171
Sutcliffe, Stu, 57, 68n6

T. Rex, 174
Tales from Topographic Oceans, 112
Tarkus, 127
"Taxman," 3, 26, 50, 112, 114, 117, 119,
    120, 124, 132
Taylor, Derek, 188
Taylor, Pam, 177
"Tell Me What You See," 78, 79
Temperance Seven, The, 58
"Thank You Girl," 61, 67, 73
Thank Your Lucky Stars, 56, 59, 100
That Was the Week That Was, 63
"That'll Be the Day," 40
"Then He Kissed Me," 60
"There's a Place," 11, 73
Thick as a Brick, 112
"Things We Said Today," 76
"Think for Yourself," 81
"This Boy," 74
Thomas, Chris, 89
Thomas, Dylan, 27
Thompson, John B., 185, 186
Thoreau, Henry David, 114, 115, 117,
    122, 132
Tibetan Book of the Dead, 17, 45, 114, 211
"Ticket to Ride," 63–64, 78, 79, 81
"Till There Was You," 74, 75
Tillekens, Ger, 127n2
Timbre, 4, 71–94
Tin Pan Alley, 39, 52n9, 57, 168
Tom Petty and the Heartbreakers, 113
Tommy, 112
"Tomorrow Never Knows," 4–5, 17, 26,
    29, 31, 45, 46, 48, 82, 83, 88, 91,
    111–28, 132, 139, 146n3
Tompkins, Jane, 6, 215–19
Tong, Rosemarie, 66
"Too Many People," 34
Top Ten Club, 57, 164, 176
Tourism, 5, 169–81
Towner, John, 180n1
Transcendental Meditation, 14–15, 67,
    104

Trident Studios, 170
Turnbull, Colin, 173
Turner, Edith, 170, 175, 180
Turner, Steve, 94n11, 130
Turner, Victor, 170, 175, 180
"Twelfth of Never, The," 61
Twenty Greatest Hits, 184, 185, 189
Twickenham Film Studios, 107
Twiggy, 67
"Twist and Shout," 60, 73, 107
"Two of Us," 90, 91
Tynan, Kenneth, 130

United Artists, 99, 109n10

Valdez, Stephen, 59, 127n2
Vanilla Fudge, 126–27
Velvet Underground, 185
VH1, 184, 188
Vietnam War, 136, 137, 140, 149, 153

Wagner, Naphtali, 127n2
"Wait," 81
Walden, 115, 117
"Walk Right Back," 58
Wall, The, 113
"Walrus and the Carpenter, The," 17
Walter, Tony, 173
Warwick, Jacqueline, 61, 62
Wayne, John, 217, 218
"Wayward Wind," 58
"We Can Work It Out," 65, 81, 197,
    209, 210, 213n9
"We Gotta Get Out of This Place," 127
Welch, Raquel, 217
Wenner, Jann, 142, 152, 204, 206,
    213n11, 213n13
We're Only in It for the Money, 137
West, Mae, 27
Whannel, Paddy, 162, 163
"What Goes On," 80
"What You're Doing," 77
"When I Get Home," 211

"When I'm Sixty-Four," 85, 86, 87, 127,
    133, 134, 138–39
"While My Guitar Gently Weeps," 17,
    50, 90, 91
Whitaker, Robert, 189
White Album, The. See under *The Beatles*
Whiteley, Sheila, 4, 55–69, 68n3, 68n4,
    69n13, 69n14, 137, 141–42
Whitley, Ed, 15, 24
Who, The, 112, 117, 127, 187
"Why Don't We Do It in the Road?,"
    28, 31, 155, 217
Widgery, David, 204
Wiener, Jon, 149, 151, 158, 205
"Wild Honey Pie," 91, 155
Wilde, Marty, 57
Wilde, Oscar, 27
"Will You Still Love Me Tomorrow?," 60
Wilson, Brian, 51, 151
Wilson, Harold, 63
Wings, 146n7
Winner, Langdon, 130
Wish You Were Here, 113
"With a Little Help from My Friends,"
    2, 47–48, 50, 87, 134, 137, 138, 142,
    216
With the Beatles, 63, 75
Withers, Bill, 120
"Within You Without You," 14, 27, 50,
    85, 86, 87, 124, 139, 140, 152
Wolfe, Arnold, 194n11
Womack, Kenneth, 1–6, 25, 97–110,
    194n7
"Word, The," 45, 80, 81, 82
"Words of Love," 77, 94n7
"Working Class Hero," 211
"Wumberlog, The," 144

Yellow Submarine [film], 4, 97, 104–06,
    109n10, 189
"Yellow Submarine," 83, 85, 86, 91, 112,
    115, 116, 123, 124, 185, 189, 190
Yellow Submarine Songtrack, 87

"Yer Blues," 15, 19, 148, 155, 156
Yes, 112
"Yes It Is," 79
"Yesterday," 29, 61, 64, 69n11, 72, 77, 79, 80, 84, 164, 197, 199, 216
Yesterday . . . and Today, 103, 109n6, 189
Yogananda, Paramhansa, 139
"You Can't Do That," 76, 77
"You Don't Know Me," 58
"You Keep Me Hanging On," 126–27
"You Like Me Too Much," 78
"You Never Give Me Your Money," 3, 25, 83, 89, 90

"You Really Got a Hold on Me," 68n7, 73, 109n7
"You Won't See Me," 20, 80
"Young Ones, The," 58
"You're Driving Me Crazy," 58
"You're Going to Lose That Girl," 63, 64, 78
"You've Got to Hide Your Love Away," 13, 45, 79

Zain, C. C., 94n12
Zappa, Frank, 129, 137, 146n8